LIVING TRADITIONS IN CONTEMPORARY CONTEXTS

Living Traditions in Contemporary Contexts

The Madhva Matha of Udupi

VASUDEVA RAO

Orient Longman

The maps in this book are not to scale. The external boundaries and coastline of India, and the boundaries of the states of India as depicted are neither authentic nor correct.

ORIENT LONGMAN PRIVATE LIMITED

Registered Office
3-6-272 Himayatnagar, Hyderabad 500 029 (A.P.), India

Other Offices
Bangalore, Bhopal, Bhubaneshwar, Chandigarh, Chennai, Ernakulam, Guwahati, Hyderabad, Jaipur, Kolkata, Lucknow, Mumbai, New Delhi, Patna

First Published 2002

ISBN 81 250 2297 X

Typeset by
Scribe Consultants
New Delhi

Printed in India at
Baba Barkha Nath Printers
New Delhi

Published by
Orient Longman Private Limited
1/24 Asaf Ali Road
New Delhi 110 002

In memory of my father
Professor M.S.A. Rao

Contents

Acknowledgements

'*Mangalacharana*' is the traditional acknowledgement in Sanskrit texts. My bringing in this term sets the stage for the task this book attempts.

For at least a decade before writing this book I had been striving to find a voice that would be acceptable to the academic world, and that would bridge the gap between the two parts of my life—what I knew in private and what I had learnt in public (embodied in degrees). I was indeed fortunate to have Professor Veena Das as my supervisor. She makes the point that even such disciplines as sociology and anthropology are themselves constructions of the west, thus making it necessary for people who wish to faithfully represent the Indian to create their own spaces within these broad genres (1995). During initial discussions, Professor Das had even said, 'some failures are better than most successes'. It is with her encouragement that I have been able to attempt the interplay of philosophical ideas with sociological reality. This study is a small representation of the voice, that I have tried to find.

To give such a voice a published form, is I think, an equally courageous act, For making this journey with me and transforming that voice into a book, I thank Orient Longman, my publisher, and Vidya Rao, my editor at Orient Longman.

Professor Thomas Trautmann went through the earlier draft and gave me valuable comments and criticisms. I cannot express how helpful the voluminous inputs have been. I thank him for his expansive generosity. I also benefited from the contributions of Professor Andre Beteille, Professor J.P.S. Uberoi, Professor M.N. Panini, Professor R.S. Khare, Dr. Rabindra Ray and

Dr. Arthur Helweg. Professor B.S. Baviskar and Professor Chandrashekhar Bhatt provided much needed support and encouragement. I am grateful to all of them.

I received excellent comments during the Friday Research Colloquim of the Department of Sociology, Delhi School of Economics, the XXth All India Sociological Conference held at Mangalore, at the Indian Institute of Technology, Kanpur and at the Institute of Social and Economic Change, Bangalore, for which I am most grateful. I am especially thankful to Professor M.N. Srinivas, Professor R.S. Misra, Dr. Robert. J. Zydenbos and Dr. Smriti Srinivas.

Part of my research was funded by a Junior Research Fellowship. Later, Professor Veena Das provided me with working space in the project on 'Social Science and Immunisation' which eased my financial burdens considerably.

Chapter 3 of this book is a revised version of a paper 'Gastromantics of the Udupi Krishna Matha', (*Sociological Bulletin* 43:2, 1994), the concluding chapter (Chapter 7) is a revised version of a paper 'Udupi Matha in Contemporary India (*Seminar*, August 1997). I am grateful to these journals for their interest in my work.

The kindness and generosity of all the *swamijis* and members of the *matha* has gone a long way in shaping this work. There are too many people involved here to name individually. Nevertheless, I would like to specially mention and thank Bannanje Govindacharaya (who incidently is the script-writer for G.V. Iyer's award-winning films *Shankaracharya* and *Bhagavad Gita*) for his scholarly guidance, I would also like to thank his student Ramanathacharya, from whom I received instructions on a text relating to the practices of *sannyasa* in the tradition. The *swamijis* of Puttige, Adamar and Pejavara matha provided accommodation and space without which fieldwork would have been impossible.

I am fortunate to have good friends Vineet, Pratiksha and Hayavadan, who bolstered my spirits wen they sagged. Srikanth my friend and student of Indian *darshanas* provided valuable assistance with his eye for detail. I am also grateful to Pradyumana Murti for sharing his computer expertise.

My love and gratitude to my mother, Saroja Rao, who knows what it takes to make an anthropologist. And to my wife, Rama, for her support and for spending our first wedding anniversary in Delhi, while I was among ascetics in Udupi.

My father, M.S.A. Rao, was my first guru—both for Vedic knowledge and sociology, although it was only after his death that I gave up a course in Engineering and began my studies in Social Anthropology. I have missed my father in more ways than one. This book is dedicated to his memory.

A Note on Transliteration

Sanskrit and Kannada words, except proper names in the text, have been used in their English version without diacritical marks and have been italicised when they first appear. The use of 'aa' for long 'a', and 'ee' for long 'i' has also been avoided. The use of 'th' is reserved for the Sanskrit aspirated form, as in the second consonant in 'tatha'. The Glossary, however, gives the word as spelled in the text, its diacritical spelling and meaning.

1

Introduction: The Inquiry and its Context

Sociology and Indology

This study aims to make a sociological investigation of the *mathas* or monasteries in Udupi belonging to the Brahmins of the Madhva sect.

Scholars from India and outside have tried to grasp the unique and the universal in India society. Some of these efforts, notably the works of Dumont (1970) and Marriott (1955, 1989), have tried to identify certain structural features that are said to hold a key to the understanding of India. Others have been less ambitious but have tried to capture contemporary changes, especially the interplay between tradition and modernity (Singer 1972, Das 1982, Khare 1970, Appadurai 1981).

There have been very few attempts to interpret the Hindu world-view through a study of the sectarian traditions in India. This has led to a peculiar situation. Indologists believe that the knowledge of Vedanta, Navya Nyaya or Buddhist epistemology can provide clues to the operation of India, of at least the period when these systems of thought were conceived and promulgated.

Orientalists feel that thus knowing the essence of Indian society, one can explain existing forms by referring to the familiar corpus of ancient lore. Social anthropologists tend to be equally naive when it comes to the acceptance of the native's representation of the tradition. The understanding of world-views and thought in complex, literary traditions is difficult to bring off. The 'cosmology' constructed from religious texts is often quite remote from the 'world-view' implicit in the conduct and thought of the individual (Redfield 1953). It is, therefore, important that the indologist and the anthropologist come together in order to report on patterns that include both the written tradition and the workings of particular traditions—a project envisaged by Dumont (1957) but seldom practised in relation to the study of sectarian traditions.

According to Milton Singer (1972), Robert Redfield's conception of a civilisation, as a compound structure of Little and Great Traditions and M.N. Srinivas's concept of Sanskritisation are both designed to deal with this problem. However, Singer contends that his conceptions have not been applied to the study of Hinduism, arguing that:

> [because] they are not usually Sanskritists and cannot often obtain the collaboration of Sanskritists, anthropologists must bypass the textual corpus and content themselves with noting references to it that turn up in their interviews and observations. The Hinduism that emerges from such studies will more closely approximate the 'world-view' of popular Hinduism than the systematic 'cosmology' of any school of Sanskritic Hinduism (Singer 1972: 39–40).

General Approach to the Study

The scriptural forms and interpretive strategies found in any tradition at any given moment may suggest a rigid set of characterising features. The emphasis on the static dimension often does not take into account the specific cultural and historical context. This ultimately obscures the dynamic and persistent pluralism of changing forms and contents. The native exegeses of the sect employ diverse interpretive strategies and understandings of the sacred text, dramatically demonstrating the amazing fluidity of the category sacred text.

The act of uttering (interpreting, teaching and learning) the text takes place in a social setting. It may support or critique the existing social environment. By supporting the social setting, it perpetuates the tradition of the sect and by its rendering as a critique it seeks to transform the tradition. In both these aspects, the texts act as a way in which tradition articulates its existence in the present world.

Besides functioning as a perpetrator of world-views, epistemologies and cosmologies, the text in the hands of its interpreters (*sannyasis* and other scholars) becomes therapeutic as well. This is the salvational or soteriological aspect of the text.

The extratextual reality of Brahman is mediated through the explication of the text and is communicated to a humanity trapped in ignorance and misery. Martha Nussbaum (1994) highlights the parallel 'therapy of desire' in Greek philosophy. For Aristotle, Socrates and others, thought defines types of existence. Correct thought leads to correct lifestyle or emotion, that is one without misery, anger and so forth. This is also the way the Madhva sect articulates the removal of misery. Madhva's statement is, 'Inquire always into the actual way things are by critiquing erroneous views, for it causes good action and thought; wrong knowledge leads to destruction' (*Anu Vyakhyana*).[1]

In modern western philosophy, the hermeneutics of Paul Ricoeur tries to focus on this relation between knowing and being. Following Heidegger, Ricoeur emphasises that to understand something implies a way of being or dwelling in this world. The concern of Ricoeur is no longer what does it mean to know, but to the ontological question, what does it mean to be? He writes:

> The first function of understanding is to orient us in a situation. So, understanding is not concerned with grasping a fact but with

> apprehending a possibility of being. We must not lose sight of this point when we draw the methodological consequences of this analysis: to understand a text, we shall say, is not to find a lifeless sense which is contained therein, but to unfold the possibility of being indicated by the text (Ricoeur 1981: 56).

In the Madhva sect's celebration of *Brahma gyana* (knowledge of Brahman) as liberating, the individual grows with knowledge and seeks to transform himself or herself into a liberated soul (depending on the capacity of the person). In the light of this understanding, it is difficult to accept any theory which stresses only the coercive power of knowledge in the formation of a certain sort of self (Foucault 1988). As Nussbaum says,

> It is questionable whether Foucault can even admit the possibility of such a community of freedom, given his view that knowledge and argument are themselves tools of power (Nussbaum 1994: 5).

The textual exegesis renders itself into various forms and these interpretations depend on specific social contexts. They can, for instance, be used politically (as in the case of articulations of Hindutva) or as performative in *upannyasa* (public lectures). The text, by its ability to be used in different ways, can have transcendental, political, philosophical and poetic manifestations, being able to express itself orally and in the written form. Jeffrey Timm claims this flexibility for the sacred-text traditions for the whole of South Asia (Timm 1992: 305). This, however, should not imply that there is no specificity to the issues discussed or that the text is a collection of inchoate views. They are all views expressed in defence of a particular standpoint and developed with a critique of opposing points of view.

The conclusions drawn from the chapters aim to subvert some accepted understanding of certain distinctions, as between oral and written, learning and instruction, and theology and philosophy. These categories take on a different meaning within the context of the mathas and to a large extent in Indic traditions generally.

For example, it is usually understood that Indian systems of thought are theological, with only the advaita (monist or non-dualist) being sometimes considered philosophical. This is because most sects ostensibly propound *bhakti*, which is often translated as faith in a personal God without much reference to philosophical inquiry. Though this may be true of most sects formed during the Bhakti movement in Indian history, one cannot bracket all Brahminical sects under this assumption. Similarly, it is difficult to club different sects under one conceptual framework. Even within a sect, specifically contextualised interpretations give rise to varied meanings and intentions. In fact, it is through a systematic study of sects that one understands that the Hindu identity is not monolithic. Across sects in India, there are some which revitalise the caste system and its hierarchy as argued by Dumont, while others contradict it with the ideology of egalitarianism (Das 1982; Heesterman 1985; Rao 1984; Van der Veer 1988). Some sects have a detailed understanding of renunciation while a few do not have renouncers at all (e.g. Vallabha, Kabir Panthis, etc.).

It is not my aim here to sketch out in any great detail the various orders or sects of India; it is rather to highlight a totally neglected diversity—that of the differentiation of the Brahminical sects. By Brahminical sects, I mean those sects which are primarily organised around renouncers who are themselves Brahmins (or are recruited from among Brahmins of a specific sect) and have lay followers not necessarily belonging to one caste (this includes the Shankaracharya mathas, mathas of Ramanujacharya and of Madhvacharya). The focus is on one such sect known as the Madhva sect or *sampradaya* in the town of Udupi[2] in South Karnataka, India.

The philosophy of Madhvacharya, along with that of Shankara and Ramanuja is Vedantic philosophy. Shankaracharya is considered the first of the Vedantic philosophers who founded the advaitic interpretation. The date generally attributed to him is 770 AD, but this date is disputed and various historians place it within 500 BC and 800 AD. It is generally agreed that the Adi Shankaracharya lived a short but productive life and died in his thirties. Ramanujacharya and Madhvacharya who followed Shankaracharya and founded the Vishishtadvaita (qualified monism) and Dvaita (dualism) schools respectively are more precisely dated. Ramanuja lived in the early eleventh century and Madhva was born in 1238 AD and lived for 79 years.

Thought and Behaviour in Context

Most of the philosophical understanding of renunciation related to sectarian institutions, and even general orientations to religious thought in India, assume an advaitic or non-dualist standpoint; fundamentally constituted as (i) the world is an illusion and (ii) the soul in its liberated state becomes one with Brahman or God who is without any attributes. This espouses a certain idea of solipsism, with a rejection of the reality of the world.

Emile Durkheim, making observations on the idea of a supreme reality in India writes:

> This supreme reality, which no longer has anything of a divine personality about it, is contained within man himself, or rather, man is but one with it, for nothing exists apart from it. To find it, and unite himself to it, one does not have to research some external support outside himself; it is enough to concentrate upon himself and meditate (Durkheim, 1961: 48).

This is a typical representation of 'Indian thought' duplicated by westerners and Indians alike, countless times in sociological and cultural studies. This picture remains only a partial representation of Indian philosophical thought and of the supreme reality since it gives only one sect's (namely the advaitic) intellectual stance.

There is another problem in the understanding of Indian 'scriptural' or philosophic thought. Most of the texts, for example the *Upanishads*, are interpreted independent of their sectarian placing. This decontextualised knowledge often gives an incorrect picture of the status of certain Upanishads. Patrick Olivelle writes:

> Most of our *Upanishads* subscribe to the advaita vedanta doctrine that the world of multiplicity and our own consciousness, as separate individuals are ultimately illusory (1992: 79).

This understanding of the *Upanishads* not only ignores the sectarian differences and the varied interpretations of the same *Upanishads*, it also without any conceivable advantage, disregards the traditional background of the understanding of scripture. The *Upanishads* are not in themselves Advaitic. The interpretation of these texts by students of Shankaracharya is Advaitic. The same statements can be interpreted to be non-Advaitic. A Vedic statement such as *Brahma eva satya* (Brahman alone is real) need not mean the rest of the world is unreal as it is made out in Advaita. The Dvaita philosophy interprets this statement to mean that the only 'independent' reality (uncaused reality) that exists is Brahman. The world is also real but not as real as Brahman because it is created, maintained and destroyed by Brahman. This dependent reality is the crucial difference. To imply this idea, the world is said to be unreal if conceived as having an independent existence. Therefore, Brahman alone is 'real' in the sense of not being dependent. (There will be occasion further on to refer to some other illustrations.)

The Upanishads and other parts of the Vedas, according to the Advaita, Vishishtadvaita and Dvaita sects, are interpreted in the light of the *Brahma Sutras*, a text written by Veda Vyasa to facilitate a correct understanding of the Vedas. Similarly, the Vedas too support contrary traditions depending on the interpretation.

The Vedas are thus organised into a system through the *Brahma Sutras* and the various Brahminical sects follow this discipline. The tendency to ignore this tradition has been going on since the time of Max Muller who also tried to read the Vedas disregarding the complex literature that has evolved in trying to interpret them. The contextualising of a body of knowledge within the sectarian tradition highlights that the knowledge of Sanskrit in itself is insufficient to understand scripture.

The Madhvas, using the same Vedas, interpret it to

understand the world as real, *satya* (not illusory) and the soul as being dependent on Brahman, who is full of attributes (*guna purna*), never becoming one with it. The reality of this world is a dependent reality; hence though Brahman and the world are real, there is a difference in degrees of reality.

The difference in the understanding stems from the difference in the interpretation of the *Brahma Sutras*. These interpretations are known as *Bhashyas* and the interpreters or the saint-philosophers who started the sect are called *Bhashyakaras* (the Bhashya-givers). It is principally this difference in the *Brahma Sutra Bhashyas* that differentiates the various Brahminical sects such as the Advaitic, Vishishtadvaitic and Dvaitic.

For the sannyasis (renouncers) and the lay followers of the Madhva sect, Shankara or Advaita is the *purva-paksha* (the prior text to be refuted). The works of the Madhva tradition seek to give an alternative meaning (which they feel is the correct one) of the *Sutra* and hence the Veda. For the Madhvas, the 'other' is Shankara and the Advaita philosophy. This opposition, along with a well-developed philosophical position and tradition, marks off the Madhva sect or the Madhva Brahmin from the other Brahmin sects. This difference is manifested in body markings, dress, eating habits and other codes of conduct. There are internal variations as well. Burghart, in defining a sect, deals with the issues thus:

> In seeking to understand the basis of the individual identity of a sect one fact of primary importance comes to mind: each sect claims to have its own founder who discovered and preached an universal message of liberation from transience, a message which is still preached by the founder's followers. Since all sectarian founders are credited with having discovered a liberating message, such a discovery by itself does not serve to differentiate sects. Differentiation occurs with the further claim that this discovery was a unique and unrepeatable event in the course of transient existence. By crediting the sectarian founder with having discovered a unique path of liberation, the sect becomes autonomous both with respect to durational time (the founder has liberated himself from transience) and with respect to rival

sectarian founders (the founder's discovery is unique) (Burghart 1983: 646).

In studying tradition through sampradaya or sects, one is able to contextualise and situate thought and behaviour. For example, the conceptualisation of renunciation has been a vexed issue in anthropology. Depending on the sect to which they belong, sannyasis have a different status and relation to the world. In understanding the various categories involved, the sectarian viewpoint establishes the frame through which one may provide an analysis. Only by understanding this can we effectively move towards the general understanding of Hinduism. It is hoped that the subsequent chapters will be able to justify this need, as well as point to other areas of inquiry not dealt with here.

My analysis has focussed on the organisation of the sect, sacred food, the transmission of knowledge and on renunciation. The different constructions of people and by the people on these topics lead to a diversity of ideas and points to a multi-layered construction of reality. The ideas and constructions need not necessarily be the same between different groups. Further, thought, behaviour and utterances are often constructed differently according to different contexts and depending on who the 'other' is.

Within the matha, sacred food is viewed and understood differently. The context and social setting in which it is eaten makes for differences. Spaces where the saints eat are more sacred than the other spaces and involve a complex ritual which is absent or mitigated in other spaces where sacred feasting takes place. Similarly, transmission of knowledge attains different meanings and utterance depending on who the audience is. There are significant differences when one is instructing students (called *patha*) and when one is giving a public lecture (*upannyasa*).

The importance of pinning down specific acts and utterances points out that languages and other symbols are not unidimensional, but are to be found in a variety of contexts with different usages. The written word ceases to be only a repository of knowledge about a particular sect's ideology and structure and instead becomes a vehicle of understanding the native's expressions about himself or herself and of those around him or her. It becomes pregnant with the possibility of many meanings, helping us to analyse the way people communicate ideas about themselves to each other and explain the similarities and differences between groups.

In many of the formulations by the members of the sect, there is a dynamic interaction between modern day institutions and values suggesting a movement in the idea of tradition. The pedagogic practices, the dramatisation and communication of Pauranic and epic materials, the bureaucratisation of the matha, and the general world-view, all incorporate elements of the modern day. In Milton Singer's words:

> These elements, as expressed in myth and legend, history and ceremony, not only represent a sense of a shared past and a common culture but also suggest that Indian civilisation is becoming more modern without becoming less Indian (Singer 1972: 247).

Life in the Udupi matha juxtaposes in itself a series of heterogeneous moments, some steeped in tradition, others, an expression of modern times and means. Together, these make up the larger world-view of the members. In this situation, one cannot expect a tradition devoid of modern meanings, nor modernity bereft of traditional moorings. And an anthropology which tackles this predicament will have to account for the introduction of the present. Marc Augé (1977) stresses the need for anthropology to forsake the nostalgia for the past (the purely exotic) and to translate its categories to take into account the experience of contemporary societies. Veena Das writes:

> Augé protested vehemently—anthropologists are not purveyors of dreams, and they are not there to answer to the demand (or the lack of it) in those who protest the present (Das 1995: 196).

In this understanding, the tradition of the sect is not a given and fixed entity but is a constantly emerging field constructed in the various articulations in equally diverse contexts. For example, Bakhtin's 'dialogic activity' provides a tool to understand utterances as being constructed as they are being uttered, depending on who the 'other' is. In the case of the exposition of the sacred texts, there is ample room for re-interpretations and modifications (defying an understanding of wisdom as static or ready-made that has to be passed on). Teachers and scholars keep devising ways to communicate the subject matter depending on who the listener is. The interaction of the Udupi matha with present-day institutions and changing values is an attempt to establish and preserve their identity. The matha is trying to survive in circumstances where the members no longer have the historically exalted status of caste superiority or religion.

In this century, the desirability of economic growth results in the assertion of economic power. In a relatively anonymous world, where what people know about each other is often limited, where the possession of consumer luxuries is valued more than spirituality and there is an increasing desacralisation of social institutions and the entire cosmos, the mathas are trying to keep their voice alive by adapting to the present. This forward movement displaces any understanding of tradition as static or 'freezed' (Goody 1968:15).

It was observed that the assimilation of various interpretations and meanings given by natives often transcends the idea or world view of the informer. Although the peoples' interpretation is the data on which one works, their perspectives on everyday life may not always converge. And again the interpretations often tend to be incomplete because the interpretations are gained in particular contexts.[3] To be able to understand meanings in different contexts is the work of the researcher; 'to formulate clearly what one has more or less confusedly perceived' (Dumont 1970:36).[4] In seeking to move beyond the native's perception 'we do not only look and listen, we also think' (Madan 1987:9).

Within the hermeneutic framework, the comprehension and explanation of reality, is an inevitable outcome of the tension between the 'self' and the 'other'. For Ricoeur (1981), 'distanciation' is the dialectical counterpart of 'belonging'. These two movements represent the twin arches of the hermeneutic bridge. When we try and understand the other, we belong to it and hence become distant from ourselves. And when we come back to our self we are more than what we were, now there is a new belonging. Such appropriation has nothing to do with the empathic intuition (putting oneself in another's shoes as in the formulation of Dilthey and other stalwarts of the *Verstehende* school), but rather involves the expansion of one's own horizon through the incorporation of a new mode of being. The next section deals with these issues relating to the movement, beyond the native's interpretation and, its incorporation in greater detail.

Some Thoughts on Fieldwork in Udupi

I began my fieldwork in May 1993 and continued until the month of November 1994 with two short breaks. I stayed for the most part in one of the mathas of Udupi, only once changing my residence to another matha.

My entry was facilitated by one of the pontiffs of the Udupi matha, who allowed me to stay in one of the rooms in the matha, free of charge. I used to eat with the students of the swamiji or at the main Krishna matha, where food is served as *prasada* (sacred food) without charge. Visits outside Udupi were usually with swamiji's travelling in their vehicle or moving in public transport or on foot, to visit places associated with the matha and its activities.

In doing ethnology one exposes oneself to an alien consciousness, time and place, in varying degrees depending on how 'exotic' the field is. In doing so there is a disappropriation from given assumptions regarding one's own immediate world. At the same time the ethnographer seeks to reappropriate this 'other' world for his or her own contemporary consciousness. James Clifford writes,

> Hermeneutic philosophy in its varying styles, from Wilhelm Dilthey and Paul Ricoeur to Heidegger, reminds us that the simplest cultural accounts are intentional creations, that

> interpreters constantly construct themselves through the others they study (Clifford 1986: 10).

In Ricoeur's understanding, one cannot give up one's own identity and become the other entirely, nor can one be indifferent to the 'opening up' of the self that takes place in such interactions. In terms of Madhva's philosophy, this is the central argument that is levelled against the monists or advaitis. One cannot give up one's identity to merge with the Absolute, as Advaita claims (*Tat tvam asi, Aham Brahmasmi, So aham asmi*— are various Upanishadic statements quoted by Shankara to prove the merging of identities). For Madhva, the self grows to become like Brahman but can never become Brahman: like = to be + not to be like.

If one translates this for the fieldworker in the field, both Madhva and Ricoeur indicate a delicate balance that needs to be achieved. In the words of Edgerbon and Langness:

> Complete involvement is incompatible with the anthropologist's primary goals, but complete detachment is incompatible with fieldwork. Successful fieldwork requires a balance between the two, a balancing act which is every bit as difficult as it sounds (Edgerbon and Langness 1974: 3).

Paul Rabinow (1977: 5–6) and Vincent Crapanzano (1980: 139), following Ricoeur, talk about the understanding of the self through the detour of the other, namely the native in their field. The predominant theme that is portrayed is the radical difference of the other vis-a-vis the self. Anne Beal (1995) criticises this approach which celebrates the shock of the unknowable other as experienced and discovered by the ethnographer:

> [E]ven sensitive works that intend to disintegrate essentialised categories of self and other can succumb to Orientalist stereotypes. Celebrating the shock of the unknowable other is perhaps a luxury that western anthropologists working in the Middle Eastern world in the late twentieth century can ill-afford (Beal, 1995: 301).

Leaving aside substantive issues, my reference to Ricoeur is situated in a different context. The field and the fieldworker do not stand in such sharp contrast and therefore the shock of the other is mitigated. The self (that is myself) and the other are not placed in sharp contrast, for in spite of my urban upbringing, I belong to the sect (though not the matha) I am studying. Therefore, although there might be separate problems with the placement of the ethnographer, the problems in viewing the other in sharp contrast may not arise. Some of the problems caused by this proximity will be discussed shortly.

An Indian studying a community within his own country has been a common, if not the only, ethnographic practice, especially since 'the other' can be encountered literally next door (Srinivas 1992: 138). Only slightly less common is the practice of an insider studying his or her own community.

Apart from the advantage of not having to negotiate the formal bureaucratic regulations of getting a research permit and the like, there are other advantages which the 'indigenous ethnographer' has (Clifford 1986: 9). For instance, I could not have had access to several sacred spaces and events had I not been a member of the sect. As one senior Indian sociologist from near Udupi, who is a non-Madhva, mentioned:

> If it were somebody else he would not be allowed easy access to the sannyasis during many of their activities. And as far as the *chowki* (the place where sanyasis and Brahmin devotees take *prasada*) is concerned, we would be denied entry.[5]

T.N. Madan's study (1965) in the village Utrassu-Umangiri is an illuminating example of an anthropologist study his own community. Madan's experience recounts the enthusiastic and cooperative response he got from his younger informants (1975: 139). In the case of elderly Pandits, the positive response, as Madan observes, was partly 'because some of them saw in the situation their opportunity to reclaim ('resocialise') me' (1975: 151).

Although both these attitudes were part of my fieldwork experience,[6] at another level, there was a reticent mood that I had to encounter. The sannyasis and other scholars were not always willing to answer my questions. Especially in the beginning, they used to give me standard replies that they were accustomed to give, for public consumption and to journalists. One particular instance highlights this reserve:

Once while I was questioning a swamiji about what he had read and how it was relevant, he said 'All that is okay, but first tell me what you have studied, what is your *adhikara* (level of knowledge and hence capacity) to ask this question? How do I know that you will understand?'

I had to convince him and many others that my study (that is my traditional instruction) of Madhva *shastra* (philosophy) and other *darshanas* (the different philosophical systems) was adequate enough for me to be able to understand and discuss Shastra.[7] This was usually done by quoting the texts and by referring to the great living *gurus* of the Madhva tradition. After this initial introduction, my participation and the discussions during patha (instruction to students) and debates must have convinced the gurus of my interest to know if not my ability. During several encounters, the use of the philosophical, technical terminology or jargon facilitated the discussions.[8] Thus, as a fieldworker, I could not have entered the field as a naive observer—I was constantly being put to test.

I realised that this was peculiar to such studies where the specialised realms of knowledge and the things of this world are not only secretive, not also necessarily sacred, but considered hard to obtain and understand and therefore unfit for the unprepared and unskilful (*ayogya*) or the uninterested (*ashradhalu*). It is not enough to be a good listener but to be an 'informed' listener to prevent the person being interviewed, from being distracted.

In these circumstances, it becomes important to sift through the various layers of meanings given and try to 'engage' the informant into moving to deeper layers, at a level which the speaker himself feels is the correct understanding. This level is difficult to explain, because the listener is often 'unprepared'.

The ethnographer in this kind of setting has to contend with a special kind of circumstance. Not only does he or she have to apply the skills of an anthropologist in understanding the complex cultural system, but he or she also needs to know the science and textual knowledge that informs the everyday life of the informants. This is similar to an anthropologist studying the natural scientist, be it an experiment in physics or medicine. This sort of fieldwork differs from the ethnography of tribal groups or peasants. In the case of scientists or other experts (or for that matter any field where there is a textual body of knowledge which informs the world-view of the informer, e.g. lawyers, engineers, etc.) it is not enough to learn the language of the native (the native's spoken language), but also to learn the language of his or her science. The latter language is '*language-2*'.

In the level of interaction with the informant and the answers the ethnographer receives, the usage of language-2 is an important factor. Many times the complexity in the level of discussion which took place amongst sanyasis or other scholars while I sat listening did not take place when I was having a discussion with them. This situation changed when I started speaking in language-2, the language of their Shastra.

In personal conversations with those who have done fieldwork among such experts or scientists of the modern world, the importance of the acquisition of language-2 was considered critical. Byron Good,[9] at the Department of Social Medicine Harvard, himself went to medical school for two years attending 30 weeks of classes. This he told us was done for two reasons. Firstly, it would enable him to know how the doctor's world was formed. But, secondly and more importantly, he wanted to overcome the barrier and difficulty that doctors encountered while answering questions asked by social scientists. He highlighted the different sort of discourses between specialists and between a specialist and a non-specialist.

In many of her interviews with microbiologists (while working on a project on 'Social Science and Immunisation'), Veena Das emphasises the need to speak in the language of the microbiologist. For example, if one is talking about cholera to an expert, one needs to be aware of new strains of the virus and their names, the way in which immunisation prevents the spread of cholera, and other such technical details. This language-2 is important for a fruitful dialogue.

I am not suggesting that fieldwork requiring language-2 is necessarily superior to fieldwork where this is not required, in less literate cultures or where informants are forthcoming about themselves (their being secretive, if at all, is not because of language-2). The study of these societies or communities may require equal if not more effort and there may be many other unique problems that such an enterprise poses.

The ethnographer's birth or caste status should not imply an 'automatic' access into the native's world-view. M.N. Srinivas's observations on the matter are very pertinent here. He writes:

> It is only when he chooses his own specific group within his own society that he might have some *knowledge* as distinct from a sense of *familiarity*. But there are *different levels of knowledge* and the anthropologist may have only a superficial knowledge of the culture of his own group. For instance, I am a Sri Vaishnava Brahmin by birth, but it will take me years to do a proper anthropological study of a Sri Vaishnava community, and a lifetime to master the complex theology and ritual of different groups and subsets among them (Srinivas 1992: 148–49).

Apart from the distance that could be overcome and access gained, there were certain other issues which could not be easily bridged. This had to do with my being an investigator trained in a university and brought up in north India. My discussions and the way I approached the various members of the sect revealed to them my status as an outsider. During my interactions with the sannyasis of Udupi, I addressed them as 'swamiji'. This term is a typically north Indian usage, with the suffix '*ji*' implying respect in Hindi. The term used by the natives is *swamigalu* or *shreeoru*. The words *swami* and *shree* mean sannyasi, while both suffixes, *galu* and *oru*, imply respect similar to 'ji'. But it is only after some time that I realised that I was using a foreign nomenclature. The sannyasis understood this was due to my north Indian upbringing. There were some others from the upper part of the Deccan plateau who addressed them as swamiji and hence the sannyasis were used to it. This, however, forced me to explore my behaviour and brought to my own attention the distinct point of view on my sectarian affiliations. In the discussions with the sect's members, this was more clearly visible.

During such a discussion with a *grihastha* (or lay) Madhva about the origins of the sect, I mentioned that if he were to trace the history of his clan he, would find that his ancestors were Advaitis or Smarthas and were recently converted by immediate followers of Madhva. This enraged him a great deal and he said in Kannada:

> You boys educated in the western way learn wrong things. We have been Madhvas all along. Dvaita existed in some guise and we belonged to it. Our *mata* (doctrine) has always been there, but you will not understand this and even if you do, your examiner will reject it.

On asking him why he thought so, he replied:

> There was a similar student doing his Ph.D. on Madhva philosophy from Mysore university. During his Ph.D. defence, he had to say many things in favour of Advaita and he felt embarrassed to say that Madhva had refuted Shankara, all because his examiner was a Smartha. You may also have to say many things to please your examiners and get your degree. You are bound to misrepresent us.

In another discussion, a scholar categorised me as an outsider because I would use the tools of modern scientific discourse rather than rely on traditional logic. His words were, 'Most outsiders do not do a complete study of Madhva's philosphy and hence give an erroneous if not an incomplete picture.' Another brahmin, after reading some sections I had written on the notions of detachment (*vairagya*), cautioned me against the possibility of political or other misuse of my dissertation.

These accentuated two things. Firstly, the anxiety of the members to expose themselves to interpretations by a person who uses techniques not learnt in the traditional set up. Secondly, it displayed my alienness from my own sect. This distance was not always the result of a subconscious or conscious application of the tools of 'science'. There were instances when the disagreement was from within tradition as will be evident in some of the discussions with the members of the matha (Chapters 4 and 5). On some occasions (wherever I thought it would not have an adverse effect on my stay in Udupi), I did voice my disagreements about the process of instruction, the way of the sannyasi and so on. For instance, a woman (whose husband had been critical of my methods in undersanding historical debates) spoke to me about her dissatisfaction with the rule excluding women from patha (formal instruction) when given by a sannyasi. She was almost in tears when she complained that her husband did not allow her to go with him to patha. She, did, however, manage to go alone to those places which were not restrictive and encouraged women's participation. I am quite certain that had any of the conservative members of the matha heard me criticising this practice, they would have been very upset. Besides this silencing, there are elements in the dissertation which could lead to certain objections.[10] I have often thought— what if this were to be read by the sannyasis—would I be forbidden to enter certain spaces or meet pontiffs even outside Udupi? This is a risk the ethnographer takes when he or she chooses to study his or her own community. In this respect, it would have been much easier studying another sect or matha. Bourdieu quotes Die Fachel who says:

> Anyone who rejects the pleasure and easy profit of long-distance criticism, in order to investigate his immediate neighbourhood, which everything bids him hold sacred, must expect the torments of subjective persecution (Bourdieu 1988: 5).[11]

While this book is not in any sense a critique of the matha, I wish to emphasise a certain tension in expression and in the process of writing. There was often a 'stuttering' before I could find my voice. The voice moves on different planes; sometimes critical, often sympathetic and sometimes without any recognisable view, the faceless voice. The representation here moves between all these various voices, depending on the context. There is no single stance that I have taken because the material is diverse, frequently moving from one conceptual plane to another.

A few words about some of the terms I have used. The word 'swamiji' is retained more for its heuristic value as it seeks to delineate the sectarian status of the Madhva sanyasis. There is a wide range of vocabulary used to denote the renouncers such as monk, mendicant, ascetic, *sadhu, bhiku, muni, swami, baba* and *sannyasi*. These contexts move from the renouncers bound by an institution to the renouncers who have abandoned the world. There is a necessity to pin down the correct usage with the type of renouncers. The other terms used for the swamijis of the Udupi mathas are sanyasi, pontiffs and *mathadipati* (the head of the matha). Similarly, the institutions in the anthropological literature are referred to as matha, monastery, *sangh, panth, marg*, sect and the like. The monastery of Udupi is called matha by the people of Udupi in Sanskrit, Kannada and Tulu. This usage is retained as it is. The caste group is spelt Brahmin, while the philosophical reference to God is denoted by the word Brahman.

Scheme of Chapters

This study consists of seven chapters including the introduction and the conclusion. The chapters deal with diverse issues, themes and concepts, and I am wary of imposing a theoretical sense of unity on them. However, each of the ensuing chapters is organised around certain major issues. The second chapter deals with the organisational aspects of the mathas in Udupi, with a special focus on the main Krishna matha.

The third chapter provides an analysis of four spaces in the main Krishna matha where sacred food (prasada) is served, namely the *mrsthanna bhojana*, chowki, ground and first floor of the *bhojanshala*. Within each space, there are differences in the variety of food and the way in which it is prepared and served. This further orders the variables such as caste, seating arrangements, dress codes, singing of *bhajans*, etc. Food/prasada does not have an unidemensional meaning even within the Udupi matha. It has different connotations for various groups such as the gods, sanyasis, the Madhva Brahmins, the non-Madhva Brahmins and the other varnas and serves different functions. An understanding of the various usages of prasada shows how food, as a medium of expressing a particular ideology, structures the Hindu community surrounding the Udupi matha.

The fourth and fifth chapters focus on the cultural production and transmission of traditional knowledge. These chapters seek to highlight the connection between what is read and learnt, and how life is lived. Again, while there are philosophers and philosophies throughout the world, it is not always easy to spot and distinguish a follower or disciple of a certain philosopher. For example, one may not recognise a 'Sartrian', a 'Merleau-Pontian' or a phenomenologist, until one reads his works or talks to him or her at an intense level. In most sectarian traditions of India (especially those that consciously attach themselves to a philosopher), one can, by and large, spot a person who belongs to the Madhva, Vishishtadvaita or Advaita sects. This is possible because of the body markings and dress codes that differentiate them.

Apart from this outward appearance, at a deeper and more conceptual level, the life led by the students of these philosophers or philosophies articulate a recognisable world-view. This orders their relations to people and things, in what they reject and what they accept.

Pierrie Bourdieu's frame of analysis helps us in understanding this cultural production of knowledge. Bourdieu criticises the scientific stance which distances the anthropologist and displays a spectacle rather than a practice (1977: 2, 26–27). According to Paul Rabinow, Foucault also stresses the same by differing from Rorty and emphasising the treatment of philosophical ideas as social practices and not just chance twists in a conversation or in philosophy (1986: 240).

Traditional knowledge and the teaching of it has been understood to be authoritarian, often stressing the authority of tradition and the *guru* or teacher. The study of the Madhva sect points to a more complex arrangement.

Knowledge and belief play hide and seek with each other in the arena of the human mind. The belief and faith in the tradition and what the guru says is countered by the intellectual tendency to question and contradict. A householder scholar of the Udupi matha went so far as to say, 'Traditional education creates a fence around your thinking. The learning is from mind to books rather than from books to the mind'. What he seems to be suggesting is the preconceived notion of tradition which presents the texts or words of the guru in an exalted mode. The non-sannyasi gurus have more freedom to change or at least modify the structure of the instruction by permitting women and non-Brahmins to become students. There is active debate on many of the issues in Udupi and outside, as a result of which, new ways of living and thinking are emerging.

Chapter 5 specifically deals with the discourses in the transmission of knowledge. Complex arguments and terse textual exegesis, often the context of patha (instruction) cannot be duplicated in a more general public lecture (upannyasa). The difference in discourses suggest that the context and the identity of the one to whom the discourse is addressed, becomes very important.

Bakhtin provides an instructive tool to analyse this 'dialogic activity'. The styles of discourse are differentiated according to the content of the utterances and this difference can create a hierarchy in terms of reality or adherence to the actual philosophy.

Often, the process of simplification which the gurus aim at in the upannyasa is inevitable and not always undesirable. But it does affect the complexity and reliability of the exegesis.

A similar movement is encountered when Indian sociologists write articles for newspapers, on the Mandal Commission or the religion of India, for example; or when a classical singer, afraid to bore his or her uninitiated audience sings light bhajans and simplified songs. The term that I use for all these adaptations of style to accommodate a particular addressee (whatever be the desired goal) is *upannyasanisation* (*upannyasa-nisation*). This usage helps distinguish those who 'belong' to the discipline or vocation and those who do not, but have a general interest (the addressee in public lectures, etc.). This distinction cannot be a straitjacketed one as a merger between these two genres is possible.

The sixth chapter deals with the understanding of renunciation as practised within the sectarian domain. It analyses the relation between the householder (mainly the Madhva Brahmin householders) and the sannyasis of Udupi.

Sannyasa is undertood in two ways. (i) It is first a 'value' which specifies a way of life and can be adopted theoretically by any member of the sect. In this sense it is synonymous with vairagya (detachment). (ii) Secondly, sannyasa refers to the sannyasi within the sannyasa ashrama. It is in this sense ashrama-bound and is a specialised trait of renouncers. This distinction emerged from the field and in interactions with the people. The chapter uses many direct quotes from the informants' speech—references from the *Bhagavad Gita*, the *Bhagavata Purana* and the *Upanishads* which were freely evoked in discussions. Renunciation is not understood so much as a negative injunction (to leave), but as a positive transcendence and attachment to Brahman.

The concluding chapter provides an analytical overview of how the matha relates to the modern world. Its interaction with contemporary values and institutions changes the face of tradition and establishes its relevance in prevailing times.

The main significance of this study, as I see it, is the analysis of Sanskritic Hinduism in its sectarian expression. By concentrating on the variety within Brahminical sects, the study underscores the plurality of the Indian world. Even within the sect, pluralism is evident in their practices and conception of food, knoweldge and renunciation.

When one talks of God, *maya*, ego or self and the relation of man to society (concepts constantly being used in sociology and related subjects), one assumes that the construction of Brahminical thought and of Indian philosophy, has been in general, Advaitic. One assumes the Advaitic standpoint to be universal. This study seeks to demonstrate that there is a need to relook at religious studies in India keeping in mind the diversity in sectarian traditions and life-style (*achara*) and philosophy (*vichara*) that go with it. This it does by illustrating what it means to live traditions and keep them alive in contemporary contexts.

Notes

1. This statement reflects Madhva's insistence to move beyond first appearances, an aspect Madhva developes with great care, but is seldom emphasised by westerners and Indians alike. It is similar to Karl Marx's statement emphasising a theory of suspicion which draws connections between practice and knowledge—'To leave error unrefuted is to encourage intellectual immortality.' In both cases it is not possible to unearth the potential of these thoughts without an indepth study of texts, whether *Das Capital* or *Anu Vyakhyana*. This is an enterprise conceivable only in philosophical discourse.
2. Udupi is also spelt as 'Udipi', however, the former spelling has been used consistently in this monograph.
3. Rosaldo underlines the nature of information that is received from a native: 'In dialogue with informants, both parties accommodate one another, in making their lives open to our questions and to form a discourse that begs for system and reflection. The natives who 'inform' us construct what are always situated and necessarily partial interpretations of more complexly textured modes of life' (1980: 30).
4. Das commenting upon Dumont's method writes that Dumont not only rejects the dichotomy between thought and behaviour but 'also insists that an explanatory model cannot be limited to a replication of observed reality… Whether one agees with the substantive parts of Dumont's writings or not, the altered conception of the nature of anthropological explanation itself constitutes a landmark in Indian sociology' (Das, 1982).
5. Of course, a study in which such access is denied could in itself provide interesting insights. *See* for instance, Frederique Marglin's work. *Wives of the God-King: The Rituals of the Devadasis of Puri* (1985).

6. I got a chance to briefly experience what the status of an outsider is in another matha or sect, when I visited the Advaita matha in Sringere, I announced myself as a Madhva. This created a certain turbulence among the administrators, the swamiji and his close associates. Although my academic investigation was smooth, there was a marked difference in the degree of acceptance and there was no effort to 'resocialise' me. I would not have been aware of this, had I not been with the Madhvas of the Udupi matha.
   The visit to Sringere also put many of the practices of the Madhvas in relief. To view contrasting behaviour made possible the explanation of the taken for granted or given.
7. With respect to that particular sannyasi the right to know was bestowed upon me after this incident. I was presented with the customary reward (*bahumana* in Kannada) given to scholars and students for their achievement in Shastra or for simply presenting a discourse. This consisted of a coconut, betel leaves and nuts, fruits, the prasada of the deity and a cash prize.
8. I have been interested in Indian philosophical systems for several years and have received training under gurus on some of the traditional texts.
9. Professor Good visited the Department of Sociology in 1995 and spoke to us about his work.
10. Kirin Narayan chooses to study the stories told by a swamiji in Nasik and avoids a life history of the swamiji. She writes, 'If I had focussed primarily on his life history, for example, I would have had to hazard psychological interpretations that may have delighted scholars but alienated me from those whom I cared about in Nasik' (Narayan, 1991: 59).
11. The process of writing reflects this internal debate between moving beyond the native's perceptions and identifying with it. Complicated by the fact that my 'self' is involved both in the subject-matter and in that which is perceived as distinct from it. This distinction takes the form of disagreement and criticism, expressed or concealed.

2

The Madhva Matha in Udupi: Social, Spatial and Temporal Organisation

Location of Udupi

Udupi is a small town in south Karnataka. When I did my fieldwork there in 1981[1] it had a population of 34,000. Since ancient times, Udupi has been known as a sacred centre because of its temples. According to Puranic tradition, the city lies in the holy land of Parashurama, an incarnation of Vishnu. The region between the Arabian sea and the Western Ghats stretching from Nasik in Maharashtra to Kanyakumari at the southern end of the peninsula is known as the holy land of Parashurama. When sage Parashurama appeared on this earth, the land he had conquered was gifted away to the great saint Kashyapa. Since Parashurama could not live on land gifted away, he created a new land for his residence by reclaiming it from the ocean. According to legend, 'Parashurama shot his arrow, the water retreated and stayed back, a new landscape appeared and this was known as Parashurama Kshetra.' (Govindachar et al. 1984: 1).

Within the Parashurama Kshetra (Parashurama's region), the area lying in the Karnataka state from Kasargod to Gokarna is known as Tulava country. In his work *Ram Sandesham*, the fifteenth century saint Rajarajeshwara wrote:

> Go to one of the horns of the high peaks of Sahyadri and look down. The clouds float about. Look down farther with your eyes wide open. That is the land known as Tulava country. The region spreading from Gokarna up to the sea is the abode of the learned people who have mastered the Vedas. This is the new creation of Parashurama, the enemy of the Kshatriya race.

Udupi is one of the seven holy places[2] in Tulunad, described as *Rupya* or *Rajata Peetha*. Both words mean the 'silver seat'. Although Udupi as a place of pilgrimage is not at par with the *sapta puri* (seven sacred cities: Ayodhya, Mathura, Hardwar, Kashi, Kanchi, Avantika and Dvaraka), it has been a sacred space famous in the past for the Ananteshwara and Chandramauleshwara (Shiva) temples. The folk tradition associates Udupi with *nagas* or aquatic divinities. However, today the town of Udupi is known for its Madhva matha or monasteries, besides of course, the Udupi hotels spread throughout India and the world. The sacred geography now surrounds the birth and activities of the founder of Dvaita philosophy, Madhvacharya, and the icon of Krishna he worshipped.

The narrative and myths surrounding sacred geographic spaces have changed over time. But geography changes more slowly than the history attached to it (Eck 1983: 36) and the sacred sites, hills and ponds in Rajata Peetha or Udupi continue to attract worshippers much as before:

> The particular myths and stories may come and go, the narrative may change or be forgotten; but the hilltop, the pool and the grave remain (*ibid.*).

I shall not expand on the sacred geography of Udupi as a town, but rather focus more centrally on the monasteries of Udupi.

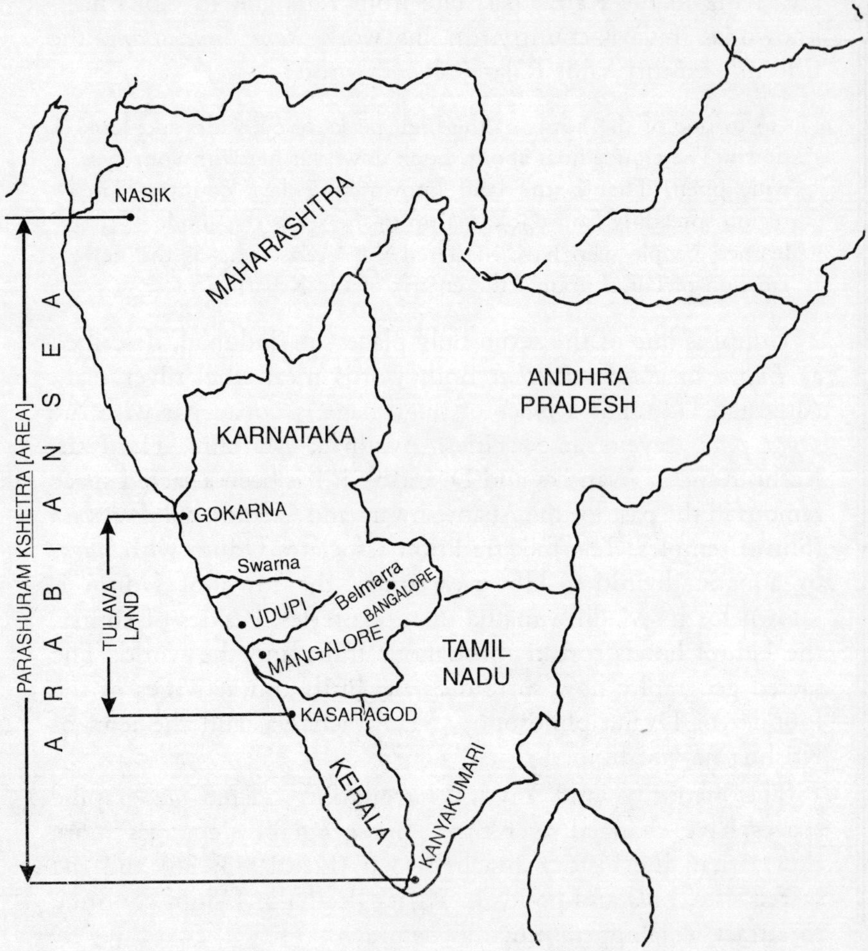

Map 1: Geographical situation of Udupi and its traditional location

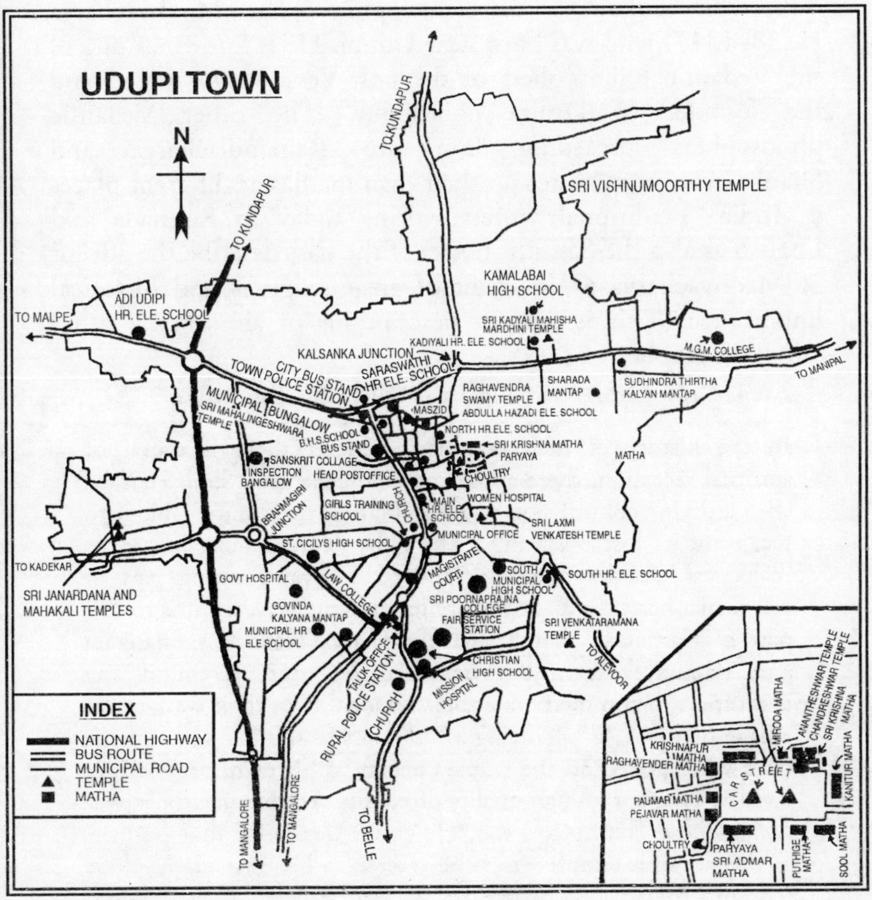

Map 2: Udupi town 1992

The Organisation into Mathas

The Udupi matha is made up of eight sub-mathas and is hence collectively called the 'Udupi *ashta* (eight) matha'. These mathas owe their origin to the saint philosopher Madhvacharya (1238–1317) who was born near Udupi. He is known as one of the Vedantic philosophers of the post-Veda Vyasa period and the founder of Dvaita philosophy. The other Vedantic philosophers preceding him are Ramanujacharya and Shankaracharya, who set up their own mathas at different places in India. Traditional writers writing today in Kannada and English as also the Sanskrit books of the past describe the advent of Madhvacharya as an event of great religious and historical importance (This is true of descriptions of almost any other saint-philosopher of India).

An Udupi scholar writing in English has this to say,

> In the history of each country whenever there is moral or spiritual recession, there appear on the scene great souls charged with a divine commission to rehabilitate society and enable it to recapture its lost position... The glory of Karnataka lies in its dialectical wealth. The tiny land of Tulavas forming part of Karnataka has thus made history in a unique way, for it is to this part of Karnataka that Sri Madhvacharya belongs... Shankara and Ramanujacharya did not feel the urge to found any institution to commemorate their personality in their own native village or town. While being a humanist in the full sense of the term who looked on the whole country as his own, Sri Madhva had the essential human quality of natural attachment to his own *janmabhumi* (birthplace) too. He chose Udupi for that purpose as the site of a temple which he erected in his own matha there for Lord Sri Krishna, where he installed an icon of the beloved of the Gopis, in one of the most bewitching poses of the boyhood of Krishna; the lord standing erect holding a churning rod in the right hand and a churning rope in the left, with a heavenly smile on the Divine lips (Keshava Das 1968).

The matha in which the Krishna icon is placed is the main Krishna matha. Spread out in a rectangular shape along Car

Street, with the main matha in the corner are the eight sub-mathas of Udupi (Map 3). Madhavacharya appointed eight of his disciples (all *bal-sannyasis*, i.e. those taking up sannyasa at a young age before marriage) as pontiff to the mathas. It is customary to call these eight mathas after the name of villages wherein the landed properties belonging to the matha were situated. Thus, the matha that had its property in the village Adamar is now called Adamar matha.

These mathas were paired by Madhvacharya that is, each of the mathas have a *Dvanda* matha (a paired matha). This was done to substitute for the responsibility of looking after the main Krishna matha in case the matha looking after the Krishna matha had any problems, or if the saint of one of the mathas died and there was no substitute, or the junior pontiff was too young. In such cases the pontiff from one of the Dvanda mathas took over temporarily.

The names of the founder disciples of the eight mathas and the present number of sannyasis in each matha are as follows:

Table 1

Sl. No.	*Matha*	*No. of swamijis in each matha at present*	*Founder saints*
1.	Phalimar matha	2	Hrishikesha Tirtha
2.	Adamar matha	2	Narhari Tirtha
3.	Krishnapura matha	1	Janardhana Tirtha
4.	Puttige matha	1	Upendra Tirtha
5.	Shirur matha	1	Vamana Tirtha
6.	Sode matha[3]	1	Vishnu Tirtha
7.	Kaniyur matha	2	Rama Tirtha
8.	Pejavara matha	2	Adhokshaja Tirtha

The other disciples of Madhvacharya, both pontifical and lay, continued the tradition and established mathas outside Udupi mainly in Karnataka with branches all over India today (not necessarily looked after by bal-sannyasis).

There is also the tradition of *bidi-sannyasis* (mostly Madhvas) or free-sannyasis who are not attached to any particular matha

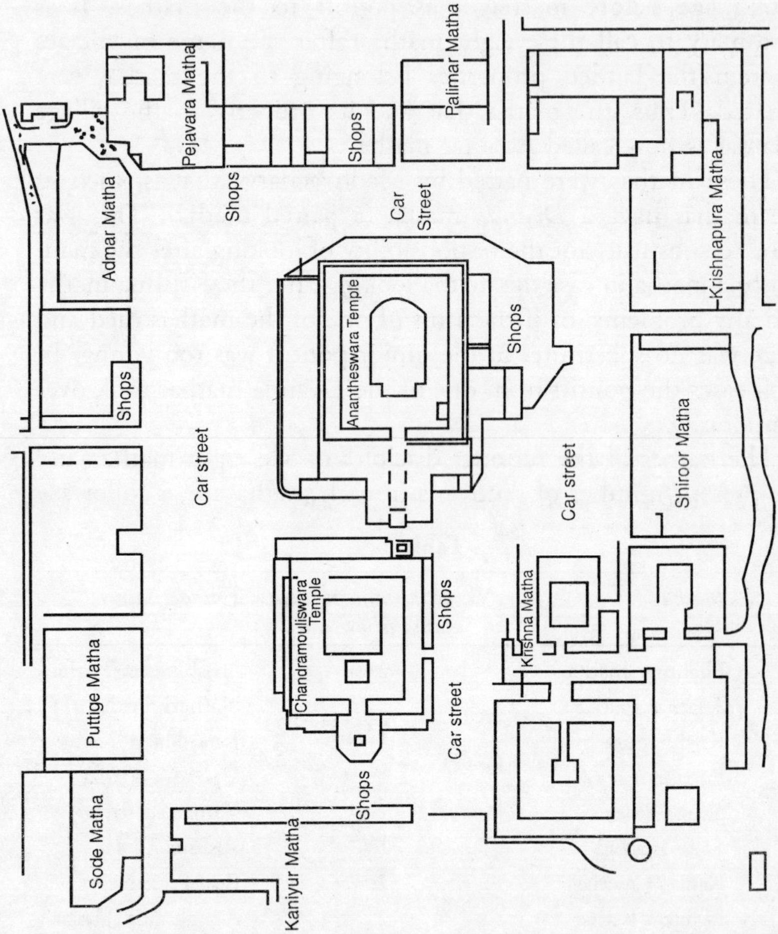

Map 3: The temple square: A sketch plan

and are free from all responsibilities of looking after the matha. Today, this tradition is not very well developed and they are not as important to the Madhva sect as the mathadipatis (or matha heads). Nevertheless, bidi-sannyasis do come and stay in the Madhva matha and participate in the activities of the matha. Those wanting to be bidi-sannyasis come to Udupi and are given *diksha* (initiated into sannyasa) by one of the pontiffs of the Udupi matha.

Table 2 traces the genealogy and development of the mathas in the Madhva or the Dvaita tradition.[4] (Acharya, 1989; Bhat 1975; Govindacharya 1985; Nayak and Gopal 1990; Rao 1989; Sharma 1981). In all there are 24 Madhva mathas. However, only the Udupi matha sannyasis have the privilege of performing worship for the icon of Krishna installed by Madhvacharya. Although these mathas have the main centre in Karnataka, their branches are spread all over India and are known by their affiliation to the main matha.

The Paryaya System

The pontiffs of Udupi undertake the responsibility of worshipping Lord Krishna and manage the main matha by rotation for a fixed period of time. This system is known as *paryaya* (succession) and the swamiji (pontiff) in charge of worship and other rituals is known as the paryaya swamiji.

Up to the period of Vadiraja Swamy (1480–1600), the paryaya took place once in two months. Thus, each swamiji or sub-matha used to get their turn once in sixteen months. Vadiraja (of Sode matha) then changed the system. He started the tradition of a two-year term for the paryaya. Acordingly, at the time of my fieldwork, each matha had completed 29 two-year terms of the paryaya. The thirtieth cycle began in 1986–87 with the paryaya of Phalimar matha and ended in 2000–2001 with the paryaya of Pejavara matha.

About four to five months before the paryaya ceremony, the swamiji goes on a pilgrimage to different holy places. This is

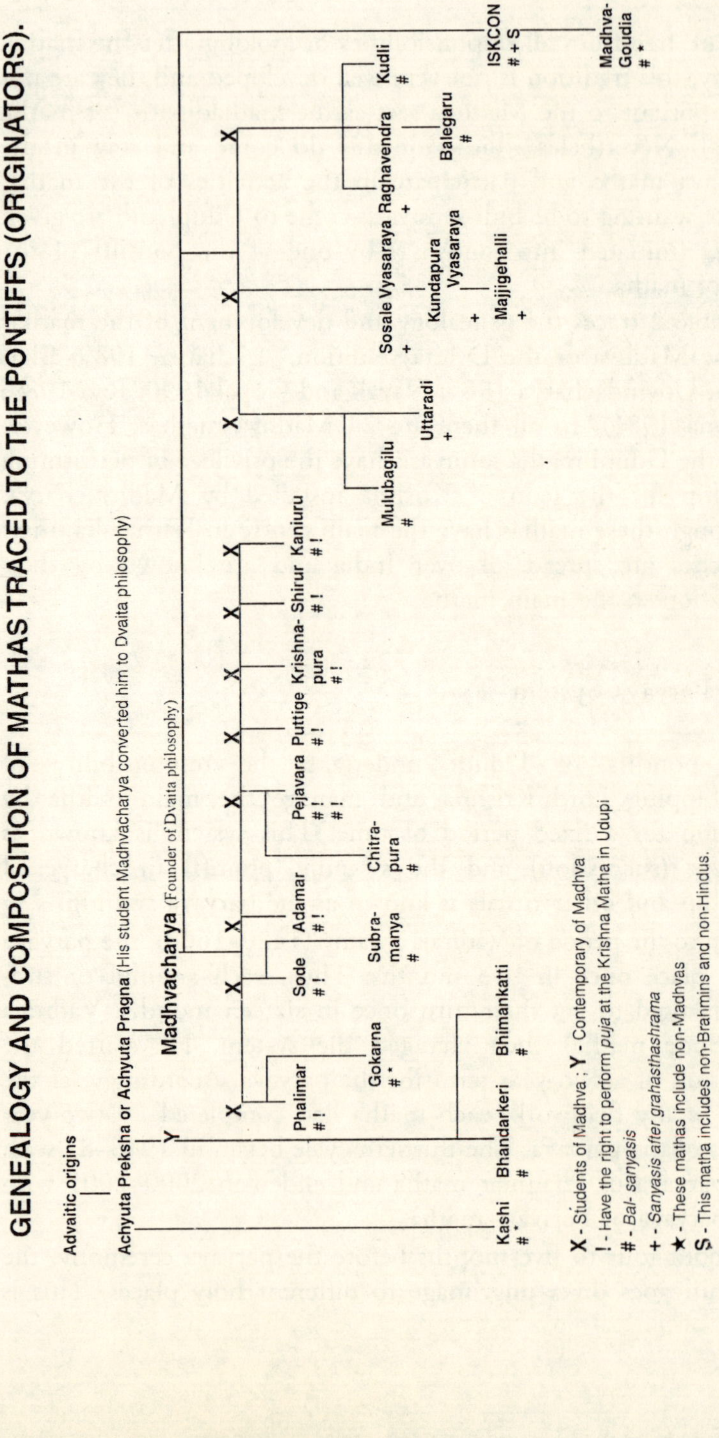

GENEALOGY AND COMPOSITION OF MATHAS TRACED TO THE PONTIFFS (ORIGINATORS).
Advaitic origins
Achyuta Preksha or Achyuta Pragna (His student Madhvacharya converted him to Dvaita philosophy)
Y
Madhvacharya (Founder of Dvaita philosophy)
X X X X X X X X X X
Kashi # *
Bhandarkeri #
Bhimankatti #
Gokarna # *
Phalimar # !
Sode # !
Subra-manya #
Adamar # !
Chitra-pura #
Pejavara # !
Puttige # !
Krishna-pura # !
Shirur # !
Kaniuru # !
Mulubagilu #
Uttaradi +
Sosale Vyasaraya +
Kundapura Vyasaraya +
Majjigehalli +
Raghavendra +
Balegaru #
Kudli #
ISKCON # + S
Madhva-Goudia # *
X - Students of Madhva ; Y - Contemporary of Madhva
! - Have the right to perform puja at the Krishna Matha in Udupi
- Bal- sanyasis
+ - Sanyasis after grahasthashrama
★ - These mathas include non-Madhvas
S - This matha includes non-Brahmins and non-Hindus.

Table 2

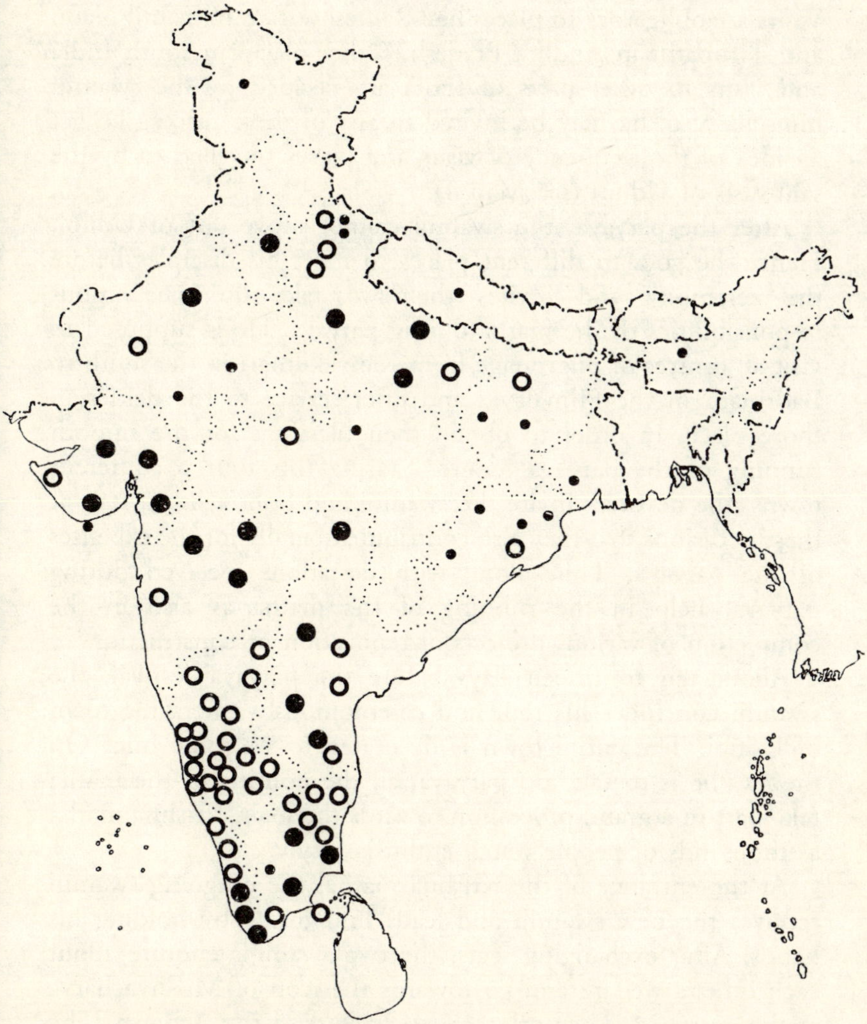

○ Visited frequently (usually for discourse or chaturmasya. Also places of pilgrimage)

● Visited sometimes (mostly during paryaya or because they are temple towns).

• Rarely visited.

Map 4: Paryaya purva sanchara

known as *paryaya purva sanchara* (the visiting before paryaya). Visits are obligatory to places like Rameshwaram in Tamil Nadu and Tirupathi in Andhra Pradesh. Other places in south India and visits to other parts of India are decided by the swamiji himself. Also, he may be invited to any of these places. To get an idea of the frequency of visits and places travelled to by the sannyasis of Udupi (see Map 4).

After the paryaya, the swamiji cannot move out of Udupi. Hence, he goes to different places to meet his disciples before the ceremony and invites them to take up the various responsibilities of the matha during paryaya. He is supposed to visit all centres of pilgrimage from Kanyakumari in the south to Badrinath in the Himalayas and offer service to the deities in those places in order to obtain their blessings for the smooth running of the paryaya tenure. During this tour to different towns, the devotees invite the swamiji and honour him. It is at these occasions that they also contribute liberally for the expenses of the paryaya. This, along with donations received during paryaya, help in the running of the matha as also in the completion of various projects of renovation or construction.

About ten to fifteen days before the paryaya festival, the swamiji concludes his tour and ceremoniously enters the town of Udupi. The entire town is decorated to welcome him. On the day he is to take up paryaya, all the pontiffs of the matha take part in a grand procession towards the main Krishna matha as thousands of people watch enthusiastically.

At the entrance of the Krishna matha, the outgoing swamiji receives the new swamiji and leads him inside by holding his hands. After exchanging seats, the two swamijis enquire about each other's welfare and go towards the icon of Madhvacharya at the entrance. They offer *arghya* (water) to the Acharya. The outgoing swamiji hands over to his successor the *akshaya patre*, the age-old vessel preserved from the time of Madhvacharya, its ladle, as well as the keys to the shrine. With this ritual, the management of the Krishna matha is officially transferred to the new paryaya swamiji.

The last programme of the ceremony is a big congregation

known as Darbar sabha at the Rajangana. All the swamijis come in a procession at about 7.00 a.m. to this auditorium, that can accommodate about twenty thousand people. By the time the swamijis arrive, the place is packed with people.

Leaders and luminaries from different sections of society felicitate the new paryaya swamiji on this occasion. The swamiji honours scholars, social workers and officials. Names of new office-bearers and employees of the paryaya matha are announced. The devotees offer their contribution to the new paryaya swamiji. After this the new swamiji conducts the rituals of the day for the first time.[5]

Each paryaya swamiji undertakes many projects that he wishes to fulfil during his tenure. These revolve around traditional education and help for the poor. In recent years, it has become customary to undertake some development project for the town of Udupi, either through new constructions or through renovation. During my stay, the paryaya swamiji had constructed a structure to mark the entrance of Udupi. He also constructed a large building called the Gita Mandir near the matha, which he intended for a museum of books, statues, paintings, etc. In order to mark out this construction as distinct from other constructions undertaken by the Municipal or State bodies, the paryaya swamiji encouraged the participation of devotees by asking them to write the *shlokas* (verses) of the *Bhagavad Gita* in a book. The participants were asked to renounce all vices before they wrote the verses. These books were later buried at the site of the building. Along with the written shlokas, the devotees also gave their contributions in the form of money and gifts. The paryaya swamiji next in line had already announced his plan to construct a bus stand along with a guest house.

Layout and Resources of the Krishna Matha

The Krishna icon in the main matha attracts devotees from all castes throughout India. This flow of devotees, as in a temple, differentiates the main Krishna matha from the sub-mathas.

Although the sub-mathas have their own gods, they are only visited by the Brahmins who are affiliated to the specific sub-mathas as sannyasis, students, administrators or guests. The presence of the Krishna icon thus brings about changes in the matha and renders it a quasi temple. However, the main door does not in any way resemble the architecture of the south Indian temples with the traditional *gopuram* (a tall structure constructed over the main gate). The board on the main door also specifies that this is the 'Shri Krishna Matha' and not a temple as given in the Karnataka State Gazetteer (Kamath 1983: 1366).

As one enters the shrine, the reception office of the matha is on the right. This office welcomes special guests. It is the place where devotees pay and book in advance for the *puja* (worship) they wish to conduct for the Krishna icon in the matha. The office provides a list (in English and Kannada) with rates of the pujas from which the devotees select (see Table 3 for a list in English).

A few yards further, a path leads to a sacred tank known as Madhva *sarovara* (Madhva lake). To the west is the entrance of the shrine which is usually closed and only opened on Vijayadashami (some time in October).

To the right, in front of the shrine, is a covered space (*mantapa*) supported by wooden columns. In between this space, and the sanctum sanctorum (*garbha gudi* or *griha*) is a small passage and a window through which visitors can look at the icon inside. This window with nine square holes is know as *navagraha kitiki* (window of nine planets). There is no entrance to the sanctum sanctorum in the front. The entrance is from the side and is restricted to sannyasis and their helpers only.

Though the main architectural pattern of the matha remained unchanged for centuries, its outer appearance has changed due to renovations at different times. To the west in front of the mantapa is a hall known as *chandrashale*. Kanaka kitiki (Kanaka Dasa's window) is on the wall of this hall. Scholars recite epics and scriptures here in the evening. In the northern corner is another small mantapa reserved for the worship of sacred texts

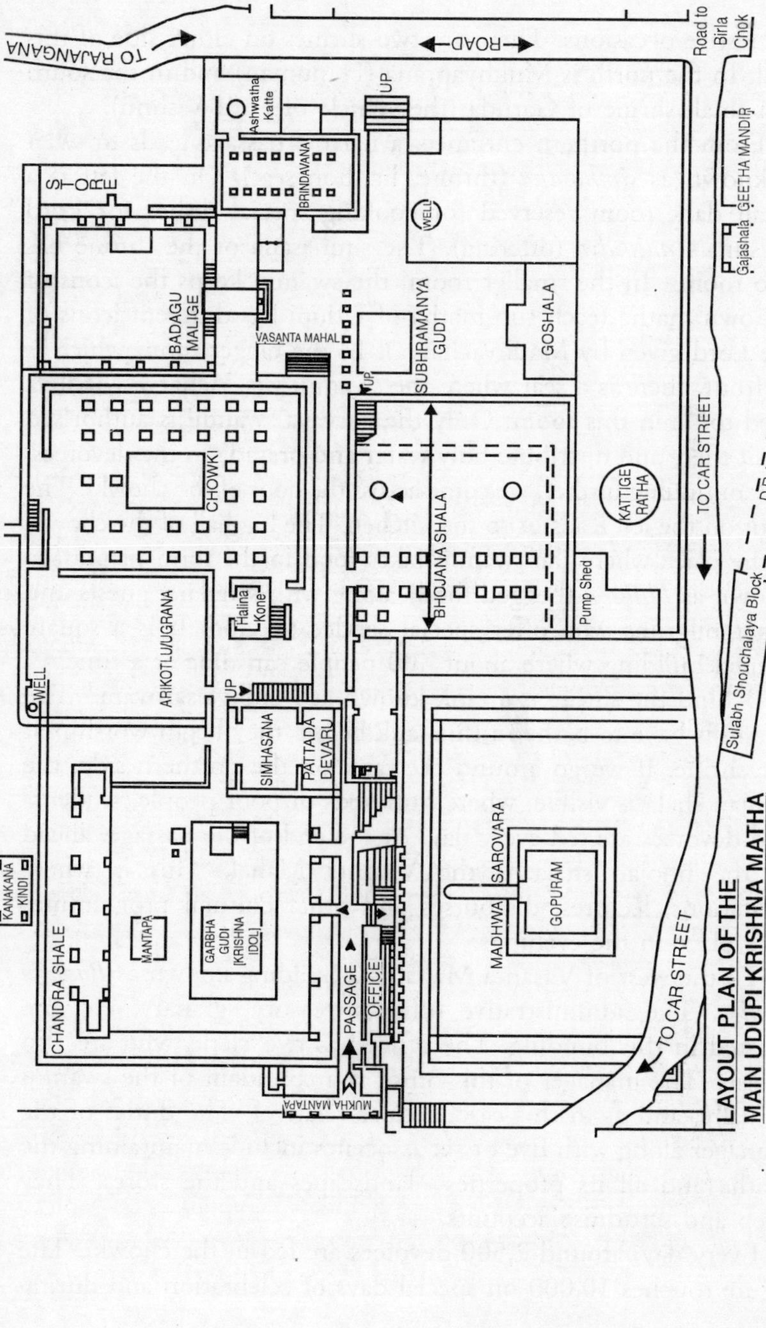

LAYOUT PLAN OF THE MAIN UDUPI KRISHNA MATHA

Map 5

on festive occasions. There are two shrines on either side of this hall. In the north is Mukhyaprana (Hanuman) and in the south is a small shrine of Garuda (the vehicle of Lord Vishnu).

From the northern entrance, a narrow passage leads to what is known as *simhasana* (throne, lit. lion seat). On the left is a small dark room reserved for cooking special dishes for Lord Krishna's *naivedya* (offering). The simhasana or the throne has two rooms. In the smaller room, the swamiji keeps the icons of his own matha (each sub-matha of Udupi has different icons of the Lord given by Madhvacharya). In the bigger room which is in front, there is a seat where the swamiji sits. Acharya Madhva used to sit in this room. Only the paryaya swamiji is authorised to sit there and distribute holy water and prasada to the devotees.

Continuing further, we come across the door of the chowki. The door on the left leads us to the kitchen. The big hall of the chowki is the place where the swamiji takes food in the form of prasada known as *bhiksha* (begged food) along with scholars, guests and other pilgrims who offer special service to God. It is a square shaped building where about 400 people can dine at a time.

Behind the shrine is a tank known as Madhva sarovara.[6] The swamijis have to bathe in this tank before they begin worship at the shrine. If we go around the tank on the northern side, the bhojan shala is visible, where hundreds of poor people, students and devotees are fed every day. At the end of the passage, ahead of the bhojan shala is the Vasanta Mahal. This is where recitations, lectures, discourses and other cultural programmes take place in the evenings.

To the west of Vasanta Mahal is a building known as *Badagu malige*. The administrative offices, treasury, granary, etc. are located in this building. The office has two clerks who are also typists. The manager of this office is a confidant of the swamiji (usually, and as in this case, a close relative). The duties of the manager along with five or six associates include maintaining the matha and all its properties—landscapes and the stores. They keep and scrutinise accounts.

Every day, around 2,500 devotees are fed in the chowki. The figure touches 10,000 on special days of celebration and during the paryaya festivities, as many as 25,000 people recieve the sacred food. A daily supply of food includes around 1,000 kg of vegetables which come either from the matha's own garden, or are purchased from the market. Apart from the resources of the matha and the money collected by the swamiji during pre-paryaya visits, devotees coming in daily give *kanike* (anonymous donations) and gifts to the matha.

Some of the other assistant managers of the matha look after the distribution of prasada. They look after the guests and screen the devotees before letting them in, either to meet the swamiji or to have prasada at the chowki. These officials are all male Madhva brahmins. The office situated at Badagu malige also issues passes to students living in Udupi and those who have their food at the bhojanshala. The sentry of the bhojanshala (here usually a non-Brahmin) allows students only after he has seen the passes. The sentry receives a fixed salary, but the other officials do not work for a salary. Working in the paryaya itself is considered to give *punya* (merit). There are, of course, non-tangible rewards in terms of control over goods and resources.

Also within the Badagu malige are rooms where the paryaya swamiji and other invited swamijis live and give patha (instruction) to the disciples. The matha runs a Sanskrit college in Udupi and the professors and scholars attached to the matha often use some of the rooms as their studies. Special places are reserved for scholars of different subjects—Vedanta, *dharmashastra, tarka* (logic) and *vyakarna* (grammar). Often the paryaya swamiji employs teachers to teach recitation of the Vedas to young boys. These teachers are usually Madhva males, but during the paryaya of my stay, the swamiji had employed a Smartha or Advaitic Brahmin and he was allowed to stay in a room in Badagu malige.

To the east of Vasanta Mahal is located the shrine of Lord Subramanya. Towards the north, behind Vasanta Mahal is what is known as *vrindavana*,[7] the burial ground of the pontiffs. There are forty-three vrindavanas. There is also a banyan (*ashvattha*) tree here. The swamijis go around this tree before they offer oblation to the vrindavana of their preceptors (not all sannyasis of the Udupi matha are buried here, most of them have vrindavanas in their mathas in the villages). From here is visible the vast level ground known as rajangana, where the paryaya festival culminates.

The Process of Worship

One of the distinguishing features of the Udupi matha is in the area of worship. While the deities of other places of worship are worshipped by non-sannyasi *archakas/pujaris* (priests), the main deity (Krishna) at Udupi is worshipped by a sannyasi (renouncer). The paryaya swamiji, apart from worshipping the icon of Krishna, also worships the icon given to his matha by Madhvacharya. All sannyasis who belong to the eight sub-mathas perform this worship to their respective icons which they carry with them wherever they go.

The difference in the process of worship by a sannyasi and a non-sannyasi can be comprehended at two levels. At one level, the worship of God by a sannyasi (renouncer) is considered as superior to that of a non-sannyasi as it is not done with any expectation other than its primary objective of paying obeisance. Corroborations to this can be had from primary sources like *Bhagavad Gita* and *Bhagavata*, among others. The state of mind of a sannyasi is best described in the *Bhagavad Gita* (2:55) by Krishna as *stitha pragnya*, one who has attained equilibrium and stability—one who has given up all varieties of desire for the things of the world.

The superiority of renouncement of desires was stressed by the paryaya swamiji, when he narrated an incident from the *Bhagavata Purana*. Lord Narasimha is pleased with the devotion of Prahlada and asks him to choose a boon. Prahlada, like a true renouncer, wishes for nothing other than a state of mind in which he does not need to ask for anything. The paryaya swamiji added that this was the only legitimate aspiration.

The sannyasi as well as others, try through their study of scriptures and practices to accomplish a tranquil mind undisturbed by worldly desires. This is why the devotees consider *puja* or worship at Udupi to have special significance since it is performed by 'renouncers'.

At the other level, the process of worship dwells on the difference in visualising the icon. Brahman and the demigods (dependent and working according to His will) are meditated upon in the icon and in the human body. This practice is called *tatvannyasa*. This is common to both the sannyasi and the non-sannyasi. However, the sannyasi visualises the icon from toe to head while the others do so from head to toe. In Brahman or in the icons of the Lord (Krishna etc.), the demigods in each part of the body are mediated upon as *ashrita* (under the Lord's protection) and within one's body, they are meditated upon as protecting the self under the guidance of Brahman.[8]

The *puja vidhi* (details of procedure) are outlined in a book by Madhvacharya called *Tantrasara*. Besides laying down the rules of tatvannyasa, it also rejects the practice of *bali* or sacrifice to the gods. Some of the sannyasis of the mathas depend on a book *Paramahamsa Nama Japa Puja Karma* (1976), which summarises the procedure. However, all recent publications are derived from the originals, especially the *Sanyasapaddhati* (apart from *Tantrasara*), by Vishnutirtha (14th century), the originator of the Sode matha.

Patrick Olivelle (1992) is of the opinion that apart from the sacrificial string and the top-knot, the renouncers also 'give up the use of *mantras*' (1992: 63). Although the sannyasis of Udupi renounce fire and other related rituals (along with sacrificial string and top-knot), they do not renounce all mantras or the recitation and chanting of verses from the Vedas, and the Smritis.

The Daily Routine

The following description of the puja performed was personally observed with inputs by sannyasis and their helpers. This matched well with the description in books (Govindachar 1984), and some souvenirs brought out by mathas.

Devotees can have most of these pujas performed in their name by paying for it. The act of worship is puja for the sannyasi, but in the devotee's usage it is *seva* (service) to Lord Krishna. Puja and *seva* both entail the act of honouring the deity. Babb's study in north India (1975) and Fuller's in south India (1992) both highlight that 'puja is, in the first place, an act of respectful honouring...' (Fuller 1992: 68).

Coming to Udupi from elsewhere is in itself an act of merit because one can have *darshan* (viewing the deity) and purify oneself. Most devotees and all Madhvas coming to Udupi first pay their homage to Krishna before going about their business, as if to be acknowledged by Him. As Eck emphasises, 'Beholding the image is an act of worship, and through the eyes one gains the blessings of the divine' (1981: 3). Seeing and being seen by the deity is the immediate way of attaining grace. The darshan of the holy brings benefit (which is why darshan of sannyasis is also valued). Some of the devotees, especially those belonging to the sect, besides going for darshan, also get a puja performed. The devotees coming for darshan or puja may or may not wish to fulfil a specific desire—completion of pending work, success in examination, career, etc.

The icon of Krishna is worshipped fourteen times a day by the swamiji. Here is a brief description. In each phase, the swamiji acts on the icon and also offers different kinds of food to match the time of worship and associated activities.

1. *Nirmalya Visarjana Puja*: The door of the shrine is opened at 4:00 a.m. The swamiji enters in a state of *madi*[9] (purity) after his bath. The purification of the worshipper and the implements of worship is an essential preliminary for beneficial contact with Hindu deities (Dumont 1959: 31). The swamiji goes on to remove the previous day's flowers, sacred leaves and sandal paste from the icon. He then removes the ornaments.

The icon can now be seen in its original form. This vision of the Lord is known as *Vishvarupa Darshana*. The food offering at this service consists of flattened rice, curd, groundnuts, ginger, jaggery, coconut and betel leaf with nuts.

2. *Ushakala Puja*: The icon is washed and sandal paste along

with *tulasi* (*Ocimum Sanctum* or sacred basil) sprouts is offered. Eight *artis* (sacred fire) are waved around the icon after food is offered. The offerings are almost the same as for Nirmalya Visarjana.

3. *Akshaya Patre Puja and Gopuja*: The swamiji now performs pujas to the vessel and ladle (akshaya patre) preserved from the time of Madhvacharya. It is believed that the Acharya presented the vessel and blessed the matha so that mass feeding (*anna-dana* or the gift of food) should continue in this holy place forever.

One of the cows housed in the cowshed is selected and worshipped after which food is offered and *arti* performed.

4. *Panchamruta Abhisheka Puja*: This puja follows the Akshaya Patre Puja and Gopuja. While the scholars chant the Vedas, the swamiji first pours coins of gold on the icon. The *abhisheka* or the sacred bath of the lord starts with ghee followed by milk, curd, honey and sugar. Banana and tender coconut water are added. The same mixture is poured on Hanuman and then distributed to the devotees.

5. *Udvartana Puja*: The act of rubbing the body of the icon to remove grease is known as udvartana. Again, food is offered and arti performed after the deity has been given a ritual bath.

6. *Kalasha Puja*: Golden pots are filled with water and the swamiji sanctifies the water by chanting special mantras.

7. *Tirtha Puja*: The water from the golden pots is poured onto the icon while the Vedic chants go on. The icon is gently wiped and one can see the devotion and love that are expressed by the swamiji's actions and facial expressions.

8. *Alankar Puja*: This is the decoration of the icon. During this time, the window through which the devotees can have darshan is closed. It is opened after Krishna has been decorated with silk cloth, ornaments and garlands. The garlands are made with great devotion, often by the women who are affiliated to the mathas of Udupi. Female relatives of the saints who often live in Udupi or in a room in the sub-matha itself, make flower garlands for the puja. The icon is decked variously on different days, sometimes as the Matsya (fish) avtar or Rama avtar. Many rulers of Vijayanagar and Mysore have offered ornaments of gold

Table 3
Sri Krishna Math
Paryaya Sri Puthige Math
UDUPI - 576 101

Puja-Anna Santarpana Sevas at Sri Krishna Sannidhi

		Rs.
1.	Akhanda Saptotsava	45,000
2.	One day's complete seva at Sri Krishna Math	15,000
3.	Sarva Puja with Brahma Rathotsava	10,000
4.	One day's Anna dana	10,000
5.	Golden Rathotsava	7,500
6.	Brahma Rathotsava	6,000
7.	Diamond Crown Alankarotsava	5,000
8.	Nandadeepa in Ghee (for one year)	5,000
9.	Godana (Uttama Kalpa)	4,500
10.	Sarva Seva (without Rathotsava)	4,500
11.	Rajata Rathotsava	3,000
12.	Nandadeepa (for one year)	3,000
13.	Garuda Rathotsava	1,500
14.	Suvarna Palaki Utsava	1,000
15.	Mahapuja Rathotsava	800
16.	Godana (Madhyama Kalpa)	800
17.	Godharma (for one day)	501
18.	Madhyam Mahapuja	400
19.	Ratri Puja	300
20.	Golden Cradle (Puja) Seva	250
21.	Alankara Puja	200
22.	Thottilu (Cradle) Puja	150
23.	Panchamrita Abhisheka	125
24.	Godana Kanike (if cow is brought)	125
25.	Avasara Sanakadi Puja	100
26.	Ushakala Puja (Vishwaroopa Darshana)	75
27.	Chamara Seva	75
28.	Kolalu Seva	75
29.	Sahasra Namarchana	65
30.	Ekanta Seva (Shayanotsava)	65
31.	Gopuja	50
32.	Ksheerabhisheka	50
33.	Halu-Benne (Milk-Butter) Samarpana	50
34.	Ashtottararchana	40
35.	Karpoora Mangalarati	20

Source: Panjaya Puttige Matha, 1993

and diamonds to Lord Krishna. On every Friday the icon is decorated with the costumes of the Goddess. The food offering and arti continue after each puja. The swamiji need not always perform this puja and he uses this time to visit and supervise the various projects that the paryaya matha has taken up.

9. *Avasara Sanakadi Puja*: During this occasion, even the swamiji stands outside the garbha gudi and the window for darshan is closed. It is believed that Sanaka and other sages perform puja of the icon.

10. *Mahapuja*: The Mahapuja is the last service in the forenoon and is the most elaborate. The drum known as *nagari* is beaten to announce the commencement of the ritual. The swamiji after performing puja to Lord Krishna, goes around the matha to worship the other gods and icons including the icon given by Madhvacharya (the matha icon). The food offerings are elaborate. Then sitting on the simhasana, he accepts holy water (*tirtha*) and also distributes it to the devotees. He then takes his food along with scholars and pilgrims in the chowki. After this, the state of purity (madi) of the swamiji ends. After lunch, the swamiji sits for a while in his simhasana and meets devotees, blessing them and offering prasada.

Later, he engages himself in teaching and scholarly discussions with students and other pandits. There might sometimes be a period of rest. At 4.00 p.m. the drum announces the commencement of the evening rituals. Scholars, on being requested by the swamiji, give a discourse (upannyasa) on topics like the *Mahabharata* just outside of the garbha griha, where any one can come and listen to them. Sometimes, after the discourse, women sing bhajans (devotional songs) in praise of Lord Krishna. The singing of bhajans reduces the sharp difference between the sexes in the participation in the worship and praise of the lord which is done usually by the recitation of Vedic chants by males. It also allows for members of non-Madhva caste to participate.

11. *Chamara Seva Puja*: The swamiji, after another bath by which he re-enters a state of madi, does *japa* (meditation and silent chanting of mantra) and gets ready to perform puja to the icon used in processions. This is the first service to the deity

(represented by the icon of Krishna) outside the garbha-griha (another term for garbha-gudi). After this puja, the icon given by Madhvacharya which is kept on the simhasana is worshipped.

12. *Ratri Puja*: As the swamiji performs this puja, there is singing of bhajans and dancing (mostly men) outside.[10] Rows of light are lit and the icon of Hanuman is worshipped.

13. *Mantapa Puja*: The moveable icon of Krishna is kept in a cradle and the swamiji rocks the cradle, putting Krishna to sleep.

14. *Ekanta Seva*: The cradle is taken around the garbha graha in a procession as bhajans are sung. The swamiji then takes the moveable icon and places it in a golden cradle. The public does not have access to this worship and it is therefore known as ekanta seva (worship in seclusion).

The swamiji now goes to the simhasana and gives prasada to the devotees. By 11.00 p.m. the matha closes (later on festival days) and it is time for the swamiji to sleep as well.

These pujas and sevas are performed every day in a sequential routine. A list of pujas is provided to the devotees so that they can make a choice. This list includes some special pujas which are also performed by saints. Table 3 gives the names of the respective pujas and the charges against each, as printed by the matha. It shows how the management of these rituals has been bureaucratised over the years.

Annual Festivals

The festivals celebrated give us an idea of the Gods, and their various incarnations worshipped in the Udupi matha. There is also the worship of Shiva in spite of this being a Vaishnava matha. It also gives a glimpse of the saints who are respected and worshipped in Udupi. The traditional Hindu calendar based on the lunar month and day is followed here. There are thirty days to a lunar month and twelve lunar months to a year. The lunar day is called *tithi*. On certain occasions, the solar month is considered more appropriate. This is a special feature of the Udupi sampradaya. The lunar months are:

Chaitra (March/April)	*Asvija* (September/October)
Vaishakha (April/May)	*Kartika* (October/November)
Jyeshtha (May/June)	*Margashira* (November/December)
Ashada (June/July)	*Pushya* (December/January)
Shravana (July/August)	*Magha* (January/February)
Bhadrapada (August/September)	*Phalguna* (February/March)

Each month is divided into two sections or *pakshas* of about fifteen days each such that the first fortnight (paksha) ends with the new moon (*amavasya*) and is known as *krishna paksha*, the dark half, while the second fortnight ends with the full moon (*purnima*) and is known as *shukla paksha*, or the bright half.

There are six seasons (*ritu*) each lasting for about two months. *Vasanta* (Spring), *Grishma* (Summer), *Varsha* (Rain), *Sharad* (Autumn), *Hemant* (Winter) and *Shishira* (cool season). The twelve lunar months are spread over the solar year which is about a day shorter (only 354 days). To compensate for this discrepancy between lunar and solar year, one leap month is added every third year. This leap month follows either Ashada or Shravana and is known as *adhik masa* (extra month).

The months of the solar calendar though rarely used are as follows:

Mesha (Aries), *Vrishabha* (Taurus), *Mithuna* (Gemini), *Karka* (Cancer), *Simha* (Leo), *Kanya* (Virgo), *Tula* (Libra), *Vrishchika* (Scorpio), *Dhanu* (Sagittarius), *Makara* (Capricorn), *Kumbha* (Aquarius) and *Meena* (Pisces). *Sankramana* is the day on which the sun (*surya*) transits from one constellation (*rashi*) to another (usually sometime between the thirteenth and eighteenth day of each western month).

After this brief description of time in the sect, I now give a list of important festivals celebrated in Udupi Krishna Matha along with their traditional monthly dates. From this we get an understanding of the main ritual activities associated with mythical/historical events. The festival days observed according to the solar calendar wherever applicable have been mentioned.

Sl. No.	*Name of festivals with a short description*	*Time of year*
1.	*Yugadhi*—New Year's day.	Lunar calendar—first day of the month of Chaitra. Solar calendar —First day of month Mesha (Aries).
2.	*Matsya Jayanti*—When God Vishnu took the incarnation of the fish (matsya).	Third day in the bright fortnight of Chaitra.
3.	*Rama Navami*—The day Rama was born.	Ninth day of bright fortnight of Chaitra.
4.	*Hanuman Jayanti*—Hanuman's birthday.	On full moon day of Chaitra (Chaitra poornima).
5.	*Akshaya Tritiya*—The day of incarnation of Lord Vishnu as Parashurama.	Third day in the bright fortnight of Vaishaka.
6.	*Vasant Utsava*—Festival of spring arranged every day of the season.	From Akshaya Tritiya to full moon day of the month of Vaishaka.
7.	*Vasant Dvadashi*—God took the incarnation of Vedavyasa through Satyavati.	Twelfth day in the bright fortnight of Vaishaka.
8.	*Narasimha Jayanti*—God took the incarnation of Narasimha (man-lion).	Fourteenth day in the bright fortnight of Vaishaka.
9.	*Bhagirathi Jayanti*—On this day, the river Ganga came down to earth at the request of Bhagiratha.	Tenth day in the bright fortnight of Jyeshtha.
10.	*Prathama Ekadashi*—The next four months are known as the period of *chaturmasya.* sannyasis stay in one town for four months or at least for four fortnights. In Udupi the sannyasis stay in one place for four fortnights.	Eleventh day in the bright fortnight of Ashada.
11.	*Jayatirtha's Punyatithi*—Jayatirtha or Tikacharya's (Commentator on Madhva's works) death anniversary.	Fifth day of dark fortnight of Ashada.

12.	*Upakarma*—The ceremony to change the sacred thread, or *Yagnopavit*. There are different days for this occasion depending on the clan of Vedic inheritance.	On sighting the Shravana star in the solar month of Simha (Leo).
	If one belongs to *Rigveda*.	On sighting the Shravana star in the solar month of Simha (Leo).
	For men belonging to *Yajurveda*.	Full moon day of the month of Simha.
	For men belonging to *Samaveda*.	On the day of star Hasta in the month of Simha.
		All the three occasions usually fall in the lunar month of Bhadrapada.
13.	*Hayagriva Jayanti*—The Lord took the incarnation of Hayagriva (man-horse).	Celebrated on the full moon day of Shravana.
14.	Anniversary of Raghvendra Swamy.	Falls on the second day of dark fortnight in the month of Shravana.
15.	*Krishna Jayanti*—Birthday of Shri Krishna.	Those who follow the lunar calendar celebrate it on the eighth day of the dark fortnight of Shravana. But in Udupi this festival is celebrated on the eighth day of the solar month of Simha (Leo).
16.	*Ganesh Chaturthi*—The festival of Lord Ganesha.	Fourth day in the bright fortnight of the month of Bhadrapada.
17.	*Vamana Jayanti*—God Vishnu took the incarnation of Vamana and conquered the demon king Bali.	Twelfth day in the bright fortnight of Bhadrapada.
18.	*Ananta Chaturdashi*—This is the day of Lord Anantha Padmanabha (The lord reclining on the seat of the serpent God *Shesha* with consort Lakshmi).	Fourteenth day in the bright fortnight of the month of Bhadrapada.
19.	*Navaratri*—The icon of Krishna is decorated with the costumes of Godesses.	First to ninth day in the bright fortnight of Asvija.

20.	*Vijaya Dashami*—This is the festival of harvest. Tender spikes of corn are ceremoniously brought to the shrine and worshipped. It is also celebrated as the birthday of Lord Buddha and Madhvacharya.	Tenth day in the bright fortnight of the month of Asvija.
21.	*Deepavali*—The festival of lights. It is on this day that Krishna had gone to Assam to vanquish the demon Narakasura. This is the reason it is celebrated in most parts of south India. In north India the victory of Rama and his return to Ayodhya is celebrated.	Festivities start from the twelfth day in the dark fortnight of Asvija (for three days).
22.	*Utthana Dvadashi*—This is the day of tulasi puja. The days of lighting one lakh oil lamps begin.	Twelfth day of bright fortnight of Kartika.
23.	*Saptotsava*—This is one of the most famous festivals of Udupi as chariots of different sizes are pulled by the pontiffs and lay men and women on car street[11] with devotees coming from all over the world.	On Makara Sankramana day (mid January).
24.	*Madhva Navami*—Madhvacharya went to Badrinath and disappeared.	Ninth day in the bright fortnight of Magha.
25.	*Shivaratri*—This is the day when Lord Shiva is worshipped.	Fourteenth day in the dark fortnight of Magha.
26.	*Holi*—The icon of Kama (God of love) is burnt symbolising the curbing of lust.	Full moon day in Phalguna.
27.	*Vadiraja Punya Tithi*—Death anniversary of Vadiraja Swamy.	Third day in the dark fortnight of Phalguna.
28.	*Vyasatirtha Punya Tithi*—Death anniversary of *Vyasatirtha* of the Vyasaraya matha (outside Udupi matha), author of several important commentaries).	Fourth day in the dark fortnight of Phalguna.

The Ashta Mathas of Udupi

All the eight mathas observe the annual festivals listed above, observed in the main Krishna matha, in their own respective mathas or sometimes together with paryaya swamijis. On special festival days some of the mathas have a greater significance attached to that day. For example, on Akshaya Tritiya day, the Pejavara matha, besides the worship of the day, has a special function to commemorate the death anniversary of the sixth pontiff in the lineage of the matha Vijayadhvajacharya (15th century). He wrote the commentary for the *Bhagavata* epic followed not only by all Madhvas but also by other sects today. On Narasimha Jayanti, the Krishnapura and Kaniur mathas have a special significance as the icon given by Madhvacharya is Narasimha. Similarly, the Hayagriva Jayanti is an important day for the Sode matha as Lord Hayagreeva was the *ishta devata* (beloved icon) of worship for Vadiraja Swami of this matha. The icon is preserved till today and worshipped with great devotion.

The ashta mathas apart from being interconnected by the chain of festivals also depend on the main Krishna matha for their daily routine. In Udupi, the saints wait for the drums to beat, signalling the afternoon *mahapuja*, before they offer food to their own deities in the mathas. When the chariots drawn on festive occasions pass the mathas lined on car street, the swamijis, if in Udupi, come out and wave the arti as it passes on. The sub-mathas otherwise are more flexible as they are not centres of pilgrimage and the swamijis of the mathas are not restricted in their movements. The mathas have their own staff and are visited by those devotees who want to meet the swamiji.

The ashta mathas of Udupi are differentiated externally by the different Gods they worship and by the body markings used by the men belonging to these mathas. Further, each matha acts as a clan so that householders affiliated to a particular matha cannot enter into marital alliance within the matha (similar to the *gotra* exogamy). Members belonging to a particular matha call their matha the guru matha.

Following is a chart outlining the icon belonging to the matha along with the differentiating body markings. The body markings are applied on the torso, arms, neck, face of men, both saints and non-sannyasis, with *gopichandana* or a ball of yellow clay. The clay ball is rubbed on the palm of the left hand with water to form a watery paste and then applied. Along with curved or straight lines moving upwards (rarely downwards), men also stamp parts of the upper body with five symbols (*mudre*)—the conch (*shankha*), the disc (*chakra*), the mace (*gada*), the lotus (*padma*) and *Narayana mudra* (symbol of Narayana). These markings in general differentiate Madhva Brahmins from Smarthas or Iyers and Iyengars.

Name of matha	*The icon given by Madhvacharya*	*The gopichandana marking (nama)*
Kaniur	Yoga Narasimha	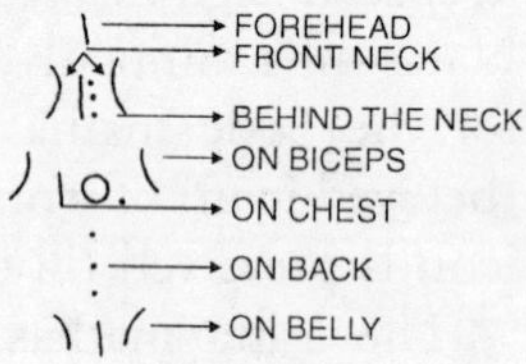
Sode	Bhuvaraha	
Puttige	Vitthala with Rukmini and Satyabhama (consorts)	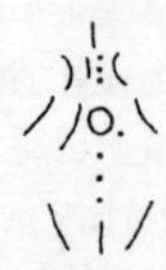
Adamar	Kaliyamardana Krishna	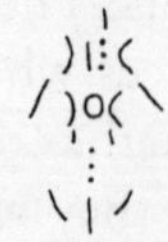
Pejavara	Vitthala with Sri and Bhu Devi (consorts)	

Phalimar	Kodanda Rama with Lakshmana and Sita	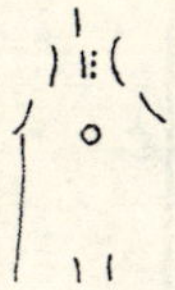
Krishnapura	Kaliyamardana Krishna with four arms	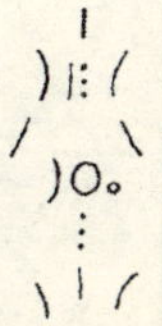
Shirur	Vitthala with Sri and Bhu Devi. The name of this Vitthala is Vamana Vitthala hence differentiating it from Pejavara matha's icon	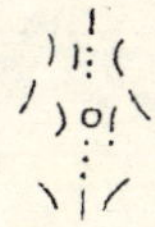

Spatial Organisation of the Sub-mathas

All the Gods in the mathas of Udupi, including the main Krishna matha face the west. This is unusual as generally the garbha griha in the temples and other mathas faces the east. Even the mathas of the Udupi matha in the villages face the west, except the one at Sode in northern Karnataka which faces the east.

As soon as one enters the richly ornamented doors of the sub-mathas in Udupi, one first encounters the offices. Further inside through another door, the garbha griha is surrounded by rooms on the ground as well as first floor. In one corner is the room (simhasana) for the swamiji, who is usually seated inside on a deer skin on a raised platform, meeting devotees from different parts of India and distributing prasada (fruits and *mantrakashe*— coloured rice). The roof, supported by a large and artistically carved wooden pillars (made of one tree trunk), is a special feature of the Udupi mathas.

As one moves through the next door, there are the stores, the kitchen, the well and more rooms. The rooms are occupied by the students of swamiji or by his mobile staff who travel with

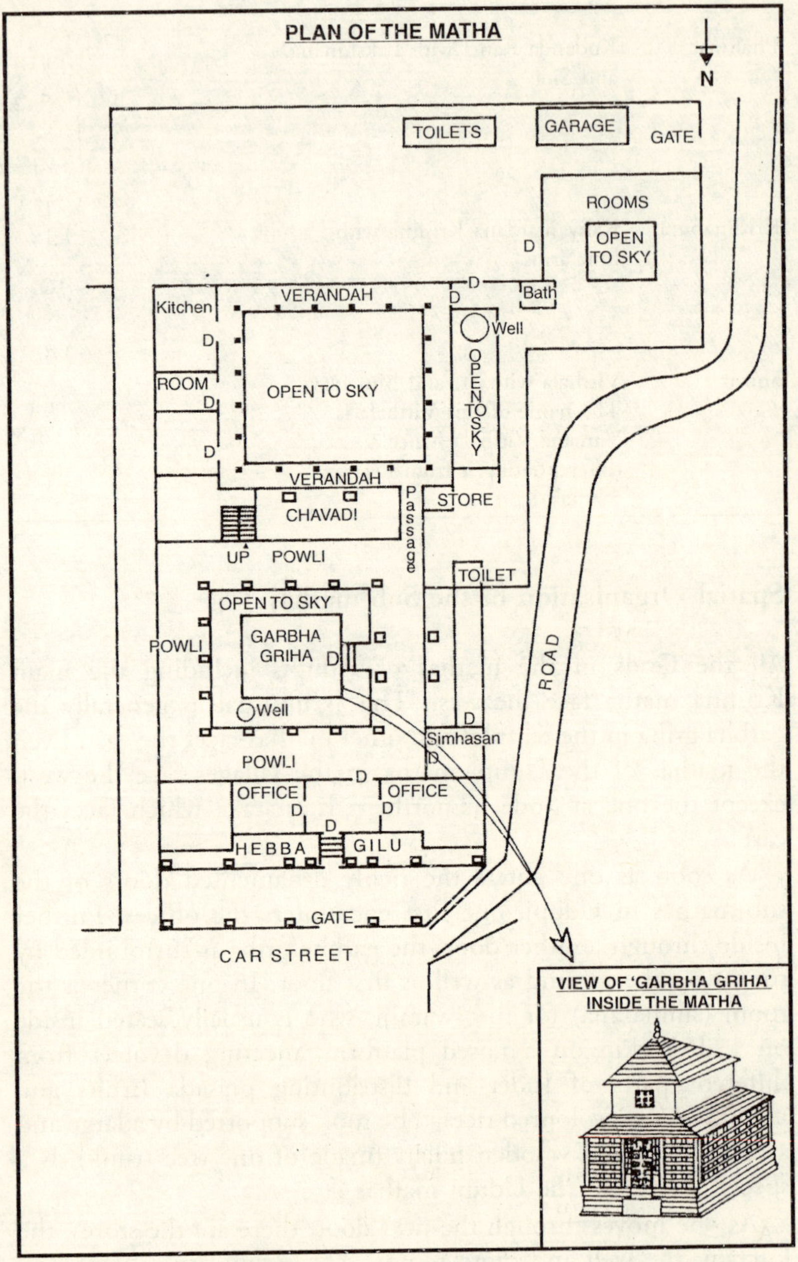

Map 6: Plan of the matha

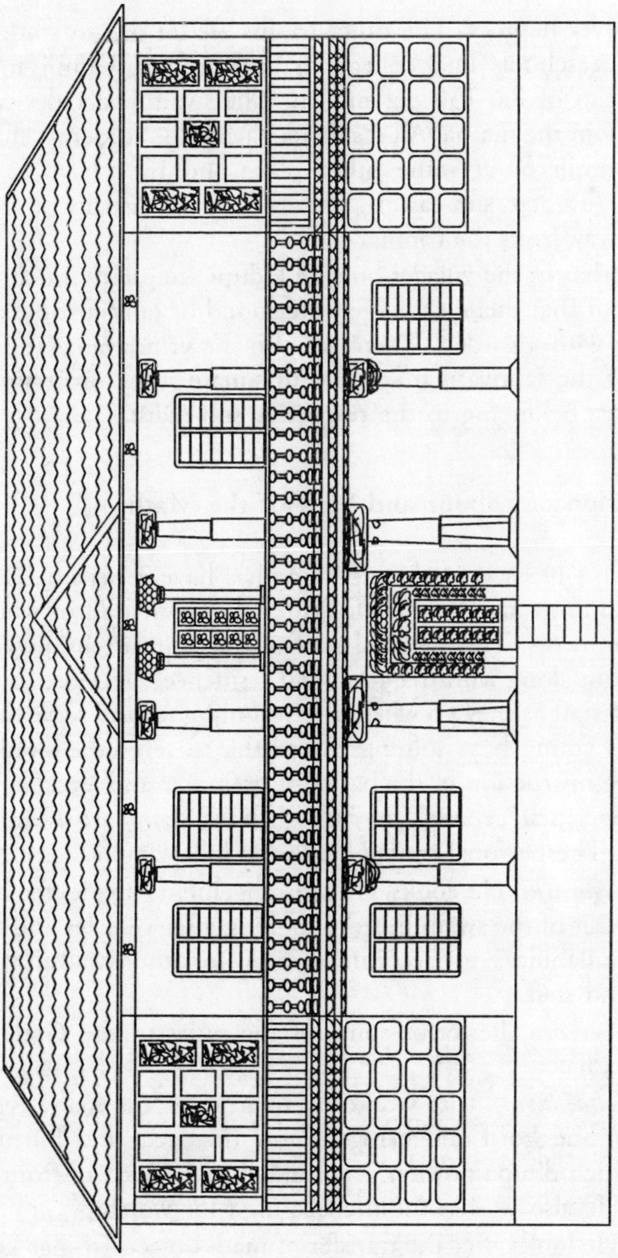

Fig. 1: Typical front view of the mathas in Udupi

him wherever he goes. The other rooms are let out to students studying in schools and college in and around Udupi for a nominal sum of Rs. 150 per month. The swamiji decides who should stay in the matha. All residents have to be students, either of the swamiji or at some other place and they have to be Brahmins (of any sub-caste). The toilets are usually a little distance away from the rooms.

The mathas in the villages outside Udupi are pretty much the same, except that there is a large water pond or tank just outside the matha with a garden. There are also the vrindavanas (burial grounds of the sannyasis marked with square stone projections) of the saints belonging to the respective sub-mathas.

The Division of Labour and Staff of the Matha

The swamijis of each of the eight mathas have a personal staff and an administrative one to look after the matha, all of whom are non-sannyasis. The personal staff of the sannyasi are given a nominal sum along with free food and residence. They are called the mobile staff as they go where the swamiji goes and serve him. Sometimes young boys joining the matha to serve the swamiji also receive instruction in the basics of grammar and Vedanta or train to be ritual experts (*purohits*). All of them are Madhva Brahmins. The personal staff include the following:

Parpatyagararu: He looks after arrangements made for the proposed visit of the swamiji, from looking after vehicles and the driver's availability, to accommodation for the swamiji, his students and staff.

Devara seveoru: Performs some of the pujas to the Gods in the sub-matha.

Benki kelsa davaru (fire worker): He arranges the many types of artis for the Lord and brings *dhupa* (incence) and burning coal on which dhupa powder is sprinkled and waved in front of the icon. He also washes the utensils used for worship.

Chitte: He looks after the transfer of madi objects (things kept in a state of purity) from one place to another, such as bringing the food from the kitchen to near the icon for offering naivedya. He is what one might call an assistant cook.

Adageoru: The head cook, who cooks for the swamiji and all those eating in the sub-matha.

Gindi: Washes the clothes of the swamiji, and draws water from the well and sometimes also heats it for the swamiji's bath.

Needless to say when serving the swamiji and God, all the staff have to be in a state of purity (madi). Sometimes a swamiji need not have all the staff, in which case one person takes on the other workers' responsibilities. And in case the person is not aware of how to perform the duty, students of the swamiji take over.

The administrative staff of the matha is also selected by the swamiji and they look after the matha in Udupi and those institutions near Udupi run by the matha. For mathas further away from Udupi, there are a different set of officials. These men need not be Madhva Brahmins. The staff is often a mix of Madhvas and Smarthas and they do not live in the matha.

Diwan: He is the manager and looks after the collection, redistribution of resources and accounts.

Bhandari: Taking care of the jewellery of the deity was the original task, but today much of his time is spent tallying accounts.

Shanbhog: The original function was to look after land and property matters, but now he too is more of an accountant. The various people looking after the accounts distribute their work by concentrating on different aspects of the matha (educational institution, land and property or donations).

Kothari: He looks after the stores and the upkeep of the rooms in the matha. He also visits and inspects those in charge of the matha land in and around Udupi.

Property and Institutions of the Mathas

The mathas traditionally owned large plots of land spread over south Karnataka. However, after the Land Reform Act in the mid-seventies, all the extra land was taken away. In return, the government paid to the mathas the amount of tax they used to pay for the land multiplied by approximately ten (depending on dry, wet and garden land) as yearly annuity.

This, the swamijis claim, is no compensation. Some of the mathas cannot continue with the present funds that the land generates, while some can. These mathas have sufficient land in villages near Udupi and sometimes as far away as Delhi and Mumbai. In the lands meant for cultivation, coconut is the main crop, besides clove, pepper, banana, mango and some vegetables. These are used by the matha and the surplus is sold in the market. There is also the non-agricultural land and forests of the matha. One of the swamijis (of the matha that claims it has very little land wealth to depend on) runs a cinema theatre in Udupi. This does raise many a eyebrow, but the swamiji justifies his actions saying that it is the only way he can survive with the matha and prepare for paryaya when his time comes.

The sannyasis explain that the money and property are not for their personal use, but are redistributed and channelised back to society. This is their justification of sannyasa or renunciation, which is to a great extent true. Almost all the mathas invest in education and as far as traditional education is concerned, they do not take any fees, providing on the contrary, free food and other help to students.

Some of the mathas are actively involved in a secular or modern system of schooling and higher education. These mathas also bring out journals, monthly magazines, souvenirs and books on philosophy in English, Kannada and Sanskrit. Besides this, they are also run orphanages, old age homes and look after destitutes and Harijans.

The Adamar matha has recently opened a school especially for the scavenger caste. The senior swamiji of the Adamar matha expresses his deep concern about the state of affairs in the country. 'The only way out is education. One has to break the cycle of corruption which the Kshatriyas and Brahmins—the rulers and politicians, have brought about,' he says.

These changes being brought about in the traditional set up

can be seen as the matha's attempt to orient itself to the modern world. An important area that demonstrates the matha's relation with the external world is in the way in which the distribution of sacred food in the main Krishna matha takes place. It orders the relationships of various groups amongst themselves and vis-a-vis the matha. The details of these sacred food events are developed in the next chapter.

Notes

1. After the urban agglomeration (clubbing of two towns or more into a city with a population over one lakh) the population of Udupi. Malpee and Manipal together is 1,17,744 (1991).
2. Rupya Peetha (Udupi), Kumaradri (Subramanya), Kumbhasi Dhvapeshvara (Koteshwar), Kroda (Shankaranarayana), Gokarna and Mukambika (Kollur).
3. The former name of Sode matha was Kumbhasi Kanara. Later on, in the time of Vadiraja, when the matha was established at Sode in north Karnataka, it became famous as Sode matha.
4. The other brahminical traditions in south India are the Advaitic and the Vishishtadvaitic known as the Smarthas and the Iyengars. It is also important to note that those in these mathas do not exhaust the Madhva sannyasis. Jayatirtha and many others did not belong to any matha. There were and still are many bidi-sannyasis (free renouncers). However, this tradition has not developed in the same way as the matha tradition.
5. I witnessed the paryaya festival in January 1994 when the outgoing Puttige matha welcomed the Shirur matha.
6. According to legend, the Ganga descends into this tank every 12 years since the time of Madhvachárya.
7. In most of the other traditions, especially Advaitic, this is called the *samadhi*. However this word was never used to denote the burial space of a sannyasi in the Madhva sect.
8. Each part of the body, the organs, limbs, etc. is governed by a demigod according to the *Upanishads*. The eye by the sun god, the nostrils by the Ashwini twins, the limbs by Indra and Jayanta and so on.
9. Madi is a state of purity after a ritual bath when one neither touches

nor is touched by anybody who is not in the same state. Therefore, all implements of worship need to be purified and later touched only by those in madi, usually the swamijis and his assistants.

10. The tradition of composing and singing bhajans is very strong in the Madhva mathas. Purandaradasa and Kanakadasa, established names in the Karnatak style of classical singing, belong to this tradition. They had close ties with the Udupi matha also. Many saints within the Udupi matha have also composed bhajans in Kannada and Sanskrit. These are popular today.
11. Swamijis do not travel in their personal vehicles on Car Street. They get down from their van or car and walk the distance to their matha, while the driver parks the vehicle near the matha.

3

Gastrosemantics within the Udupi Krishna Matha

Introduction

The anthropological study of food in India has demonstrated how eating and feeding involve, in complex ways, social rank, sectarian affiliations and even certain philosophical presumptions (e.g., Appadurai 1981b; Dumont 1970; Khare 1976; Khare and Rao 1986; Marriott 1968, 1974). The studies have dealt with these practices at various levels and institutions such as the village, the domestic sphere and the religious sphere.

The focus on sacred food or prasada in the religious sphere has taken on many connotations, from a gift or communion to the grace of the divine. Sociological and anthropological studies from the 70s up to recent times have discussed the hierarchy-asserting (Appadurai 1981; Breckenridge 1976; Toomey 1986) or hierarchy-neutralising effects (Babb 1975; Cantlie 1980; Khare 1976; Toomey 1986) of sacred feasting in temples or within sectarian traditions. However, most of these studies portray prasada as an undifferentiated concept, having a common meaning and function for all these involved in a given space.

The present discussion revolves around the sacred food events at the main Udupi Krishna matha. Gastrosemantics[1] in the matha takes on a more focussed meaning when compared to its distribution in temples. It allows for ritualised manipulation of prasada and the complexities of philosophical reasoning that can be played out by the followers of the sect's ideology.

As we have seen, the Udupi matha is managed by the sannyasis who belong to the Madhva sect. They are distributed across the eight sub-mathas. Every two years, the pontiff of one of the eight sub-mathas takes over the management of the Krishna matha on a rotation basis. This two-year tenure is called paryaya. The worship of Krishna can be performed only by the sannyasi in charge of the main Udupi matha.

The tradition of public feeding (prasada) which is a full course meal, is the responsibility of the pontiff in charge of the Krishna matha. Apart from the prasada that is distributed as a meal, a preparation of wheat and sugar is also distributed in packets. The distribution of this prasada does not differentiate between castes and is considered secondary to the main prasada. Along with the *Nada Brahman* (musical Brahman) of Pandharapura and the *Kanchana Brahman* (golden Brahman) of Tirupati, the Krishna icon in Udupi is called *Anna Brahman* (food Brahman).

As the pontiff heading the Krishna matha is about to finish his tenure, preparations for the mass feeding for the next paryaya begin. Plantain groves are formally set up to provide the leaves to eat on and the collection of rice starts from the harvest time. From about six months before the commencement of the paryaya, the sub-matha that is about to take over starts collecting firewood, which is built into a huge and artistic wooden chariot. All this is collected through donations made by the devotees and the funds available with the matha.

Food/prasada within the Krishna matha is served in four spaces namely the mrsthanna bhojan, chowki prasada, ground floor bhojanshala and the first floor bhojanshala.

Everyday, except on *ekadasi* (the eleventh day of every lunar fortnight, which is the prescribed day for fasting), cooked food is offered to Krishna (naivedeya) during the mahapuja (grand worship). On ekadasi, an offering of rice gruel is made to Krishna but is not consumed as prasada by the sannyasis and Madhva Brahmins who observe a fast. The mahapuja or worship is performed by the paryaya sannyasi in the afternoon, after a ritual bath in the tank. As the puja begins the drum outside the matha is beaten to convey the message to the entire town. Those who desire to witness the puja start coming towards the main Krishna matha. The deity is washed and dressed after which naivedya is offered. The offering consists of rice, pulses, sweet pudding, sweet bread, porridge, milk, curds, fruits, coconut, betel leaf and nuts. On special days such as the Krishna jayanti (birthday of Krishna), after fasting for the whole day, puja is performed at midnight and the offering consists of an elaborate cuisine prepared and offered on a grand scale.

The food as prasada is served during the mahapuja called the *mrishthana bhojan* and after the mahapuja in the chowki, where the sannyasis eat with the Brahmin devotees. The food served in both the spaces has sweets along with rice, pulses, vegetables and yogurt. A bit of jaggery is also added to servings of *saru* (pulses in spicy tamarind gravy) or *huli*, more popularly known as *sambhar*, which is eaten with rice. This incorporation of vast quantities of sweets into the Brahmin diet has caused problems for devotees suffering from diabetes. As Toomey points out (1986: 77), 'Krishna's sacred cuisine in Govardhan may have enhanced the occurrence of diabetes among the Brahmins.' The emphasis on sweet food was explained by one of the Brahmin scholars with a quote from Ayurveda: '*Shat rasan madhura prayan, nati druta vilambitam*'. On translation it would mean—among the six *rasas* (flavours) in food, sweetness should dominate. One should eat neither too quickly nor too slowly.

This, he elucidated, calms the mind and helps control anger. Besides the two places mentioned above, food, though offered to a different deity (Hanuman) is also served as prasada in the ground and first floor of the bhojanshala. The prasada here has no sweets and the dishes are limited to rice with saru, sambhar and buttermilk. The method of cooking food is also quite different from the food offered to Krishna and served to the sannyasis and devotees in the chowki and the mrsthanna. In the latter places, food is to be cooked in madi or purity by male Madhva Brahmins. The cooks rise in the morning and after a bath, wearing a wet *dhoti*, perform their *sandhyavandana* (daily worship). They then start cooking the food on a firewood *chulha*. They are in a high state of purity and should not touch or be touched by anybody until they have finished cooking and serving the food.

In the bhojanshala, the food is cooked by male Madhva Brahmins in madi but by modern methods of cooking. Food once offered need not be served by Madhva Brahmins only. non-Madhva Brahmins who are Smarthas or Sri Vaishnavas (Iyengars) also participate in distributing prasada in the bhojanshala.

The entry to the ground floor is generally restricted to three categories, viz., (i) students who have been issued passes by the matha authorities, (ii) Brahmin devotees who reach too late for the chowki prasada or have not got any special puja performed and are therefore not allowed inside the chowki, and (iii) poor local Brahmins without any other source of livelihood who do odd jobs at the matha. It is only in the ground floor bhojanshala that prasada is served in the night as well. Sannyasis have only one meal a day and restrict themselves to fruits or other uncooked varieties of light food in the night.

The first floor permits all non-Brahmins to enter. The matha is open for Krishna darshan to people from all castes from all over India. However, the distribution of prasada segregates the non-Brahmin castes and restricts their entry to the first floor bhojanshala. Brahmins can also go there and take prasada, but they rarely do so. Though prasada for the followers of the sect's ideology as elsewhere is related to proper health, long life, pure mind and *gunas* (disposition), the analysis here is to see how food/prasada has different connotations for gods and different categories of human beings such as the sannyasis, the Madhva

Brahmins, the non-Madhva Brahmins and those belonging to other varnas. The focus is also on the various types of interactions between saints, God and society.

Food for the Gods

Food when offered to God is naivedeya and when retrieved is prasada. Let us analyse what prasada means to a sannyasi. Sannyasis or swamijis here as in most other sects seek to set an example. The followers too look up to them and the swamijis believe that their superior understanding can lead others to bliss and happiness.

The sannyasis of Udupi spend most of their time either studying or teaching the Vedas, the *Brahma Sutras* and the various commentaries. However, during the two-year paryaya, when they are responsible for the worship of the Krishna deity, the teaching/learning schedule is relaxed. All the sannyasis of the Udupi matha have students studying with them besides those students in various *gurukulas* (traditional schools for learning) run in the name of the matha. This pre-occupation with the study of Shastra makes it important for us to know how the sannyasis and their students understand prasada as enunciated in the Dvaita philosophy of Madhvacharya.

'Prasada' in the texts (*Brahma Sutra Bhashya, Nyaya-Sudha* and *Tattva Prakashika*) signifies the grace of Brahman. Madhva's Bhashya (commentary) on the *Brahma Sutras* states: '*Yato Narayana prasadantre na moksha.*' This means that there is no release from bondage and misery without the grace of Narayana (Brahman). Further, this prasada is caused by knowledge produced by inquiry. Thus, knowledge in itself does not cause release. It is the prasada of Brahman, where knowledge or *jignyasa* is the language, the medium that causes *moksha*. When translated, it means that the giver of life and energy is Brahman and food is the medium through which one gets energy and life. And therefore food is prasada. Eating itself does not give

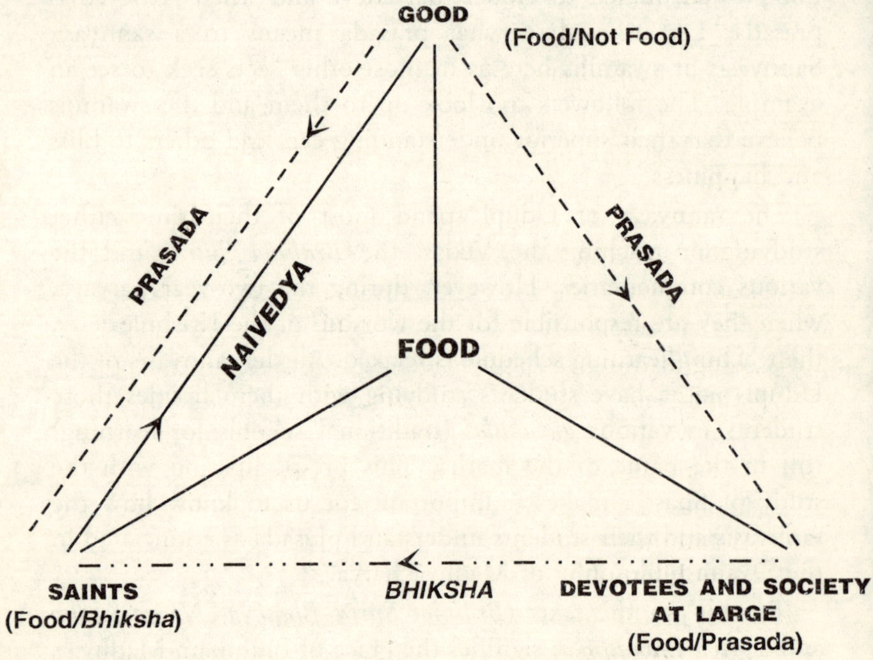

Fig. 2: Relationship with, and meaning of sacred food for various groups.

moksha, but it is a medium, understood as giving energy, etc. to attain moksha.

The relationship between Brahman and man is that of dependence. All human activities and desires are directed towards Brahman in Dvaita philosophy. To highlight these concepts, a swami of the matha quoted and explained the first stanza of the *Ishavasyopanishad*:

> *Ishavasyam idam sarvam yatkimdra jagatyam jagat, ten tyaktena bhunjitha ma grdhah kasya sviddhanam*
> (Whatever exists is for the residence of the lord. Therefore, enjoy the wealth given by Him, lust not after any man's possession).

This was explained as follows:

> This world is incapable of movement by its own independent volition. It is for of this reason that it requires the indwelling of Brahman in it. This world is dependent on *prakriti* (nature with all its abundance). Prakriti is dependent on Brahman. All are dependent on the Lord for their movement. Hence the world belongs to Him. Those who are other than Brahman, being dependent have no power to give gifts. Therefore, live by the wealth gifted by God. Do not beg from others as if they are the givers.

Audrey Cantlie (1981: 57), in a study of the Assamese Hindus emphasises that:

> For the true Vaishnava, therefore, all food is assimilated to the category of prasad... To eat without knowledge is a physiological act, but for a man of understanding it is a religious experience in a sacred world.

The offering of food to God (naivedya) and then it being retrieved as prasada symbolises that man is not the producer of food he eats. Rather, Krishna gives the food. the cosmic secret of creation (of food here), which is not visible, is made manifest by the keeping of food in front of Krishna, as if to say, 'What seems to be our creation is actually Yours.' Prasada in this sense is understood as the leftovers of Krishna. Applying here what Clifford Geertz says of Balinese cockfights, prasada too is not merely 'a reflection of a pre-existing sensibility analogically represented; it is a positive agent in the creation and maintenance of such sensibility' (Geertz 1971: 28). However, this sensibility is only present among the sannyasis and some students of Dvaita philosophy. Among others, prasada could mean the food blessed by Krishna that creates well-being and *sattvika* (good) disposition or the direct cause of moksha.

This shows that in the present context, the anthropological writing which views food/prasada as co-produced, requiring mutual interdependence (Appadurai 1981); as a concept of gift (Ferro Luzzi 1978: 86); and as a requirement since gods do not eat on their own but must be fed by humans (Manuel Moreno 1992: 148) does not hold true for all categories in the society.

Manuel Moreno (1992), by drawing support from the *Taittriya Upanishad*, feels justified in reversing the hierarchy and says that it is humans who feed the gods, instead of the other way round. The interpretation is based on Nikhilananda's version of the *Upanishad* which states that giving away food is the only way of preserving it, this preserves life. However, the interpretation for the same according to K.T. Pandurangi, a member of the Madhva sect is that what is given away or distributed is the knowledge of Brahman and what is preserved is his glory (Pandurangi 1990: 102).

Moreno further draws support from Manu's injunction: 'He who prepares food for himself (alone) eats nothing but sin' (Buhler 1886: 96). The continuation of the text from Manu's laws specifies that: 'Food which remains after (the performance of) the sacrifices shall be the meal of virtuous men' (*ibid*).

The text that lays down the laws for the sannyasis in the Madhva sampradaya written in the 14th century, also stresses that eating food which is not offered to the gods first (naivedya) is a sin and it adds: 'If food is offered to the God before consumption, one shall be rid of the misery in this world' (Vishnutirtha, reprinted 1931: 67). Though the implication is the same as in the laws of Manu, it does not mean that the gods cannot eat on their own. The laws stress the need to recognise the producer of the food and to acknowledge the dependence.

Krishna's disinterest in food is emphasised by Vadiraja Swamy (1480–1600), one of the sannyasis of the Udupi matha in his book *Rukmanisha Vijaya.*

> Having eaten kilos of butter he also ate the same amount of mud…and those who hid their butter [from Him] lived in ignorance. Is there any desire that He needs to satisfy?

For Krishna then, food as we understand it, loses it significance and food is really not food.

Food for Sannyasis and the Followers

Traditionally, the sannyasis of Udupi used to beg for food from vegetarian households in the town. The practice of collecting alms has been specified in the book of codes for the Madhva sannyasi, referred to earlier. Accordingly, the sannyasi must beg small amounts of food from each household and after offering it to God, eat it. This way of bhiksha is called *madhukara vritti* (the bee's livelihood) by Vishnutirtha, the author of *Sannyasapaddhati* (1931: 134). The often quoted example of a saint who performed it to perfection is Jayatirtha or Tikacharya (1365–88), the author of *Nyaya Sudha*—a sacred text for the Madhvas. It is said that after begging a handful from no more than five houses and having put it in a cloth, Jayatirtha used to wash the food in the flowing river, so as to remove all the spice from the food. The food was then spread out on a rock and offered to God before consumption.

Today, the concept lingers on and the food eaten by the sannyasi is still called bhiksha (alms), although food is not collected by literally begging from each household. Without going into the details of a historical investigation, one can agree with the reason given by the sannyasis themselves for this change; that over the years, the sannyasi has become more and more involved in the perpetuation of the matha and the responsibilities it entails. This no longer permits him to roam as a mendicant.

The paryaya swamiji, for the period of two years, does not go out anywhere and so he has his bhiksha in the chowki. He can and should invite other swamijis of the sub-mathas if they are in Udupi. The swamijis of the other seven sub-mathas are not bound and do go out when invited to Brahmin households on condition that the house has a well. The sannyasis are only allowed to use water from a well or a river for bathing and cooking.

The swamiji sits down in a state of madi (i.e., a state of purity—having had a bath and having worn clothes that are not touched by anybody as they are drying), to eat the bhiksha. Every day, before the sannyasis eat food, their students recite this mantra:

> The rice/food shall be like a mountain and the water shall reach the sea. Where the sannyasi eats, there God too eats; and where God eats, all the three worlds are satisfied. If food is given to a *brahmachari* then there is no addition. If given to a householder then it is like giving food to two. If a *vanaprastha* eats then hundreds eat, if given to a sannyasi it becomes infinity.

Here too food/bhiksha is an offering, but the connotations are very different from the food placed in front of Krishna. The food is not retrieved and the sannyasi does share an interdependence with society. He distributes knowledge, holds public lectures and helps in the running of various institutions. In turn, the society consciously tries to repay this by feeding the sannyasi and by making donations.

The sannyasi takes the prasada but it is called bhiksha. This brings in the factor of prestations. The food of the sannyasi gains an ambivalent meaning. Prasada, the gift of God moves into the hands of the devotees and they supply or 'convey' the food to the sannyasi. This is society's way of getting grace and repaying the sannyasis. Thus, the notion of gift enters the food given to the sannyasis. At another level however, bhiksha loses the significance of gift. This happens because the sannyasis believe that the giver only conveys prasada and hence is not bound by reciprocity implied in prestation. At this level of understanding, there is a parallel between offering to God and offering to a sannyasi, as also implied in the mantra recited before the sannyasis eat.

Audrey Cantlie (previously Audrey Hayley) rightly criticises Babb's interpretation of prasada that rests on the assumption that the giver is superior to the receiver. She writes, 'The Hindu gift is grounded on the opposite assumption that gifts pass from inferior to superior' (1980: 114). However, she notes that there are no counter-prestations among the Assamese Vaishnavas. Even if the recipient makes a gift to the donor, its connection with the original gift is denied. Parry (1980) and Raheja (1988) in their studies discuss the evil that goes along with the gift. In Banaras and Pahansu, where Parry and Raheja respectively were engaged in fieldwork, the acceptance of gifts involves the risk of contracting the evil or the inauspiciousness of the donor, which is passed on through the gift. Raheja stresses that the acceptor is reluctant to accept the gift as he fears the loss of *shakti* (power) and *tej* (lustre). This is the reason why there are no counter-prestations as it would mean returning the evil.

Ostensibly it may seem that the perception of evil or inauspiciousness in the gift prohibits a counter-prestation while its absence permits a counter-prestation. This equation is not relevant for *kanyadan* (gift of the maiden) in marriages. There is no evil perceived and yet in most cases, there is no counter prestation. For example Trautmann, while discussing the notion of kanyadan as a pure gift (1981: 277–315), feels it is a potent force in arranging marriages in India. He writes:

> ...kanyadan in the *Dharmasastras* is a gift that must not be repaid and this ideal in practice is evidenced in the asymmetrical relation that gift-marriage inaugurates between the contracting parties, with its etiquette of superordination and deference would cancel itself out were it to follow the cycle of marriage back to its point of origin (*ibid.* 293).

Thus, the ideology of the gift cannot be reworked through a single principle of exchange.

In the Udupi Krishna matha, the sannyasis, however, do give gifts in return to pandits (scholars who teach the scriptures) and guests of honour. All those who eat in the chowki are given dakshina (gift) on behalf of the sannyasi and the matha. These prestations and counter-prestations entail no exchange of evil or inauspiciousness. Raheja does cite Fuller's study of south Indian notions about *dan* which are not tainted by evil or sin. She suggests that this 'may simply be an artifact of his [Fuller's] focus on temple and temple worship' (Raheja 1988: 36). Further, she also distinguishes the gift (dan) in Pahansu, *carhapa or pujapa* from *bhik* or *bhiksha* (alms) and prasada. But more generally, Parry and Raheja attribute a singular meaning to 'gift' which is applicable to diverse contexts. Exchange of food in the Udupi matha, demonstrates that meanings differ according to contexts. Thus, exchange takes on multifarious meanings according to the diverse contexts, a fact which is often blurred in the English equivalent—gift. It is in this light that one needs to contextualise a gift in order to analyse its ramifications, whether it is dan carhapa, prasada, bhik or bhiksha.

Returning to our field, the Smartha and Madhva purohits (ritual experts), *vidwans* (scholars) and Madhva Brahmins who teach in Sanskrit colleges can eat prasada at the chowki. The chowki is also open to those Madhva Brahmins who have performed a puja in the matha. At times, the staff and others also join in. Some time ago, only Madhva Brahmins were allowed to have prasada here. Recently, Smarthas and Sthanika Brahmins have also been permitted entry. The Gujarat Brahmins and the Gaud Saraswat Brahmins are still refused entry and there is much ill-feeling among them about this. For the Madhva Brahmins, all Madhvas are at the top of the Brahmin hierarchy. Next come the Smarthas or the Iyers, at par with the Shri Vaishnavas or the Iyengars, and then the Sthanika Brahmins followed by the Gaud Saraswat Brahmins.

The guards at the door are experts at detecting a non-Madhva. When I asked these expert detectors, they told me,

The yagnopavit (sacred thread) is the hallmark of a Brahmin and we can see that easily because men do not wear stitched garments on their upper bodies. Even if the Brahmins are wearing trousers and not a dhoti, they are asked to go to the bhojanshala. Further, when the *sankalpa* (a preliminary ritual before the puja) is conducted, the *gotra* is asked. If they are unable to say it or they stutter, we know that they are non-Brahmins or non-Madhvas.

My informant added,

I can generally make out by asking them their mother tongue. We also do not allow Konkanis who are generally Gaud Saraswat Brahmins.' Besides these, in an unspecific way, the colour of the skin, the marks on the forehead etc., do act as clues in helping the guards to detect the caste/ sub-caste origin.

In case a VIP comes for darshan, he or she is given a warm welcome with expensive gifts. But if the males are not wearing a dhoti and cannot remove the upper stitched garment or they belong to the non-Brahmin caste, they are served food separately in a decorated enclosure. However, to save himself and the matha from embarrassment, seldom does such a VIP devotee come to the matha during the distribution of food/prasada.

As the distribution of prasada is about to take place in the chowki, the sannyasis sit down on wooden mats with the devotees but in a separate row perpendicular to the rows where all the others sit. The first two rows are generally reserved for the learned and the old. Special places are kept for devotees who have performed a major puja. Women generally do not sit in the first two rows. All the men have a dot and a black line that resembles an exclamation mark on their forehead. Such a mark denotes that he has had his meal.

After the sannyasis start eating their bhiksha, the devotees start eating their prasada. The food/prasada is served in a particular order with buttermilk coming towards the end. The eating process is accompanied by a person reciting the *Bhagavata* (on the mike) which reiterates its meaning as prasada. Dakshina is given by the staff on behalf of the paryaya swamiji to all who are eating in the chowki, usually one rupee for lay followers and up to ten rupees for the scholars. The matha staff also supervises the serving of prasada and asks the devotees to eat leisurely. Left overs on the leaves on which food is eaten is given to the cows.

Prasada in the chowki is usually a heavy meal, but during four months in a year called the *chatur masya vrata* (four months of abstinence), it becomes simple and often bland. In the first month, food/prasada does not include pulses, vegetables and fruits. No seasoning, other than pepper is allowed. In the second and third month, yogurt and milk is banned. In the last month, pulses and some vegetables are disallowed.

The vrata begins in grishma ritu (the summer season) and in the month of Ashada on the *dvadasi* day (the twelfth day of the lunar calendar), which usually falls in the month of July (See Table 4).

Table 4

No.	*Months*	*Type of food*
1.	Mid July-mid august (Ashada–Shravana)	No pulses except horsegram, no vegetables, no tamarind souring, however, raw mango souring is allowed. No fruits except mango, pepper is the only spice allowed.
2.	Mid August–mid September (Shravana–Bhadrapada)	Yogurt is prohibited.
3.	Mid September–mid October (Bhadrapada–Ashvija)	Milk is not allowed.
4.	Mid October–mid November (Ashvija–Kartika)	Some vegetables and all kinds of pulses are disallowed.

The mrsthanna bhojana is similar to the chowki prasada. It is reserved for special Brahmin invitees and is less crowded. The person guarding the door has a less arduous task of screening the individuals.

Let us now study the ground floor bhojanshala. Here, as mentioned earlier, food/prasada is served in the morning and in the evening for students staying in Udupi, whether studying in the secular institutions in and around Udupi or in the Sanskrit college run by the Udupi matha. The students and others who eat prasada at the bhojanshala have to be Brahmins. The upper stitched garment in case of men needs to be removed. Apart from this there are no specifications. The food cooked and not offered to the main Krishna icon is relatively simple. The people who eat here do not put the traditional mark on their forehead before eating. Vrata is not observed in this place and the same type of food as mentioned in Table 5 is served throughout the year.

The guard at the door has traditionally been a non-Brahmin and is required to check the passes before letting the students in and the puja receipts before letting in the devotees later for the chowki prasada. The local Brahmins who eat regularly or a lurking anthropologist are all easily recognised.

For the students, prasada essentially means free food that greatly helps them in channelising their scarce funds into education. The students staying in the Udupi mathas are required to serve the guests on special festival days and look after the inventory. They are paid a nominal sum for their services. In the paryaya festival, the Brahmin students help in a major way by looking after the organisation in all its aspects. Thus, the interdependence between the Udupi matha and the students of Udupi gives rise to a strong bond and many students develop a strong commitment towards the welfare of the Udupi matha.

The first floor bhojanshala permits entry to all the people who have come for Krishna darshan. Brahmins do not go there for prasada and their absence saps from the prasada its highly ritualised preparation. The people taking prasada in the first floor bhojanshala have minimum interaction with the Udupi matha and are not integrated within the sect's ideology. This is in spite of certain attempts made by Vadiraja Swamy in the 16th century to include Kanakadasa belonging to the shepherd caste into the mainstream ideology.

It is reported that till the mid-16th century, the Krishna icon was not open to all castes. It was Vadiraja Swamy who introduced other castes into the matha for darshan. The story that surrounds this event involves Kanakadasa, a devotee belonging to the shepherd caste. He was disallowed entry into the matha and used to watch the worship of the icon from a window outside the matha. His devotion or bhakti was so great that it made Krishna turn inside the matha so as to face the window in order to give darshan to Kanakadasa. The songs he composed about Krishna are sung even today by the Madhvas. In today's times, the practice has continued and one can view Krishna from the 'Window of Kanaka'—*Kanakana Kitiki*. Vadiraja even introduced into the offering the rice gruel that Kanakadasa used to offer from outside the matha. This is served as prasada.

Based on 'historical' evidence, sannyasis nowadays argue that Krishna did not turn and the matha was constructed in this special way, facing the west. The matha, by catering to different meanings, accommodates the various castes and this becomes important for the perpetuation of the matha.

Food in the first floor bhojanshala is in many ways similar to food in a restaurant, while the chowki food is similar to that served in traditional Brahmin households (Table 5).

The food served in the first floor of the bhojanshala is still sacred and is prasada. Unlike in a restaurant, it is not paid for and variety in the cuisine is absent. However, as in a restaurant, caste, age, and sex segregation is not prevalent. Dress codes and body markings are not emphasised. So, in comparison to the other three places of rating in the matha, one can say that the first floor bhojanshala is most similar to a restaurant.

In Udupi, Madhva Brahmins hardly invite each other for a meal except on ritual occasions such as a wedding. Most of the Madhva Brahmins who do not eat in the chowki cook their own food and those who do not cook are expected to eat in the matha. In contrast, the non-Madhvas who are not allowed inside the chowki invite each other for food. This establishes that the free distribution of prasada reorders the social interactions outside.

The three places of eating—the mrsthanna, the chowki, and the ground floor bhojanshala, structure the food rituals around

Table 5

Variables within the specified spaces	*Spaces*					
	Mr	*Ch*	*Gf*	*Ff*	*Bh*	*R*
Caste/sub-caste distinctions (within Brahmins or non-Brahmins)	–	±	–	–	–	–
Sex segregation	+	+	+	–	+	–
Age—the older seated first	+	+	+	–	+	–
Men with greater learning seated first (within the sub-caste)	+	+	–	–	+	–
Vrata	+	+	–	–	+	–
Nutrition in food during first month of vrata	*	*	**	**	*	***
Nutrition during non-vrata months	**	***	*	*	**	***
Number of dishes (vrata and non-vrata)	**	***	*	*	***	***
Irreversible order of serving	+	+	+	+	±	–
Absence or presence of upper stitched garments for men	–	–	–	+	–	+
Traditional Madhva mark on forehead during eating	+	+	–	–	+	–
Dakshina given to eating Brahmins	–	+	–	–	+	–
Hospitality	–	+	–	–	+	+
Guard	Brahmin	Brahmin	non-Brahmin	non-Brahmin	no guards	no guards
Singing	+ (mike)	+	–	–	+	–
Sacredness	!!! (madi)	!!! (madi)	!! (modern	! cooking)	!!(!) (madi)	– (profane)

Key: Mr—Mrishthana, Ch—Chowki, Gf—Ground floor bhojanshala, Ff—First floor bhojanshala (non-Brahmin), Bh—Brahmin households, R—Restaurant.

+ Considered (present)

– Not considered (absent)

± Sometimes considered

!!!, !!, ! Degree in sacredness

Brahminised practices. All the four spaces become an arena where a complex set or symbols play, to give prasada a special significance.

Prasada in all the four spaces ceases to be an undifferentiated entity. Unlike in places where the social function of the prasada is mainly to produce a bond of social cohesiveness among the devotees across the caste and class differentials (Babb 1957: 60, Khare 1976: 99), in the present context, food/prasada has varied meanings and sociological usages in different spaces, among different sub-castes and groups in society.

The food events in the Madhva sect assert the hierarchy of the caste system through its commensal practices. Sacred food as a framework for analysis expresses the sectarian social structure. It highlights that within the sampradaya, what you eat, how you eat and with whom you eat plays an important role. Food in India is much more than a material substance. It defines the internal and external states of one's being. The study of food events in different contexts can therefore provide us with a useful yardstick to understand the continuities and changes in a sect with respect to the society at large.

The conceptual stress that there are various levels of meaning depending on the context, will be maintained in the subsequent chapters. Concepts in their concrete contents diverge from one another in accordance with differing social positions. The same word or concept whether it be prasada, the soul or renunciation, as we shall see, mean different things when used by different people under varied circumstances.

This chapter also highlights that the meaning given to sacred food events by saints and others in the Udupi ashta mathas is derived from a textual corpus of a specific traditional knowledge system. The preparation of food as a marked category exemplifies how the matha tries to portray various everyday acts in a special way. It would be useful therefore, to see how this knowledge system which informs the everyday life works. Before asking what are the ways in which traditional knowledge is articulated and transmitted to various groups, let me first introduce the process of learning.

Notes

1. Gastrosemantics may be generally defined as a culture's distinct capacity to signify, experience, systematise, philosophise and communicate with food and food practices by pressing appropriate linguistic and cultural devices to render food as a central subject of attention (Khare 1992: 46).

4

The Cultural Production of Knowledge

The aim of this chapter and the next is to study the transmission, reproduction and assimilation of knowledge along with the communication of tradition within the Udupi ashta matha. The communication of traditional knowledge takes place in a particular cultural context and involves processes that are continuous, creative and inventive.

Introducing the Pedagogic Practices

The pedagogic process in the matha is located within the sect's ideological framework. Apart from the transmission of the philosophy of the sect as its major function, it also aims to produce a certain transformation of the individual—a self-realisation or understanding.

Each sub-matha operates at two levels. It is first and foremost a definite territory wherein the activities of the matha are circumscribed. At this level, the mathas act as a space for the dissemination of knowledge by the sannyasis who belong to the matha and the scholars who are invited to the matha to teach.

In addition to the localised sphere of action, there is also a wider sphere within which the sannyasis travel. They go on tours and live in other mathas or in the host's house but retain their membership to the matha and are known as belonging to that particular matha. Due to this combination of localised and dispersed sites over which the activity of knowledge takes place, transmission is not necessarily restricted within a particular space, as in a *gurukula* (traditional residential schools).

The Philosophy and Texts of the Madhva Udupi Sect

The saints and pandits of Udupi are predominantly engaged in the study of Shastra, which is primarily understood as *pramana*, a source of correct knowledge.[1] Shastra as a collective body of knowledge aims at fixing the meaning of the Vedas. In this sense, it has its origin in the *Brahma Sutras* (an aphoristic treatise composed by Vedavyasa) and follows the *sutra-nyaya* or the reasoning and logic of the *Sutras.* Shastra encompasses the various schools of thought that have tried to interpret the Vedas and *Smritis* and includes a critical study of the *nastika* thinkers as well. The nastikas as opposed to the *astikas* are those who do not accept the Vedas (or *Shruti*) as pramana. It would be incorrect in this tradition to characterise the astikas as theistic and the nastikas as atheistic. Thus, the major content of Shastra is *Brahma-vidya* (the knowledge of Brahman).

In the context of the mathas, Shastra is constructed centrally around the texts of the Madhva tradition. These texts are written by the scholars, most of whom are sannyasis of the Madhva sect (not necessarily belonging to the Udupi ashta mathas). The Madhva sect, as was described earlier, arose primarily due to disagreements over the earlier interpretation of the *Brahma Sutras* and the Vedic sentences.

It is the uniqueness of the interpretation of the *Brahma Sutras* that differentiates this philosophy of the sect from others. Accordingly, the principle texts out of which the sannyasis and scholars of the sect make sense and give meaning to the world centre around the commentaries on the bhashya or interpretation of Madhvacharya (1238–1317). He is called *bhashyakara* (bhashya maker) by the Madhvas. The astika Indic tradition divides Shastra into three parts of *prashthanas—Sutra, Upanishad* and *Gita Prashthana*. Madhvacharya composed works to amplify the teachings of the *Prashthanas*. His work on the *Sutra Prashthana* seeks to understand the *Brahma Sutras*. Likewise, the *Upanishad Prashthana* highlights the philosophy of the *Upanishads* as also the Vedas in general and the *Gita* prashthana deals with works on the *Bhagavad Gita, Mahabharata* and the *Bhagavata Purana*. In all, there are 37 works attributed to Madhvacharya, collectively called the *Sarvamula* ('the Originals').

Within the Udupi matha, although most of the texts are referred to, only a few are studied in detail. A student of Shastra needs twelve to thirteen years of rigorous study before he can claim to have understood the philosophy of the Madhva tradition. Any study of a text requires more than one commentary, sometimes those of several authors, on the *Sarvamula* while it is being explained and understood.

After the initial training in Sanskrit grammar (usually soon after the *upanayana* ceremony), the biography of Madhva (*Madhva-Vijaya*) is taught to solicit the grace of the first guru. The next step is the reading of Valmiki's *Ramayana* and Vyasa's *Mahabharata*. This is followed by a study of the *Upnishads* along with the study of tarka (logic), *kavya* (poetics), etc. All this is studied with the help of Madhva's bhashya or its commentaries. This prepares the student for an advanced study of Madhva's texts, usually the works of the *Sutra Prashthana*. It culminates in a commentary by Jayatirtha (1365–88) called the *Nyaya-Sudha*. It is a commentary on one of Madhvacharya's bhashya on the *Brahma Sutra* called the *Anu-Vyakhyana*. Jayatirtha is responsible for bringing to light and systematising Madhva's philosophy. In all, he has written commentaries for 18 of Madhvacharya's works. A saying among the Madhvas highlights the importance and complexity of the text, for it is said that one should either study the *Sudha* or rule a kingdom; implying that both require enormous and erudite skills. A Madhva who has studied the *Nyaya-Sudha* is highly respected and is eligible to become a teacher. All the senior sannyasis of the Udupi matha, along with many other scholars, have studied the *Nyaya-Sudha*. The younger sannyasis as a rule will be required to end their studentship with the study of the *Sudha*.

Table 6 is a genealogy of some of the important texts, which are emphasised as cardinal in the sect's ideological framework. It also outlines the succession of disciples. These texts are hierarchically ordered in the mental construct of the Madhva. The apex is formed by the authorless Veda followed by Badarayana's text, (Badarayana is considered to be the avatar of Brahman by the Brahmin sects). Madhvacharya's works, after the Veda and Badarayana's, are supposed to contain the highest level of maturity of thought and word, and Madhvacharya is considered by members of the Madhva sect to be an avatar of Vayu (the wind god) after Hanuman and Bhima. As the hierarchy moves downwards, each commentator pays obesience to the earlier commentator right up to Badarayana or Vyasa who is God Himself in the form of the guru. This section, called the *mangalacharana*, ensures a continuation of traditional thought. As Halbfass points out,

> They [the commentators] do not present their own points or reference, but instead adhere to the medium of commenting and explicating, and link up with the given stock of tradition (1988: 363).

The philosophy contained within the texts is known to the Madhvas as well as outside as the Dvaita philosophy or Dualism. However, it is only recently that this name (Dvaita) has been attached to Madhva's philosophy. Madhvacharya and his immediate followers did not coin this term. The term suggests a theory that admits of two independent and mutually irreducible substances. Nothing can be further removed from Madhva's point of view.

The problems of using the term Dvaita were first brought to the notice of the English-speaking world by H.N. Raghavendrachar during the middle of the 20th century. He preferred the term

Brahma-mimamsa (inquiry into Brahman) to Dvaita. B.N.K. Sharma (1981) suggests the term '*Svatantra-advitiya-Brahmavada*' (the doctrine of the unparalleled independence of Brahman). We shall nevertheless retain the term Dvaita because of its popular usage.

Madhva's philosophy accents the nature of the dependent world in its relation to Brahman. In contra-distinction to Shankaracharya's *Nirguna Brahman* (God without qualities), Dvaita interprets Brahman through the Veda as *Guna-Purna*, full of attributes and infinite.

Table 6

This table traces the genealogy of only the principal texts and their authors or gurus. Each text in the vertical movement downwards is a commentary of the one above it. The authors are at the end of the row in the last column. The author placed below successively considers all the authors above him to be his gurus.

Texts						Authors
Brahma Sutras				*Bhagavad Gita*	*Bhagavata*	Vedavyasa (Badarayana)
Brahma Sutra Bhashya	*Anu Bhashya*	*Anu Vyakhyana*	*Bhasyas* on the ten *Upanishads*	*Gita Bhashya*	*Bhagavata-Tatparya Nirnaya*	Madhvacharya (Anandatirtha) 1238–1317
Tattva Prakashika		*Nyaya-Sudha*		*Pramaya Dipika*		Jayatirtha (Tikacharya) 1365–1388
Tatparya Chandrika						Vyasatirtha (Chandrikacharya) 1478–1539
Prakasha	*Tantra Dipika*	*Parimala*	*Khandartha*	*Gita-Vivarti*		Raghavendra Tirtha or Swami 1623–1671

The world is not *maya* or illusion and the *jiva* or soul is ever distinct from Brahman the infinite. Madhva rejects the distinction made by Shankara between *gyana-kanda* (knowledge part) and *karma-kanda* (ritual part). For Madhva, the entire Veda in all its parts denotes one single entity—Brahman. To realise this is the source of *ananda* (joy). Gyana (knowledge) and bhakti (devotion) go hand in hand; more knowledge leads to greater bhakti.

There are two important ways in which the sannyasis and scholars of the Udupi matha seek to transmit and reproduce Shastra. The distinction emerges between patha[2] (study) on the one hand and upannyasa or *pravachana* (lecture or talk) on the other. Both these methods use Sanskrit and Kannada as a medium of transmission and exegesis. In patha, the listeners as distinct from the audience in upannyasa are referred to as students or *shishyas*. This structure entails the communication of Shastra in a pedagogic practice where the principal actors are the teachers and the students. For the present, I shall elaborate on these and analyse some of the rules that bind the imparting of traditional knowledge. I shall return to this topic again in the next chapter to talk about the upannyasa.

Gurus or Teachers

Three types of gurus can be discerned within the Udupi ashta mathas. (a) The sannyasis who belong to the mathas and hence have a right to perform Krishna worship at the main Udupi Krishna matha during their paryaya, or tenure. (b) The bidi-sannyasis who are affiliated to the Udupi mathas but do not have the right to perform Krishna worship. They may have been *grihasthas* (householders) who have taken up sannyasa or bal-sannyasis (sannyasa at childhood) like the Udupi ashta matha saints. Usually, the bidi-sannyasis who want to take up sannyasa ashram are given sannyasa by the sannyasis of the Udupi matha. They are free to roam about as they please and are not restricted by the responsibilities of the matha. They often come to Udupi and stay at their guru-matha (the matha that has initiated them into sannyasa and to which they are affiliated). (c) The non-sannyasi (grihasthas and brahmachari) scholars staying in Udupi. They give patha to the students usually in the matha premises or in their homes. These scholars also belong to the Udupi mathas. For each Brahmin, besides his gotra, the matha also is an exogamous unit to which he or she belongs. Sometimes gurus are invited from other mathas and sects. All established gurus of the Udupi matha are male Madhva Brahmins.

The eight sub-mathas within the Udupi matha and the distribution of the sannyasi teachers and those who are also learning is given below.

Table 7

Name of matha	*Numbers of pontiffs*	*Involved in teaching*	*Also learning*
Adamar	2	1	0
Kaniuru	2	0	1
Krishnapura	1	1	0
Pejavara	2	2	1
Phalimar	2	2	0
Puttige	1	1	0
Shiruru	1	0	1
Sode	1	1	0

*This was the position at the time of my fieldwork.

All sannyasis except the Kaniuru junior and the swami or saint of the Shiruru matha have completed their study of *Nyaya-Sudha*. The Shiruru swami and the Kaniuru junior swami are undergoing instructions from a sannyasi of another matha (Uttaradi Matha) in the Madhva sect. The Pejavara junior swami, although has finished the *Sudha* patha, receives patha in *Sama Veda* from a grihastha scholar and on the *Anu-Vyakhyana* from the Phalimar senior swami.

Each of the pontiffs involved in teaching have a group of students at various levels of learning who stay in the matha with the sannyasi-guru and travel with him. Those sannyasi-gurus who have a senior swami looking after the administration of the matha are more intensely involved in the teaching of students. A typical example is the junior swami of the Adamar matha who spends most of his time teaching, as the senior swami looks after the running of the matha along with other activities.

Vishvapriya Tirtha, the junior swami of the Adamar matha took sannyasa at the age of 14 on 1 June 1972. He was selected and initiated into sannyasa by his senior swami, Vibhudesha Tirtha. After being trained in the ways of *anhika* (meditation), rituals of cleaning the body, and customs and codes of conduct of a sannyasi, he received patha. He completed his studentship with the *Nyaya-Sudha* at Adamar village under the sannyasi-guru, the senior Phalimar swami.

The Adamar junior swami is considered an excellent and erudite teacher by the members of the sect and attracts students from all sections of the Madhva community. On a normal day, Swamiji starts taking classes soon after his morning meditation and worship. The details given below change as new students are taken in or the old ones progress to different subjects and topics. Given below is an example of a typical day during the researcher's stay.

In between the patha, people come and meet the swamiji and on certain days, there are quite a few interruptions, especially in the evening. When Swamiji is on Sanchara (travel) outside Udupi, the patha is spaced out and not so rigorous. Some of the guru-sannyasis also run gurukulas where they appoint and invite teachers.

Of the three categories of gurus mentioned, the sannyasi-guru is most revered as he is considered to be the best possible instructor; he is an individual totally devoted to Brahman and also his life is the exemplar of the detached mode of existence in the texts.

The second category of gurus, the bidi-sannyasis, are visitors to the Udupi matha who, because of their learning and because they formally conduct classes, attract students. The students do not live with them and the patha is for a short term. For example, one of the bidi-sannyasi affiliated to the Phalimar

Time of day	*Students*	*Patha on*
8.30–9.30 a.m.	These students have just joined and are the youngest among his students.	Sanskrit grammar and vocabulary (*Amar Kosha*, etc.)
9.30–11.00 a.m.	These are slightly advanced students, but still learning the basics of Dvaita philosophy.	*Mahabharata Tatparya Nirnaya*
11.00–12.00 noon	Advanced students, some joining after retirement, but having received preliminary training in Shastra. There are some who live in Udupi and come at this time.	*Nyaya-Sudha*
Bath and bhiksha (food of the sannyasi)		
1.30–2.00 p.m.	*Chintane* (in-depth re-thinking) i.e. revision of earlier Sanskrit patha for the students learning grammar and vocabulary.	Sanskrit grammar and vocabulary
2.00–2.45 p.m.	Revision (chintane) for *Mahabharata Tatparya Nirnaya* Chintane for advanced students also implies a test of their understanding of the earlier patha.	*Mahabharata Tatparya Nirnaya*
2.45–4.30 p.m.	The students studying *Mahabharata Tatparya Nirnaya* are given lesson in tarka (logic)	*Shabda Bodha*
4.30–6.00 p.m.	Those *Sudha* patha students staying with the swamiji receive additional instruction and revise their works.	*Nyaya-Sudha*
6.00–6.45 p.m.	Students staying with the swamiji as well as those living in Udupi attend.	*Tattva-Prakashaka*
8.30 p.m.	*Phalahara* (eating fruits). Swamiji takes uncooked edible food. He prepares for lessons and sleeps.	

matha gave patha on the *Upanishads* during the four month stay in the rainy season (chatur masya). There were four students living in Udupi who came to him for the four months. The tradition of bidi-sannyasis is not developed to the same extent as the traditional matha sannyasis. Often, bidi-sannyasis are not as learned.

The third type of guru is the non-sannyasi scholar. He can conduct classes either in his house or in one of the mathas; usually the one to which he belongs. These gurus have most of their students living in Udupi. They also conduct classes for students who live outside during specific times of a year. These gurus have an active relation with the sannyasis of the mathas and show reverence to them. The sannyasis often ask them to conduct classes in the mathas and to give public lectures (upannyasa). They also teach at the traditional gurukulas run by the matha or are asked for their services during their matha's paryaya (the two-year tenure when the matha pontiffs are entitled to look after the main Udupi Krishna matha). In return, the sannyasis offer them help with library books or provide assistance for their publications. However, a chance to give upannyasa or patha is itself considered an honour by the non-sannyasi scholar.

Gurus whether sannyasis or non-sannyasis are viewed by many as benevolent figures. Goldman (1978) suggests a relation of tension and restraint due to Oedipal conflict, present in a disguised form, involving the guru as a surrogate father figure. Although this cannot be denied, it is balanced by a guru who is seen as compassionate. The guru is viewed by students as one who offers blessings in the form of knowledge for liberation.

Shishyas or Students

This section deals primarily with the students of the sannyasis. There are some differences when it comes to students of grihastha gurus of Udupi which will be dealt with later. The usage of the word 'students' denotes a learner in a system of the transmission of knowledge through a pedagogic process and differentiates this context from those in which there are 'disciples' but no imparting of knowledge.

Most of the students of the sannyasi-gurus of the Udupi matha live with their guru, serving them and travelling with them on sanchara. Each sannyasi-guru has about eight to ten such students. They usually join at a young age and stay with the swamiji until their studies are over. Sometimes, the swami also gets students who join him to learn after retirement. Usually, such Madhva members have had initial training in Shastra and come to study the *Nyaya-Sudha*. The other younger students may not stay until they study the *Sudha*. Many have families to support or find the study of Shastra too tedious. Such students take up *paurohitya* (the conducting of rituals) and often couple their training in the conducting of Vedic rituals with the study of astrology. They do this after they have studied with the sannyasi-guru for six to seven years.

There are also a few dropouts (three during the year of my stay). On one occasion, a student of a swami had gone to see a movie, which is not allowed, and could not attend his class. The swamiji came to know of it and gave him a good scolding. However, the student was more interested in acting and soon left the matha.

Those who come to study the *Sudha* with the swamiji need to be motivated enough to stick it out through the gruelling years. An example of such devotion to learning is H.P. Achar, a retired professor of geology with a Ph.D. from the U.S.A. He had requested the Adamar junior swamiji with whom he studies, to teach him. The Swamiji when he was asked about the incident replied, 'Yes, he came and was highly interested… Of course, he had preliminary knowledge of Shastra as he had studied with a pandit in his home town.' He went on to tell me the type of students who come:

> Often I receive requests to teach young boys. I see whether they are interested enough and take them on as students. However, during their study, many drop out as they feel that this study of Shastra is not for them.

To return to H.P. Achar, he has been given a room at the Adamar matha at Udupi. He has earned the trust of the Swamiji and looks after the accounts whenever the swamiji is travelling.

Each of the students has a special duty to perform while the swamiji is either away or in a festival of the matha. They also recite Vedic mantras and get *dakshina* (gift of money, coconut, etc.). Besides the students who stay with the swamiji, there are those who stay in Udupi and come to study with him. They do not get to have an informal relationship with him and do not participate in the festivities of the matha with equal fervour.

The students or shishyas of bidi-sannyasi and the non-sannyasi guru do not live with them. The students of bidi-sannyasis live in Udupi and become students when they come to Udupi, usually in the rainy season, when sannyasis are forbidden to move out of one town. The patha is often extensive and goes on for long hours as the bidi-sannyasi has little else to do. There are fewer students as compared to the sannyasis of the mathas and the non-sannyasi gurus.

The non-sannyasi Brahmin gurus are usually householders (seldom Brahmacharis) and since they stay in Udupi, they attract students from within Udupi and from outside (during specific times in a year). The students go to the matha or the guru's house, wherever the guru conducts classes. Among all others, it is the non-sannyasi guru who attracts students from a wider range. Recently, one of the grihastha gurus also had a foreign student who was studying the *Bhagavata*. Teaching, when conducted by a Madhva householder, does not involve rigid and debarring pedagogic processes.

Reserving a detailed discussion for later, let us turn to the students of the matha, especially the younger ones, who undergo a special type of training in tradition. Some of the sannyasi-gurus, besides taking classes or patha for the students living with them and running gurukulas in the name of the matha, also conduct camps called *shibira* for a specific number of days each year (15 days). This can be considered an isolate of traditional cultural values. A shibira is a camp where crash courses are given in sandhyavandana (the daily rites of a Brahmin), Vedic recitation and ways of performing worship. These are usually for children soon after their upanayana (thread ceremony), so that the age group is 8 to 14 years. It is conducted free of cost.

Such a shibira was held at Adamar matha in the village of Adamar. The publicity for the shibira was done by word of mouth, mainly by the pandit teachers of the matha. There were 17 students who came from the nearby villages and all of them were Madhvas (the non-Madhvas seldom send their children to these camps). The junior swamiji was there to supervise.

The students got up at six in the morning. After having their bath, they first learnt the sandhyavandana. They were usually divided into two or three groups and a young boy who is a senior since he participated in the shibira last year, trained the novices. After they finished this morning ritual, the students sat in front of the worship place and watched as the swamiji did puja and his students recited the Veda. Some students complained of being bored. However, most of them started enjoying themselves after a couple of days.

After the puja, silence stood in sharp contrast to the clanging of bells still ringing in the ears. The sun's rays filtered down over the roof tops and the students scurried away as it was time for breakfast—rice gruel with pickle. The head teacher hurried them up—'Come on, eat quickly, I am waiting to teach you'.

The medium of instruction was Tulu and Kannada. The first batch comprised students who were attending such a shibira for the first time. They were taught the importance of Vedic knowledge and learnt the names of months according to the Indian calendar, the Indian rivers and such general information. Later, they were to be taught Vedic recitation.

The second batch comprised students who had attended the previous shibira. The teacher was a student of the swamiji. He was teaching *devara puja vidhi* (the way of performing puja or worship to the gods). There were six students who had a book of scripture in Kannada in front of them which the teacher sometimes explained.

The third batch comprised the senior-most students. They were learning the *Bhagya Sukta* of the *Rig Veda*. It was at this stage that Madhvacharya was accepted as an avatar of Vayu by the students. Each sentence of the text was repeated twice by the students. The teacher emphasised correct pronunciation and aspirations. The scripts were translated into Kannada with markings for intonation.

All the students and teachers had markings of gopichandana. The paste was applied as a *tilaka* (vertical line), on the forehead, the arms and torso, twelve in all. Marks of the conch and disc were stamped onto the body. They also had a necklace made of tulsi beads and the sacred thread. These distinguished Madhvas from non-Madhvas as also from those who had not yet had the upanayana ceremony. They wore a small dhoti without any upper cloth. Some had their ears pierced.

At 12:30 p.m. there was a break for lunch. Lunch consisted of rice, two 'side-dishes' and sweets. The students began to eat after the swamiji took the first morsel. Before eating they observed the traditional brahminical ritual of setting aside some rice as an offering, and chanting the Gayatri mantra. By so doing they emphasised that the food was prasada.

The students were then allowed to rest till two o'clock, after which the patha continued for another hour and a half. In the ensuing break, hot milk was served to all. Swamiji went around distributing almonds to the students. They resumed the patha that went on till 5.00 p.m. After that, it was time for fun. They slept after dinner, as Vasudeva, the name of the icon in the matha, looked on. It reminded one of what the senior swamiji of the Adamar matha had once remarked:

> The icon of Vasudeva here which dates back to times before Madhvacharya favours education. This matha has seen the growth and maturing of many swamis and learned men.

The Sphere of Cultural Production

In understanding the transmission of knowledge, the practice of teaching and learning and how tradition shapes it, it is useful to use Pierre Bourdieu's (1930) analysis of practice or action. Bourdieu considers action and practice not in terms of conscious intentionalities but in terms of an imbibed mode of existence. This is the habitus that is formed in a relation with a structure or field which distinguishes itself from others. Agents in a field imbibe the subtle ways of living life, the capital of that community through cumulative exposure and because what one imbibes fits with the objective and visible observance of social practices, the learning or imbibing process is forgotten and the habitus is rendered natural, or as given. Thus, habitus is not just a matter of cognitive understanding. It is a process of socialisation whereby the dominant modes of thought and experience inherent in the social and physical world (both of which are symbolically constructed) are internalised by social agents.

In the present context, Udupi matha may be considered the field in which habitus is formed. A field may be represented as a patterned system of objective forces. As Wacquant puts it:

> ...much in the manner of a magnetic field, a relational configuration endowed with a specific gravity which it imposes on all the objects and agents which enter it (Bourdieu and Wacquant, 1992: 17).

It is also a space where conflicts are played out and there is competition in which participants strive to gain control over the species of capital effective in it.

The gurus, or those in a position of authority, reinforce the structure of the matha by perpetuating the sect's philosophy and ideology primarily through the transmission of knowledge. They are the generators of internal dispositions that make up the habitus of the agents. For, along with the gyana (knowledge) that they impart, they are also responsible for constructing the world of customs and norms.

The subject matter of patha in terms of knowledge statements imparts the philosophical wisdom of the texts and promotes the need for inquiry against a stand that justifies belief. These knowledge statements cannot be abstracted from the sectarian customs and values and in actual practice interact with belief statements. These belief statements prescribe the pedagogic process, the way of learning and teaching and to whom it should be imparted.

For Bourdieu, belief is an inherent part of belonging to the field. Faith becomes the condition of entry and it is tacitly regulated by sanctioning and debarring those entrants who would 'destroy the game' (Bourdieu 1990: 67). This debarring process takes place tacitly in the rejection of any non-Brahmin male, and females of all castes. The unconscious preference for Madhva Brahmin boys is evident from the background of the boys in the shibira and for that matter any student of a sannyasi-guru. Both non-Brahmins and women would 'destroy the game' as the customs, habits and the faith specific to the practice of Madhva sect could not be taught to all. (I will discuss later, the patha given by a grihastha in which these other groups participate to illustrate the changes in the pedagogic practices.) It is believed that the practice of convention that is universally accepted would be disputed if the participants and rules of the game change. For example, these groups would have to be taught though they do not have the yagnopavita (sacred thread). The shared set of values, reverence, history and emotions would be destroyed. It should be kept in mind that the selection of the type of participants in the field does not take place by the sannyasis only. The non-Madhvas and the non-Brahmins also do not send their children to these camps, but send them to the camps and centres organised by their sect. The Smarthas send their children to the camps organised by the Shankara mathas and the Lingayats send them to specialised camps organised by their matha.

This logic of the field which restricts entrance is essential for its functioning. The natural mode of existence cannot be entered into by a conscious will to do so. Bourdieu further emphasises the necessity of 'doxa'. Doxa is that which is beyond question and to which each agent tacitly accords by the mere fact of acting in accord with local convention. As Bourdieu says:

> That is why one cannot enter this magic circle by an instantaneous decision of the will, but only by birth or by a slow

process of co-option and initiation which is equivalent to a second birth (1990: 68).

Entrance by Birth

Both the alternatives, birth and second birth, have resonances in the notions of the agents in the Udupi matha. Birth was often cited as the way in which one could determine the status and path of an individual's life. For a student of the sannyasi, it is birth that gives the point of entry into the knowledge system of the matha. All students in the shibira, and of the sannyasis are male Madhva Brahmins. The reason for restricting entry to a select few was given by the sannyasis through the concept of *samskara*, a free-floating concept echoing the conceptualisation of habitus by Bourdieu. Samskara may be understood as the impressions that are formed due to associations and the habitual reaction formed by one's past. The proper samskara would be a state of mind receptive to traditional knowledge and transcendental ideas.

Yet, in the traditional system of transmission of knowledge, birth itself is not sufficient. There has to be another birth. This is symbolised by the upanayana ceremony often performed for the male Brahmin between the ages of 8 and 10 years. The upanayana is the inauguration of the relationship between the student and the teacher. The student is considered twice-born (*dvija*) after this, for the guru, by giving him knowledge, gives him a second birth. The *Satapatha Brahmana* (xi, 5.4) says:

> Holding the pupil within him as a womb, [the guru] impregnates him with his spirit and delivers him in a new birth.

Faith in the traditional value, and rationality is brought about by the hidden persuasion of an implicit pedagogy. The Vedic statements pronounced by the guru regulate custom and order patterns of behaviour. Many of the utterances of the guru are intended to result in a particular behaviour of the student.

The Function of Utterances

Bourdieu's analysis of doxa, habitus and the field has many parallels with Austin's (1962) understanding that utterances are not just words, but have a force which evinces emotion, prescribes conduct and influences attitudes. For example, the elocutionary act of saying 'my horse is not fully fit' might suggest a warning and induce the listener to change his view as to the likely winner of the race and also perhaps deter him from betting on my horse. *In* saying that my horse is not fully fit, there is a warning and this has illoctionary force and *by* saying that and deterring the listener from betting on my horse is what Austin calls the perlocutionary force of an utterance.

In the matha, the guru might, for example, quote the *Taittiriya Upanishad* and explain how the student needs to approach the guru with humility and with folded hands, asking the guru to teach him. In saying this, the gurus prescribe an attitude for the student in their presence. In practice, the perlocutionary force is tacitly incorporated and evidenced in the reverence to the guru that is expressed through the bending of the body to touch the guru's feet, followed by linguistic utterances. In the way the student stands and speaks to the guru, or presses his feet out of reverence, while he is relaxing, a whole modality is displayed within which speech becomes meaningful and acquires force.

Venkatesh, a young student studying the *Nyaya-Sudha* has the same feeling of reverence towards his guru. He is a shishya of the senior Phalimar swamiji (80 years), a guru who is widely venerated for his knowledge and scholarship. Venkatesh is relatively young to be studying the *Sudha* as he is just 18. The guru found him brilliant and felt that he could skip the reading of *Tattva Prakashika* (another commentary by Jayatirtha on the *Brahma Sutra Bhashya* of Madhvacharya. It is studied before the *Sudha*) and move straight on to the *Nyaya-Sudha*. This explains the young age at which the student is receiving instruction in *Sudha*.

The student and teacher have a very affectionate relationship.

Soon after the swamiji has conducted the morning rituals, Venkatesh goes to him for blessings. He clasps his guru's feet while the guru recites a special mantra with rice (*mantra akshate*) in his hands which he then places on Venkatesh's head. The mantra is a prayer to give to the student sharp intellect and the unflinching devotion to Brahman.

Similar to the utterances and quotations from texts which specify behaviour in front of sannyasi and non-sannyasi gurus, the first guru of the sect, Madhvacharya, has a special place for the members. The teachers of Udupi stress that Madhvacharya is a great soul because he is the avatar of Vayu (the wind god). They say, 'He is the third avatar after Hanuman and Bhima. He is one with your breath.' In saying that Madhva is a demigod of the stature of Vayu, the gurus not only mean that he should be respected and worshipped, but also that his texts have a special status.

Austin insists that every utterance has a certain feature. In saying that something is done points to an analysis which not only concentrates on the 'constative' or descriptive utterances in terms of true or false, but also on the force that utterances carry. Here, it is profitable to view the propagation of Madhva as Vayu in terms of the affect it has, rather than to see it as a true or false statement.

In terms of a re-formulation of the self, Shastra consists of utterances which set standards and ideals for the novice. Such an illustration of the force that words carry is embodied within the philosophical discourse where there is an elaboration of the *uttamadhikari*, the student of philosophy who has the highest ability. The gunas (qualities) of this greater level of *adhikara* (ability) are enunciated and described in detail to differentiate it from the middle (*madhyama*) and lower (*adhama*) levels of adhikara. Adhikara at the *uttama* level means the person is *shanta* (the mind fixed in Brahma and therefore peaceful), *danta* (non repressed control over the senses born out of understanding), *uparta* (being withdrawn from the objects of the world), *titikshu* (not mere tolerance, which often is a sign of helplessness, but indifference) and *samahita* (the ability to evaluate and move beyond the cause of misery).

The utterances of the guru explaining these qualities are not meant to be a mere description of an uttamadhikari. More importantly, these qualities are stated to induce changes in the students, to set ideals and standards. A sannyasi who had heard this as a boy said it had great effect on him and had influenced his perception on life since he wanted to be similar to the adhikara of the great sages and demigods (who are known to be madhyama and uttamadhikaris).

The guru is seen as an intermediary between the subject matter Brahman and the wish or will of the student to understand Brahman. The Shastric texts lay down the qualities that are necessary in a guru who is expounding Shastra. They are an important factor in the pedagogic process for the Madhvas of the Udupi matha.

A guru should have (i) *vivaksha*—the desire to tell, and teach the student; (ii) *vivaksha artha tattva gyana*—be well-versed in the subject he is going to teach; (iii) *karna pathava*—the sense organs should function properly—a guru with impaired speech, hearing or eyesight cannot function with ease; and (iv) *avipralipsa*—the teacher should not intend to cheat the student. He must not hide his knowledge or misrepresent it. These qualities are what a student looks for while selecting a guru and the gurus strive to show these traits. The guru, in laying out these qualities of a teacher, expects the student to examine his teacher and then respect him for these qualities.

The gurus on their part desire students who are brilliant and devoted to God. A saint said, 'This will ensure that the philosophy of god (*Bhagavat Shastra*) is kept alive and it shall also make the guru famous.' Something similar is stated in the *Taittiriya Upanishad*:

> O Supreme God designated as Svaha! May the disciples come to me from all sides, the disciples who have control over their senses and are deeply attached to God come to me. May I have

reputation as a good teacher among people, may I be happy all along (I–II).

Shastra in its philosophical enterprise attempts a re-formulation of the self. The notion here is that saying something will often, or even normally, produce certain consequential effects upon the feelings, thoughts or actions of the audience. The act of locution or the act of speech produces results by what is said and this is the prelocutionary force of utterance.

This implies that the guru's word carries weight not simply because he has authority, but because he deals with words in a system of values and tradition. Most of the understanding of the pedagogic process assumes a simplistic notion of authority resting in the personality of the guru or teacher. The analysis here aims to point out that the processes involved are much more complex. This tradition which forms the field in which words are uttered and have meaning is manifest most forcefully in and through the body. Faith in traditional values being incorporated first and foremost into the body becomes the expression of the state of mind.

In the shibira, in the patha by various gurus, and generally among the Madhvas, markings on the body are a symbol of shared culture and tradition. A mark distinguishes a Madhva Brahmin who has had his upanayana ceremony from those who have not and also in general from all non-Madhvas. These gopichandana marks are applied after each bath and before the ritual of sandhyavandana. These marks also give rise to a state of mind, an understanding of oneself as a Vaishnava. The vertical marks on the forehead and the body as explained, denote the movement upwards—the striving to move beyond misery and bondage.

The dress codes during instruction are also strictly followed. The teacher and pupil wear a dhoti and an unstitched cloth over the upper body. The upright posture of sitting cross-legged without stretching one's legs is a way of showing respect to the teacher and the text. This creates dispositions:

> A durable way of standing, speaking, walking and thereby of feeling and thinking and further, most of the words that refer to bodily postures evoke virtues and states of mind (Bourdieu 1990: 70).

The Division of Time for Study and Non-study

The social order, besides using the body as a depository of thoughts, sanctions and orders the temporal dimension as well. Collective rhythms play an important part in the structuring of various groups. The organisation of time or days for study and non-study for patha as distinct from its temporal dimension in upannyasa sets off a separation and hierarchisation between the two. Bourdieu stresses that temporal forms structure not only the groups' representation of the world but the group itself. This is because the group orders itself in accordance with this representation (Bourdieu 1986: 163).

There are specific days that are proscribed for instruction or patha. These days are the new or full moon day and the next day following these days called *pratipada* (the day one of the fifteen-day lunar cycle). The days of ritual impurity are also days of no study for the non-sannyasi students and teachers. (There is no ritual impurity for the sannyasis.) On the fourteenth day of the fortnightly lunar calendar and on the eighth day, the teaching of an *apaurushya* (authorless) text, the Veda, is prohibited. However, any other authored text can be taught. So in effect, there are two days every fifteen days when no patha is offered, called days of *anadhyayna* (no study). To stress the importance of anadhyayna, a sannyasi guru of the Udupi matha quoted a sentence from Valmiki's *Ramayana*:

> *Pratipat patha shelasya vidya eva tanutam gata*. (Like a person's knowledge shrivels up if he gives or receives patha on pratipada, the first day after the full or new moon, so was Sita shrivelled up.)

The sannyasi explained that this was how Hanuman described Sita's state to Ram on his return from Lanka.

However, Upannyasa or lectures for a general audience can be given on the days of anadhyayna. This does not involve formal teaching. Though a text is discussed by the guru, it is transmitted to an audience who are not formal (initiated) students who come to listen to the public lecture if they wish. The upannyasa does not have the classroom structure of patha and is therefore relaxed in its rules of transmission. (This structure will be analysed in the next chapter in detail.) A text called *Yogadipika* written by Narayanpanditacharya, the author of Madhva's life-story specifies:

> *Srimadbharta tataprya nirnayadhyam samthyset anadhyaye na tat kuryad vyutpanno nyayahikshanam.* (The *Mahabharata Tatparya Nirnaya*—a bhashya on the *Mahabharata* by Madhva and such other books should be read properly on anadhyayna days, as there is no patha on these days.)

Taken for Granted?

These divisions of time, the relation between dispositions and body postures, body markings and behaviour are taken for granted by the gurus and students in the matha. Bourdieu teaches us that this happens because of the correspondence between real divisions and practical principles of division, between social structure and mental structures (1984: 471).

None of the actors, the gurus or students could explain their codes of conduct and modes of behaviour, except through an implicit recourse to habit or at best by stating the alternatives followed by other caste or sub-caste members and emphasising that those practices 'are not for the likes of us'—the exact words Bourdieu uses to show how habitus without violence or argument tends to exclude:

> All the extravagances ('not for the like of us') that is all the behaviour that would be negatively sanctioned because they are incompatible with the objective conditions (1990: 56).

This understanding of the social order as self-evident or given is a feature that has crept in despite Madhva's insistence on examining all aspects of life and encouraging a reflexive attitude. The Dvaita polemic takes great pains to refute the understanding of Advaita that calls *chit* or consciousness, that is the same as Brahman, as self-evident. By introducing the doubtful nature of the subject matter of Shastra, Dvaita Vedanta seeks to bring in strongly the emphasis on *jignyasa* or inquiry. And this practice of questioning and probing is very much part of the learning process of the student. Yet, this reflexivity does not seem to go beyond the limits of philosophical discourse or textual understanding, for inside the matha, one does not see a Madhva Brahmin taking up Shankara's philosophy openly because he or she feels it is better, correct or simply beautiful. On the other hand, there are no known Advaiti students today who would convert to Dvaita openly, because they feel it is the truth or because Advaita cannot reply to the objections raised by Madhva. Even if such an Advaiti wanted to take up the learning of Dvaita philosophy, the sannyasis would not allow it. Madhva himself convinced and converted many Advaitis in his time and this practice continued for a while, but this is not the case today. The Madhva sect makes philosophy non-philosophical, for, it takes an intellectual output (say, for example the *Brahma Sutra Bhashya*) as a matter of faith.

Nevertheless, if philosophical thought exists and is expressed only through practice, then there is another expression of Madhva's thought within sectarian limits. The difference comes about due to the type of students some of the grihasthas have. What follows is a portrayal of a progressive grihastha scholar who is quite popular in Udupi and in the sect by and large. Other grihastha scholars are influenced by him and the changes he advocates, though some outside Udupi are critical of his methods. It is not so much the content, as the position and participants within pedagogic patterns that changes.

Entrance by Choice

The students of this grihastha Madhva Brahmin in Udupi include both men and women. He has also had some students from USA and UK. He explains this openness by saying that 'knowledge is open to all provided there is a keen urge to know'. He feels that such practice should be encouraged and 'it is the only way thought can survive in our present world. One cannot shut it and let it suffocate.' This is the same scholar who feels that rules of conduct that are laid down in books are like the constitution and need constant amendment (see Chapter 2). He himself wears a shirt, has no top knot and often sits on a sofa while teaching.

The teaching sometimes takes place in his house, but more often in a matha of Udupi that supports his viewpoint (I shall shortly describe the reactions of sannyasis to his methods.) When I was doing my fieldwork, there were many students who came intermittently to Udupi for patha. There were three regulars receiving patha on the *Bhagavata* (having earlier done the *Purusha Sukta*—an important Vedic hymn). Among the students was a Madhva Brahmin girl who was about 23 years of age. She was an active participant and studied the texts diligently. She felt more women should be encouraged to study the Shastra and that this expended on the view of the guru. 'There are many misconceptions about *Brahma Vidya* and unless you study, you cannot remove them.' She was not against marriage and wanted to marry a man 'who was not after the materialistic things of the world'.

One of the male students who was a school teacher studying with her also wanted a wife who would 'walk with him on the path of Brahma gyana'. He proposed to her and they decided to get married. The union was easily sanctioned by the elders in both the families and the guru was one of the important figures in the marriage. All rituals were conducted in his presence and he even gave a lecture to the gathering on being a grihastha.

Besides this female student, there were other women who visited this guru and expressed their wish to learn. He removed their apprehensions by saying, 'No, I do not agree with the rules that are laid down or followed by others. Each must find their own reason to live this life.' He also specified that he was not encumbered by notions of madi (purity). These other women had come to Udupi with their husbands who in turn had come for a darshan or to receive patha on some text or the other. This prevented them from becoming long-term students as they would have to go back after a month or so with their husbands. Nevertheless, they did attend the public lecture that this guru gave which was open to all, irrespective of sex or caste.

Some of the women accompanying their husbands were critical of the pedagogic practice, while some accepted the situation and encouraged their husbands. For instance, a woman staying in the matha with her husband said, 'I cannot study these difficult texts even if I wanted to; at least let my husband study them.'

The sannyasis have a mixed reaction to all of this. All the sannyasis are at least overtly supportive of a guru encouraging females and non-Madhva students to learn, but they themselves do not want to openly accept such students on a long-term basis. It is also to be noted that the grihastha scholars have greater freedom than the sannyasis-gurus and do not share the same degree of responsibility in maintaining tradition.

During the paryaya swamiji's time, women were allowed to sit when patha was specially organised for the chatur masya. This was being conducted by the invitee swami of the Phalimar Udupi matha. There were two or three women who came to this gathering and did participate by asking questions about the text. The senior Phalimar matha swamiji was at first hesitant in answering, but got used to their questioning and later accepted their presence. The paryaya swamiji encouraged women to write the shlokas of the *Bhagavad Gita* and sing bhajans in the main Krishna matha, but he did not have any women students of his own.

Returning to the grihastha guru and his students, there was one student from the USA who had come to learn the *Bhagavata*. The student is now teaching the text to his own students and according to the guru has a mixed group of Indian Brahmins and other castes (the teacher was not specific as to the exact caste status, nor did he know if there were any women students) as also some foreigners. One can expect his teaching though further removed from the 'binding' practices would reach a larger audience.

In the methods of the progressive guru from Udupi, one can find that Shastra is transmitted without traditional bindings. There is no need for a person to be a male Madhva Brahmin. In accepting women students, the 'second birth' or upanayana ceremony, is also done away with. The dress codes and body markings are relaxed or not specified. The important thing is having shraddha (devoted interest) towards the subject-matter. The students still have reverence for their guru and his words carry the same perlocutionary force. The division of time for study and non-study are also followed.

This pedagogic method makes thought more accessible and universally applicable. There is a separation of achara (traditional practice and custom) from vichara (thought process). Another grihastha guru who shares the viewpoint that knowledge should be accessible to all said, 'Philosophy (Madhva Shastra) is liberating, one needs to concentrate and direct one's energies to understanding rather than physical preparation for understanding.' This modifies the disposition of the actors involved. Transcendental knowledge can be gained without adhering to notions of purity and dress codes. Birth need not be the characterising feature of a *gyani* (a knowledgeable one). Traditional habits are replaced by a new regime which offers scope for incorporating many modern values. They seek to break the doxa, the taken for granted.

For Bourdieu, the agent is not condemned to act in accordance within the construction of the field or structure. He calls for a reflexivity which exposes the nexus between habitus and the field. It entails a 'return' to and an exploration of the

> unthought categories of thought which delimit the thinkable and

predetermine thought [Bourdieu, quoted in Wacqanut (1991: 40)].

In this regard, the grihastha scholars who have female students or non-Madhva students are not apologetic in their stance. It is not as if they have modified some of the processes to 'survive' the onslaught of modern existence. It is rather a firm decision to change outdated practices and engage actively in the world as it is. However, there are only about three or four such gurus in and around Udupi. The core of the institution, the matha, their pontiffs and some of the non-sannyasis may want changes, but cannot implement them and at the institutional level, there are very few modifications in the pedagogic practices.

In this cultural production of knowledge, the content or the interpretation of texts is also constructed and controlled by the institution. Institutions are not only responsible for the way in which knowledge is transmitted, but also for what is transmitted. The institutionalisation of thought involves a process of selection. The tradition of the matha specifies the interpretation to be accepted or the range of changes possible in the interpretations of the texts of Madhva. This depends on the affiliations of the people who head the matha to particular interpretations. This is what I turn to in the last section of this chapter.

The Politics of Traditional Continuity

In the matha, the gurus in a position of authority perpetuate the theory of knowledge and its content in the process of selection and transmission of texts. The interpretation is grounded in the words of the guru who gives the exegesis. The reverence the guru demands and his interpretation is institutionally sanctioned. A variant is dismissed as a wrong interpretation and thus reinforces the power of tradition and doxa. These symbolic systems are not simply instruments of knowledge, they are also instruments of domination.

Truth is constructed institutionally and traditionally and there is an effort, a tacit and subtle one, to obliterate differences in interpretation and understanding as error. In the matha, as Bourdieu says, any epistemology is also a political theory. For him, the theory of knowledge is an aspect of political power where the symbolic forces construct types of social reality (Bourdieu 1986: 165–66). The agent's disposition and what he or she takes for granted depends on the stability of the objective structures and their ability to reproduce themselves. This is why systems are preoccupied with maintaining structures of thought and behaviour. It is again reflexive thought that exposes the modus operandi of doxa, that which is taken for granted. This exercise exposes the orchestrating forces in the field.

In trying to promote this reflexivity, some scholars, mostly non-sannyasis have tried to establish an interpretation of Madhva's philosophy removed from interpretation and understanding established in the pedagogic practices which seek to maintain a chain of thought and logic. X—one of the grihastha scholars of Udupi long with a few others and their students differ slightly in the historical and philosophical analysis. On the birth anniversary of Jayatirtha (author of *Nyaya-Sudha*), during the exposition of Jayatirtha's life, the swamijis and some grihastha scholars talked about the myths and miracles performed while the grihastha pandit X stressed the uncertainty of traditional dogma due to lack of historical records. He asserted that the proof of Jayatirtha's greatness lies in the text *Nayaya-Sudha*, not in his power to perform miracles.

On the philosophical front, there were a few differences with a particular sannyasi's interpretation. The word *adhina* in Sanskrit implies dependence of the world on Brahman. A sannyasi of the Udupi matha during patha differentiated two shades of meaning. He said adhina is implied in two senses: creation and destruction (*shrishti* and *samhara*), i.e. dependence on Brahman for creation and annihilation and secondly, in the sense of maintenance (*niyamana*). All things except the jiva (soul) and similar *nitya* objects (time, space) are dependent in the first sense. The relation of soul to Brahman is of dependence of the second kind, that is niyamana. 'Brahman does not create, he only maintains the soul, for the soul is everlasting'. Scholar X disagreed with this bifurcation when I posed it to him. For him, adhina implies wholesale creation of all entities of this world. He emphaised, 'The world is adhina in all the three senses. All the entities are dependent on Brahman who is *svatantra* (independent) for their creation, maintenance and destruction.' However, on further prodding, X could not categorically say that the jiva (soul) or *jiva svarupa* (jiva's essence) is created. This problem remained unresolved. This shows that there are disagreements and also some dark areas which are not readily resolved. Well, that is the process of jignyasa or inquiry, where a philosophical doubt is followed through in the texts. It is also important to note that X explained his particular interpretations as a result of a break from a rigid and dogmatic following of the guru-shishya tradition. Though X was instructed by grihastha and sannyasi-gurus, he gained 'deeper insight through self-study.' He stressed that one's own interpretation, freed from the shackles of dogmatic tradition is the way for reflexivity. 'You see, it is very difficult to disagree with your guru openly. One must learn as much and then later move towards a thorough reading in the light of present-day circumstances,' he said.

These disagreements in the understanding of certain concepts do not become major confrontations. There seems to be a certain degree of flexibility granted in interpretation. Some deviation in interpretation is permitted. Those matters that produce confrontations relate to rules and regulations in the running of the mathas.[3] The differences in interpretation seem to fall well within the ambit of the Udupi matha's philosophical framework. These varieties of interpretation flourish because they are institutionally supported. There is nevertheless, a particular variation in the understanding of Madhva's philosophy that is unacceptable to the present-day sectarian philosophy and is therefore boycotted.

In his erudite study of Dvaita literature, B.N.K. Sharma talks of a few scholars whose ideas have ceased to survive (1981: 551) due to the unorthodox relation to traditional interpretation. He is mainly referring to the works of H.N. Raghavendrachar

(1895–1966). This circumstance had prompted me to trace his students way back in 1985. At that time, my teachers had advised me not to study the corrupt interpretations of H.N. Raghavendrachar which perhaps further fuelled my curiosity. There were indeed, a few students of Raghavendrachar spread out in India and the USA, but mainly concentrated in Karnataka. A reading of his interpretation of Madhva's philosophy along with the interviews of his students revealed that the same texts of the Madhva sect, outside the tradition, could exist in the form of a distinct interpretation, claiming to be the correct one. Raghavendrachar's work also evolved after the initial traditional training and later from 'self-study'. His works forced a debate among the Madhvas of that time (1941–1966) and in the end the orthodox tradition did not accept his views. However, it did survive during Raghavendrachar's lifetime and till a little later as an alternative interpretation. With the passage of time, the gurus of the orthodox tradition, both sannyasis and grihastha gurus, were able to institutionalise their interpretation through students who became pontiffs of the various mathas of the Madhva sect. On the other hand, most of Raghavendrachar's students did not become heads of mathas, instead they took to other 'modern' professions.

In the Udupi matha, most of the sannyasi gurus are direct disciples or the students of direct disciples of a sannyasi guru (including B.N.K. Sharma who disqualifies H.N. Raghavendrachar) who had entered into debate with H.N. Raghavendrachar. This fact was ascertained through the gurus present today and also from the unpublished and unfinished autobiography of H.N. Raghavendrachar, written in Kannada.

During my stay at Udupi, I tried to raise some of these debatable issues, now long forgotten. Following is the extract from the interview:

VASUDEVA RAO (VR)—Are you aware that there is an alternative theory of Madhva which says the *jiva-svarupa* (essence of the soul in effect the soul itself) is created?

(Most of the sannyasis were unfamiliar with this thought.

Some of the older sannyasi gurus were aware that such an interpretation existed, but had not studied any of H.N. Raghavendrachar's works. They all rejected what tradition had taught them to reject).

SANNYASI GURU (S)—(coolly) How can we accept anything that is against *siddhanta* (established doctrine)?

VR: How do we know which is the correct doctrine?

A (retired Air Force officer, living in the matha and close to S): No, there can't be difference in interpretations.

VR: Is it not true according to *savishesha bheda* (according to Madhva, the substance and its attribute are identical but separated in usage) that any change in the attribute implies that it is a new substance, hence created. A pot is not mud, although made out of it, as it has a different existence (*satta*) and function (*pravritti*). If the fact that the pot is made of mud and hence non-distinct (from mud) is emphasised, then one cannot posit differences between objects. Is not the pot 'created'?

S: All that is okay but how can the soul or its essence be created? It is *nitya*, everlasting. Does not this in its very usage mean the uncreated?

VR: We know of many substances that are called nitya because of *samakarsha nyaya* or the dearth of language. Don't the *Upanishads* say Brahman is *Nitya nityanam* (the nitya of the nitya things, or the everlasting essence of everlasting entities)? There is a difference of *nityatva* between the soul and Brahman, just as you accept a difference in the degree of reality between Brahman and soul. Further, how can you limit the Vedic statements which impute 'all' creations to Brahman, or condition the *Sutra Vakya* (the aphorism of the *Brahma Sutra*)—*Janmadasya yatah aum* (All this is created and so on—by Him)?

S: (A little irritated): You don't understand, how can you say the jiva is created? If you say so, then there is a problem. Why did God create 'him' as bad and 'you' as good? Will this not imply that Brahman or God is prejudiced and is partial? It is the *karma* that defines the nature of existence. If the karma is bad then the person suffers, is evil, etc. Good karma leads to good birth. The karma of the soul defines the type of life one is to lead. Brahman maintains and sees to it that each gets the fruits of his karma.

VR: This formulation of yours itself denies what the Veda seems to teach. For according to you, the Veda instead of saying Brahman is the *sarvakarta* (all doer), and Brahman is responsible for all that happens, the Veda and Sutras should say, karma is the most important thing. Karma (one's own action) and not Brahman is responsible for this world. Does this not deny Madhva and his philosophical thrust. (*Veda pramana*, Brahman *sarva svatantra*, independent unaided creator of all, and so on). Is it not better to retain the unconditional agency described in your daily recitation *Naham karta, Hare karta* (I do not do—God acts or does)] of Brahman and to somehow explain the evil and goodness of this world, rather than deny His creatorship and eventually Brahman by your false theory of karma?

The discussion after this turned into an argument and I ceased pursuing the matter any further. The retired Air Force employee seemed to be somewhat influenced by the debate and could accept an alternative, and said he would study and research the matter. [The points raised by me are stated in H.N. Raghavendrachar's Kannada book *Madhva Siddhanta* (1945)].

However, as of today, H.N. Raghavendrachar's thought does not survive and is not accepted by any of the pontiffs of Udupi matha or of any other mathas of the sect. If this thought were institutionalised, then there could have been greater reflexivity.

Bourdieu points out that a thought cannot survive without an institution that informs the habitus of agents. By creating an institutionalised support, one can enhance reflexive thought. For Bourdieu

> social laws are temporarily and spatially bound regularities that

> hold as long as the institutional conditions that underpin them are allowed to endure (Wacquant 1992: 53).

Recently in the Udupi matha, one of the scholars, with the permission of the pontiff, took a team to a site described in the *Sumadhva Vijaya* (the life story of Madhvacharya written by Narayanpanditacharya). According to the text, this is the place where Madhva buried some of his works which will be unearthed by Vishnutirtha (the younger brother of Madhva, who also took sannyasa and is, according to tradition, doing *tapas* or penance and inquiry into Brahman in the Himalayas. It is believed that Vishnutirtha will return when Madhva's thought has been so corrupted that it will require the genius of Vishnutirtha and Madhva's originals to disprove the false interpretations. Scholars from Udupi went to that particular site and tried to dig, but could not, as wherever they dug they encountered solid rock, as if a huge slab had been stretched over the buried works of Madhva.

The scholars returned after the unsuccessful attempt. On inquiring, one of them answered:

> It was clear from the experience that I do not have the capacity (*yogyata*) to uncover the works. It must wait for Vishnutirtha.

So it seems, tradition has its own way of providing scope and flexibility; however, not in the present. The acceptance of the possibility of error in interpretation is hinted, but this will be recognised only when the tradition's history unfolds in the future, 'as was predicted'.

These voices challenging interpretations could be seen as rupturing and hence threatening the idea of a doxa which reproduces the matha intellectually and ideologically. The revered tradition of gurus is threatened as it could be proved that their version is not just a variety in interpretation, but invalid or wrong.

The present-day environment in the matha also seeks to mask differences in an attempt to give a picture of unity which is perceived as important for the present-day followers. This sense of homogeneity and harmony is an attempt to perpetuate the matha and its tradition.

On the national level, the differences among sects is being underplayed in an attempt to portray Hinduism as one, without sectarian quarrels and hence worthy of respect (for the lay followers). Some of the sannyasis of Udupi have participated in such forums where heads from different sects meet on a common platform. There seems to be an inevitable tension between the two efforts of emphasising oneness on the one hand and plurality on the other. Some lay members in the matha feel that diversity is a sign of decay. They fuel this view when they say, 'They themselves are not united, how can they guide us.' But, seen from inside, differences continue and many viewpoints have their own adherents implying an acceptance by lay followers of the variety in opinions and world views. This acceptance is, as Singer (1972: 396) observes, an orthogenetic process: an indigenous innovation which does not pose a threat as any alien idea would. The embracing or rejection of modifications or diversity therefore, does not mean the rejection or acceptance of all the basic values and traditions of the system.

I have so far concentrated on the types of actors in patha and the codes of conduct and the modes of behaviour that distinguish the realm of pedagogic practices. Let me now turn to the actual process through which knowledge is transmitted, and analyse the contents of utterances which occur during communication of traditional knowledge in different contexts. For this purpose, two genres of reproduction of knowledge mentioned earlier will be taken up; patha and upanyasa.

Notes

1. The three major *pramanas* are *prattyaksha* (perception) *anumana* (inference) and *agama* (verbal testimony). The *Shrutis* and *Smritis* fall under the third category.
2. Patha in literal translation means recitation but in Udupi, the term

denotes the process of instruction from teacher to pupil involving study of the meaning and relevance of philosophical concepts.

3. There is active disagreement as to whom and when sannyasa should be given. Foreign travel is objected to although one of the sannyasis has been to the USA. There is change which shows that the tradition is not very rigid about practices (more about this in the concluding chapter).

5

Styles of Discourse in the Production of Knowledge

Introducing Patha and Upannyasa

The two genres, patha and upannyasa, are employed in the reproduction of knowledge in Udupi. In patha, the students are initially required to learn by heart certain portions of the text that are important. Those students who want to specialise in conducting Brahminical rituals need to learn greater portions of the ritual text by heart. The emphasis in normal patha is not on learning the scriptures or Veda by heart but on the understanding. William Graham (1987), in his study on the oral aspects of scripture, stresses that patha means recitation of the sacred texts. His interest is to prove that in the Indian or the Hindu world, recitation and memorising is the primary intent of the student of sacred literature; he calls this the south Indian conception of patha (1987: 72). In view of the Madhva Udupi matha, this leads to a misleading generalisation. Jack Goody (1968: 14) also gives primary importance to rote learning. He says, 'Books... have themselves to be committed to memory before they are considered read.' He adds, 'Book learning takes on an inflexibility that is the antithesis of the spirit of inquiry which literacy has elsewhere fostered.'

In the Udupi matha, books such as the *Tattva Prakashika*, the *Nyaya-Sudha* and many more which are taught in the patha are not memorised. In its principled form, the philosophy of Madhva initiates forcefully a spirit of inquiry, rejecting other schools of thought precisely because of the neglect or absence of the will to inquire although as one saw, the spirit of enquiry is controlled in several ways in the everyday life of the matha.

Patha could, in literal translation, mean recitation, but it involves the component of instruction as well. One of the sannyasi teachers, when asked why recitation in the Madhva sect was not given importance, said: '*yastan na Veda kim richa karishyati*' (without knowing the meaning, what can the Rig Veda do or how can it be functional?). Another saint used stronger words and said: 'To merely recite without understanding is to be like a donkey carrying a load of sandalwood without realising its fragrance or importance.'

Graham makes a valid point about scripture being relational, that is, having meaning and sacredness only for particular groups of people. Given this position, it is surprising that he treats the 'Indian Paradigm' as a monolithic entity devoid of sects and hence different relational possibilities. It is also evidence of his equating Hinduism with Advaita or Shankara's philosophy. In this case, it has led the author to ignore patha as exegesis.

When a student of the matha sits for patha, he or she sits with a paper and pen along with a copy of the text. The teacher keeps the text and commentaries around him for cross referencing while teaching. The student is often seen making notes for later reference. This shows that the oral tradition is oral not because knowledge is transmitted orally, completely from memory, but because it requires a guru who translates the form of the written word into the oral medium. The written text is transmitted orally by the guru—it cannot merely be read. The guru is understood as necessary in the process of understanding and internalising the text—in the process of self-realisation. He is able to expose the connection between philosophy and life. A saint-guru specified that teaching or lecture needs to evoke bhakti (devotion) towards Brahman. The significance of the text is brought out through the human word of the seer, prophet or spiritual master, not through a manuscript, even when the latter is important.

Jack Goody terms this as 'restricted literacy' (1968: 13). The guru tradition is characteristic of situations of restricted literacy, where the role of the teacher as the mediator of knowledge is given pre-eminent importance. The guru through his instruction adds charisma to book-learning.

The pupil, when he is receiving instruction, sits on the floor while the sannyasi-guru sits on deer skin with a *Vyasa peetha*, an X shaped desk on which to place the book. At the end of teaching, the student usually offers his *guru-dakshina* (return gift to the guru). It is usually in the form of the student's first earnings and part of his subsequent earning to the matha or to the guru if he is a grihastha.

The conditions under which upannyasa is given are quite different. Let us first get introduced to the genre. The upannyasa or pravachana is given in a large room where a number of people, both male and female and belonging to various castes, are seated. Dress codes are not strictly observed. The student-teacher relation does not exist and the people disperse without any necessary verbal interaction with the lecturer. Thus, upannyasa is basically a monologue. The favourite topics for the Madhvas are the *Mahabharata*, the *Bhavagad-Gita* and the *Bhagavata Purana*.

The sannyasi or the pandit of the Udupi matha is invited outside the town as well to give lectures on these topics for a period of seven to ten days. The *Bhagavata Purana* is usually spread over seven days, together called the *Bhagavata-Saptaha* (the seven days of Bhagavata), a feature common to Vaishnavas all over India.

Jack Goody correctly points out that where writing and therefore reading is limited to a minority, there the art of narration flourishes (1965: 19–20). Here, the minority is made up of those who have had formal training in Shastra that is difficult to obtain as it needs a guru. The monetary benefits or opportunities of such training are absent in the present-day modern structure. Besides, the subject-matter itself is difficult to understand, and the orthodoxy surrounding it does not attract the modern-day youth. We see here another example of how a 'field' (Bourdieu) nourishes or does not nourish a way of being in this world.

The Understanding into Specific Genres

A genre is a set of stable utterances born in a 'dialogic' activity. This view stems from Mikhail Bakhtin's understanding of the characteristics of genre. By definition, the world is unlimited, endowed with innumerable properties; genre makes a selection among them, sets a model of the world and breaks up the infinite series. Genre originates in the dual orientation of every utterance. A generic type is determined by its orientation first to the listeners and recipients and secondly by the thematic content of the work or text. Bakhtin specifies:

> Every genre has its methods, its ways of seeing and understanding reality and these methods are its exclusive characteristic. The artist must learn to see reality through the eyes of the genre (quoted in Todorov 1984: 83).

Each utterance is born of a 'dialogic' activity. The 'dialogic' discourse for Bakhtin is a way of being in this world: I am conscious of myself and become myself only while revealing for another, through another and with the help of another. Bakhtin, who deals with Dostoevsky's works, emphasises the artistic visualisation rather than developing his ideas as a philosophical theory. Although Bakhtin opposes the 'dialogic' with the 'monologic' discourse (that expects no response from the other), this distinction collapses in his insistence that even a monologue recognises in its utterances the presence of the other. Todorov highlights that distinction cannot sustain itself in an omnipresent dimension of dialogism—'In a very broad sense even the monologue is dialogical' (Todorov 1984: 63). Ken Herschkop

(1989) agrees and shows how in the various definitions of dialogism, the monologistic differentiation that Bakhtin draws is often subsumed to accommodate the various perspectives.

> Dialogism must then be redefined to accommodate its various manifestations; as the constant mixing of intentions of speaker and listener; as the way an utterance acquires meaning by inflecting past utterances; as the need of each form of speech to position itself stylistically among other existing forms. Dialogism at this level of definition denotes a transcendental principle of discourse, the very condition of communication and of the creation of meaningful utterances. (1989: 6).

So, utterance in its dialogic mode is not a mirroring of a ready-made truth. It is, on the contrary, the processing or construction of truth within a distinct temporal and spatial world. Utterance depends on the addresses.

The Socratic Genre

The patha as a generic type corresponds to what Bakhtin calls the Socratic genre. At the base of this genre, says Bakhtin, lies the dialogic nature of human thinking about truth. Truth is not self-evident, nor is it ready-made, to be passed on from one individual to another.

> Truth is not born nor is it to be found inside the head of an individual person, it is born between people collectively searching for truth in the process of their dialogic interaction (Bakhtin 1984: 10).

Both these ideas are present within the sects' philosophical framework. The self-evident nature of the subject-matter of Shastra is rejected. On the contrary, Shastra is regarded as a problematic object of inquiry at the outset. The interpretation of *Brahma-Sutras* stresses the *samdigdha* or doubtful nature of Shastra and hence promotes jignyaṣa or inquiry. The understanding of the *Taittiriya Upanishad* highlights the dialogic activity in patha.

> *Athadhi vidyam. Acharya purva rupam. Anteyvas uttara rupam. Vidya sandhi. Pravachanagum sandhanam. Ityadyadhirupam.* (In matters concerning knowledge, the master is the first form, the disciple is the latter form. Knowledge is the link. Exposition is the point of linking).

The guru giving patha includes a conscious critique of the opponents' position. The exposition is detailed. For example, a verse from any *Upanishad* will first be split up into specific morphemes with a philosophical semantics. For example, the difference between *sah atma tatvam asi* (your soul is the same as that) and *sah atma attvam asi* (your soul is not the same as that). This is called *anvaya. Khandartha*, given by Raghavendra Swamy provides the meaning of the split up words. Next, Madhva's bhashya or interpretation is taken up, which unifies the thought of the *Brahma Sutras* and develops a critique of various positions involving a dialogic contact with history. This is further elaborated by the commentaries on Madhvacharya's bhashya by Jayatirtha. Students ask questions and clear their doubts. The guru also evaluates the students' understanding from time to time.

Bakhtin contrasts this genre with the carnivalistic genre. As compared with the Socratic genre, the specific weight of the comic element is generally increased in the carnivalistic genre. It is free of a rigorous textual exegesis. Often, there are oxymoronic combinations and contrasts such as the combination of foolishness and wisdom in one person. There is use of everyday examples to facilitate provocative laughter. The stories are filled with public decrownings of kings and sudden twists of fate are highlighted. There is play of different levels of consciousness of this world and of the world beyond. This is only an analytical distinction as it is neither possible nor desirable to completely separate the two genres. As Bakhtin says, the genres interpenetrate and often overlap.

Let us look at some examples from the field. What follows are transcriptions from tapes and notes made during patha and upannyasa.

Patha

The examples are taken from all the three *prasthanas* (parts) of Shastra, the *Upanishad, Sutra* and the *Gita* prasthanas. It also includes as illustration a separate text written by Madhvacharya which is not a bhashya.

Example 1

The swamiji sits against the wall in his matha while half a dozen students surround him. The swamiji is conducting patha on *Ishvasyopanishad*. The class is about to begin and the students have gathered discussing parts of the text. As they sit down for the class, the students take out the text and a notebook.

Swamiji: *Harih Aum Sri gurubhyo namaha* (respects to the Guru —implying Vedavyasa) *Srimad Anandatirtha Bhagavat Padacharya gurubhyo namaha* (respects to Anandatirtha guru; i.e. Madhva).

The swamiji begins by asking one of the students (who has not got a chance yet to do so) to sum up the previous shloka (stanza) of the *Upanishad*.

Student 1: (recites the *Upanishad* mantra, *yasmin sarvani...*) for one who knows that in all existence there is one lord, (looks at his notes) he has knowledge and is a gyani (wise). How shall such a person, who sees oneness, ever have grief? This means that to know Brahman to be the in-dweller of all is to be removed from attachments and grief.

Swamiji: Good. Now we move on to the next shloka. (He recites the shloka.) Some of the students who are already familiar with it, as they have earlier learnt it by heart, recite with him. *Sa paryagat shukramakayamavaranamasnavirgum shuddham apapam viddham kavir manishi paribhuh svayambhuh yathata thyato rathan vyadadhat shasvatibhyah samabhyah.*

The swamiji goes on to give the detailed meaning of this shloka.

Swamiji: The anvaya of this shloka is like this: (this orders the verse and breaks it up into separate words) *Sa paryagat shukram akayam avranam asna virgum shudham apapa vidyam kavih manishi paribhu svayambhu yatha tatyatah arthan vyadadhat shashvatibhyah samabhyah.*

The khandartha is as follows: (khandartha gives the meaning of each split-up word. Both anvaya and khandartha are followed according to the version given by Raghvendra Swamy. He provides the meaning as he claims in line with Madhva's commentary and thought). The students are ready with their note books. The swamiji goes on;

Sah—A person who has adhikara or capacity, i.e. a wise man.

paryagat—having reached Him, (such a person) becomes detached. How does this come about? It comes about through attaining similarity with Brahman. The next few words highlight the liberating attributes of Brahman.

Student 2: (A little confused) Does not being similar mean becoming Brahman, and is this not Advaitic in spirit?

Swamiji: No. The shloka does not imply becoming Brahman, but becoming similar to Brahman. Anyway, these points will be discussed in the shloka—

yo sao-vasau purusah so ham asmi.

(He who is the inner ruler of all resides as my inner ruler) (The swamiji continues with the khandartha).

Shukram—without grief.

Akayam—one who has no *lingasharira*, a body similar to ours, capable of being afflicted by suffering.

Avranam—completely perfect.

Asnaviram—One who is bereft of a physical body made up of the elements. Brahman's body is full of bliss and wisdom.

Shudham—pure.

Apapam viddham—without inauspiciousness.

The Lord (*Paramatma*) is free from all delusion and sorrow. The soul having attained the similarity to the Lord becomes free from sorrow and delusion. This Vedic pramana (evidence) shows how Brahman is not *nirguna* or attributeless as Shankara says.

Let us see further:

Kavih—the omniscient

Manishi—the inspirer of all souls

Paribhu—He has held everything under his control. The world is dependent on him, not like a puppet as many people think, for he is also the creator of the puppet. Therefore, 'dependence' as a concept should be understood through a philosophical discipline. People should be careful while giving examples.

Svayambhuh—He is *svatantra*, i.e. independent and does not rest on any other entity.

Yatha tathyta—in reality/truth

Arthan—the objects

Vyadadhat—(He) creates

Shavstibhyah samabhyah—since time immemorial, without beginning and end, He exists—implying that the process of creation (and also destruction) is going on endlessly.

Let us see what the last few words highlight. The advaitis say that the universe is superimposed on Brahman as the illusory silver in a seashell. This world is illusory, and hence there is no creation of it. This mantra, using the words *yatha tathytah*, refutes the conclusion by affirming the real creation of the world. Thus, as it has been stated in the previous mantras, the real and correct knowledge of the Lord is a result of moksha, not the false theory of illusion, however attractive it may be.

(Swamiji addresses the student who had asked a question earlier). To come to your question, similarity means that there is distinction. Shankara and his followers say that when water from one vessel mixes with water in another, it becomes one. Ha! (Addresses Student 3). H knows this is not true. (The swamiji and student 3 had apparently discussed this example from the feature film *Madhvacharya*). Why don't you explain to us? (Other students nod their heads.)

Student 3 recollects the example and narrates the story: A great Advaitic scholar had come to Madhvacharya and posed this problem to him. Acharya instantly sought to remove the doubt in the mind of the Advaitic scholar. He took water from a vessel and poured it into another vessel containing a small amount of water and simply said, 'If the two waters have become one, how come there is an increase in volume?' (Some students make noises of appreciation, others have a frown on their faces.)

(Swamiji further elucidates the concept and concludes the discussion).

Swamiji: Thus, you have seen how important it is to have correct knowledge of the Shastras.

The question asked in the beginning of the class had

ostensibly haunted the swamiji. As Bakhtin points out, utterance always answers a question.

What the khandartha implies is tested in the utterer—the guru. The guru justifies his stance by often refuting or corroborating from earlier sources and thus constantly addresses the thought as articulated in earlier times. Bakhtin points out that in the dialogic testing of the idea, the person who represents it is also simultaneously tested (1984: 112). There is a free creative development against a dialogising background of other ideas. The Socratic genre makes possible the dialogue with history, bringing it within the reach of the present.

The dialogues in the sect's tradition, Halbfass claims, lack the 'systematic and deliberate openness for questions and problems which may be found in Platonic dialogues' (1988: 362). However, unlike Halbfass's claim that the guru (one of the participants in the dialogue) possesses the complete knowledge and ultimate truth, in the sect, there is an emphasis that no complete knowledge is possible. The gurus are hierarchically placed according to the degrees of knowledge. Even in actual practice, no guru claims a complete knowledge of the truth.

Example 2

Let us take another example of patha given by another sannyasi-guru. This is a patha for advanced students who have studied the *Upanishads*, preliminary logic and the study of epics. One student has come from outside Udupi as well. A couple of students are retired and aged above sixty. There are five students in all.

The text being taught is *Tattva Prakashika* written by Jayatirtha or Tikacharya. It is a commentary on the *Brahma Sutra* bhashya of Madhvacharya. The presentation here is an abridged and simplified version of two days of patha. The list of arguments as given by the guru and the student's interventions and reactions are highlighted.

The guru begins the patha with the mangalacharana (mantras

of invocation and homage) of *Tattva Prakashika*, the text to be taught. There are six verses in all. Sticking to tradition, Jayatirtha, in the first verse, praises Brahman and sets out the discipline for achieving Him. Next, he praises and pays homage to Vedavyasa or Badarayana as the author of the *Brahma Sutras*. Then Bhashyakara, i.e. Madhvacharya or Anandatirtha is praised. It is his grace that has yielded knowledge. Finally, Jayatirtha bows to Akshobhya Tirtha, his own teacher and claims in all humility that his own work (the *Tattva Prakashika*) is an assimilation of his guru's speech in the light of Anandatirtha's interpretation.

The mangalacharana is recited by all the students before each class of *Tattva Prakashika* commences.

Presently, the section being taught is the *Jignyasadhikarana* of the *Brahma Sutra*. The section deals with the discipline and science required to study Brahman. It lays down the epistemology of Brahma Mimamsa or Dvaita philosophy.

The class has by now moved towards the last quarter of this chapter or *adhikarana*. The sutra that is being enunciated is the first—*Athato Brahma jignyasa aum*. The bhashya written by Madhva is studied with its commentary, the *Tattva Prakashika*, and other subsidiary texts. The word Brahma is being explained and the bhashya connected with it is expounded.

> Swamiji: What is the meaning of the word Brahma, one may ask. We are confronted with various interpretations today. Some say Brahma is without gunas (attributes), i.e. nirguna, others hold He is limited by *prakriti* (nature). There are some who say both positions are wrong and that He is full of attributes and complete (guna-purna). So there is doubt as to the correct position and we have seen that inquiry and philosophy is initiated by a doubted position.
>
> Acharya's (referring to Madhvacharya's) bhashya is
>
> *Bhashya—Brahma shabdascha vishnueva*
> (The word Brahma or Brahman is used only in the sense of Vishnu)

Tattva Prakashika presents the significance of the whole idea as:

> *brahma shabdasya anekarthatvepi tasya vishnaaveva mukhyatvat mukhyasyaiva grahyatvat sa eva Sutrakaara vivaksito jnayata iti bhavah.*
>
> (Though the word Brahman has many meanings, it attains its primary meaning only when it is used in the sense of Vishnu. Further, only the primary meaning deserves to be recognised. For these reasons, it is understood that by the word Brahman, the Sutrakara Vedavyasa means Vishnu. This is the significance of the bhashya).

This clearly is our position. Brahman is full of attributes, infinite and limitless, and that is why he is Vishnu.

(Addressing student 1) Can you tell me the position of Shankara on the word Brahman?

(The swamiji does not have anything personal against Shankara whose position is examined with academic detachment similar to arguments against rival schools of thought in universities.)

Student 1: They say that Brahman is attributeless (nirguna).

Swamiji: Yes, that is correct. But to be precise, they say Brahman is *akhanda* (partless). To make matters clear, let us examine this position and see how it difers from ours.

(Swamiji opens another text called the *Chandrika* written by Vyasa Tirtha, a commentary on the *Tattva Prakashikā*. The text also includes a commentary on the *Chandrika* called the *Prakasha* by Raghvendra Swamy. Swamiji reads out a sentence from *Chandrika*).

Swamiji: *Para-pakshe akhandasya brahma-pada lakshyasyaiva jignyasa-tvat Sruti-Sutrastha mukhyatha-tyagah.*

(By the position opposed to Shastra, akhanda the partless, that which is only pointed to by the word Brahma is taken to be the subject-matter of jignyasa. For this reason, there is rejection of the primary meaning of the world Brahma itself as expounded by Shruti and Sutra.)

(The advaitic account of Brahma as akhanda is presented through *Chandrika's* quotations of advaitic texts and comments along with the commentary by Raghvendra Swamy called *Prakasha*).

Swamiji explains Advaita: Brahman is akhanda (uses text to substantiate). Brahman cannot be limited by jiva (soul) or objects for example, a jar. He is not limited by these external things. The jiva or soul, because it is non-distinct from Brahman, is not external. Hence, Brahman is not limited by souls. He is also not limited by external objects and is partless because the external objects are unreal. Brahman is nirguna (attributeless) because all gunas in the external world are unreal.

(Students ask questions in the middle for clarification and scribble notes.)

(Swamiji continues and gives the relevant statements of *Chandrika* and *Prakasha* to refute the advaitic stance. He then briefly gives the simplified argument).

Swamiji: As mentioned in the *Chandrika*, let us take the example of silver in a seashell. A person who mistakes the shell for silver and later realises his mistake sees the difference between the real shell and the unreal silver. The difference is as real as the shell. Similarly, if the world is unreal and Brahman is real (according to Advaita), then the difference between them is as real as Brahman. So, there is the limitation of Brahman from the reality of differences. One cannot avoid limitation. (Swamiji deals with the question of identity of jiva in another class).

However, does this mean that Brahman cannot be limitless or partless? No.

(The arguments go on to show that difference and limitlessness have nothing to do with each other. A student asks swamiji to repeat.)

Swamiji: The idea that difference (bheda) is limitation ought to be abandoned. (Swamiji goes on to give the position of Madhva.)

Swamiji: Having shown the fallacies in *para-paksha* (the opponent's view) *Chandrika* concludes by saying:

> *Tasmat deshatah kalatashehaiva gunatashchiva purnata brahmatta natu bhedasya rahityam brahmatesyate*
>
> (Therefore, completeness from the point of space, time and attributes is what constitutes Brahman-hood. It is never non-difference that constitutes Brahman-hood).

Student 3: What is the literal meaning of Vishnu? Is there any etymological reason for selecting that word?

Swamiji: Yes, (enthusiastically and gesturing to show that it is a good question), there is a specific reason.

The word Vishnu as meaning completeness and as meaning Brahma is well supported by pramana (i.e. the Vedas).

Prakasha explains—

> *Vistr-vyaaptau ityasya knu-pratyaye rupam vishnuriti*
> (The root *vistr* means pervasion. To this root the suffix *knu* is added. Vishnu is the resultant form).

Prakasha further elucidates—Brahma as meaning Vishnu is needed to make the completeness of attribute (*guna-purnatva*) intelligible to the student and further to justify that the word Brahma is capable of giving rise to the idea of completeness of attribute (*guna-purti*).

(Swamiji clarifies the position of Madhva.)

All-exclusiveness, *akhandatva*, does not lead to infinity or completeness; rather, it is all-inclusiveness that leads to limitlessness. For example, each attribute of Brahman, though mentioned separately, should not be understood as being exclusive of other attributes, for then attributes limit one another and therefore, completeness in the full sense cannot be arrived at. Hence, the expression means that each attribute is complete and is therefore inclusive of other attributes. So, Brahman conceptualised may be unlimited in spite of being different from particular entities. This is the significance of insisting that Brahma is Vishnu. We are Vaishnavas because we support this view.

(The discussion on Vishnu ended here and the students dispersed after bowing down to their guru.)

These students will meet again with their guru at a different time the next day for *chintane* (revision). This is conducted to test the understanding of the students before the next class begins and a new subject is opened.

The students gather around the sannyasi-guru as in a patha and the guru or swamiji starts by asking one of the students to summarise the main arguments of the last class. The student uses the text and explains how the correct meaning of Brahma or Brahman is arrived at.

The students, before sitting down for chintane, have re-studied the text and discussed the interpretations among themselves. One of the students, V, lives with the swamiji and travels with him. All the others come for the class whenever swamiji is in Udupi. Student V is also the youngest of all students.

Just before the chintane is about to start, V is making his final revision of the previous day's patha.

The swamiji arrives and chintane begins. Swamiji asks V to explain how Brahman need not be limited by space, time and objects. V attempts an answer—

V: Brahman is complete and therefore is not limited by space, etc.

Swamiji: But how is Brahman not limited? If you say because he is complete, that does not answer the question.

V: Brahman is not limited because (the voice trails off and the student looks at his notes).

Swamiji: Do you think Brahman is limitless because the objects are unreal?

V: No! No! That is the position of para-paksha (the antithesis).

Swamiji: Good! So that means the objects are real and different from Brahman. So, does this cause Brahman to be limited?

V (trying another train of thought): Vishnu means complete, full of attributes, so how can Brahman be limited?

Swamiji: No. You are making a circular argument. You are saying He is unlimited because He is full of attributes and He is full of attributes therefore limitless.

(V is silent).

Swamiji (explains): Brahman is limitless and complete from the standpoint of space and time does not mean in all space and in all time. Such a view would make Brahman dependent on space and time and Brahman cannot in this case be complete. So the expression 'limitless' is justified because Brahman is the very source of space and time. It is all-inclusiveness that make Brahman limitless, although there is difference.

Swamiji asks V to meet him after he has studied the relevant portions again.

The swamiji appeared a bit disturbed, probably thinking about his student. On questioning him, he confided that he was not very happy with V and would have to repeat some of the classes for him individually. The sannyasi-gurus, besides this daily check on understanding, also conduct a test at the end of the patha on a particular text. Usually, one or two grihastha scholars along with sannyasi-gurus from the mathas are invited. There are two or three problems that are posed to the students who try to answer them. The final answers are given by one of the scholars or sannyasis. This is not a test of passing or failing, but rather a function arranged to show the other scholars and to announce that this batch of students has completed the text or studentship (as this is usually done after the completion of *Nyaya-Sudha*, a text that ends formal instruction by the guru).

The next example of the Socratic genre is a class conducted by a grihastha-guru.

Example 3

One of the grihastha scholars, Ramanathacharya, travels from Udupi to Phalimar (a village near Udupi) to give a class once a week on the *Tantrasara*. This is a text by Madhvacharya, which deals with the procedure of making icons, temples and for meditation. It takes Ramanathacharya about two hours and changing two buses to reach Phalimar, where the older branch of Phalimar matha is situated. The Phalimar matha runs a gurukula here called Yogadipika. Ramanathacharya pays his bus fare. On inquiring about the returns he gets for the expenditure of money and energy he said, 'Well, the swamiji also helps me sometimes. The swamiji (junior Phalimar swami) had got hold of a rare *Bhagavata* edition, which he had given to me for consultation. I have benefited immensely from it. It has been with me for five years, and swamiji has not yet asked for it.'

After reaching Phalimar, Ramanathacharya hurries towards the matha, as it is almost time for his class. On reaching the matha, a student of his inquires, 'Today you are a bit late?' Ramanath answers, 'I had some guests.' As the student announces his arrival, all the others (age group: 16–18) get ready. All Ramanath has to do after washing his feet is to take off his shirt.

Ramanathacharya sits on a wooden seat on the floor and his 8 students, all male Madhva Brahmins sit around him. The class begins and Ramanath speaks in Kannada. Sanskrit used is mostly contained in the text. The students are first cross-questioned; a discussion of the topic then takes place while the students take notes.

There is also a blackboard which Ramanath uses to explain calculations in the book. Ramanath also has his favourite student who seems to be making a lot of mistakes today, but to whom Ramanath addresses the complex parts of the text.

Halfway through (at 3.00 p.m.) there is a break and the students have milk. They offer milk to their guru, and with some amusement to the researcher. In such gurukulas run on behalf of the matha, there is a more systematised way of examining the students at the end of each academic year. There are written exams. It is essential that the students pass these before they move on to more advanced levels.

The final example involves women students of a grihastha scholar who is conducting classes at his home in Udupi on the *Bhagavad Gita*. The students include two women and three men, all middle-aged Madhvas, living in Udupi or nearby towns. This is a patha that is for a fixed limited duration; it has to finish within two months, after which both the teacher and students will become occupied with other things. The students have their work and family to look after, while the teacher will have to travel as he has been invited to other places. This type of fixed course of patha provides a practical way of learning Shastra for those who cannot become full time students for a longer period. The patha in this case tends to focus on finishing the text within a time limit and is often to the point, avoiding lengthy elaborations and classes for revision.

Example 4

The patha on *Bhagavad Gita* has started about a week ago and on this particular day, the focus is on the second chapter when Krishna begins to instruct Arjuna (*Bhagavad Gita* 2.11). The class begins with the mangalacharana which Madhva has written for his bhashya. This is in praise of Brahman or Narayana and expresses Madhva's humility in the presentation of his bhashya.

The guru recites the shloka (verse) *Ashochyan anvashochas tvam*... (2.11) and begins to explain. First, he gives a gist of the shloka and then begins to give the meaning of the words. This shloka, the guru emphasises, marks the beginning of *Brahma Vidya* in the *Bhagavad Gita*. Below is an extract from this patha. The guru is addressed as acharya (also a term for a scholar or teacher).

> Acharya: *Pragnya vadamsh cha bhashase* implies that Arjuna is giving his own limited understanding. The bhashya is *svamanishotha vachanani*. Tikacharya (or Jayatirtha) explains this in his *Prameya Dipika* (a commentary on Madhva's bhashya on the *Gita*).

Some of the students have a copy of the text which has both the bhashya and the *Prameya Dipika* commentary. They look into their text as the acharya elaborates.

> Acharya: What Arjuna is saying is not based on the understanding of *Brahma Vidya* or knowledge of Brahman as laid out in the Shastras. Tikacharya says, *na tu Shastra acharyopadesha praptani*, which means that Arjuna's argument (*vada*) is neither based on the understanding drawn from Shastra nor from the instruction of teachers who have that understanding. Our argument and justification in life should be based on study. Only after the study of Shastra under the able guidance of a guru can one hope to achieve a mind beyond duality (*dvanda*) and sorrow (*dukha*).

One of the women students, interrupts at this moment and asks the acharya a question:

Woman student (WS): But acharya, what about women who are interested in reading more about Brahman and want to study Veda, etc. As you know guru N and swami M do not encourage women to learn Shastra. They feel Vedas are not for women. The *Bhagavad Gita* can be read and recited by women (slightly agitated), but what if I want to read the *Upanishads* and other parts of the Veda.

Acharya: Yes, you are right. Some of these people do not accept women students, but this was not always practised in the past. Gargi, Sachi and others had knowledge of the Vedas. In fact, the *Vyomasamhita* says women can study the Vedas and Madhva endorses this view.[1] (After pause) Ah! Why do you worry, I shall teach you.

The acharya goes on to explain the shloka and the class ends with a discussion on Arjuna's need to overcome grief and the 'war' going on within himself.

This example reveals the underlying tensions in the pedagogic practices which tend to exclude certain groups. The woman student later went on to study the *Kena Upanishad* under another guru in Bangalore. She said she had started with the *Kena Upanishad* as, 'In this *Upanishad*, the student is a woman' (Shiva instructs his wife Parvati about Brahman in this *Upanishad*).

Although in pedagogic practice, women students are an exception, the interpretation and adaptation of Shastra to new circumstances stress the inherent flexibility in the practices. The patha on such occasions involves a discussion on the status of women in tradition. It gives a chance to women to articulate their voice and express their dissatisfaction. This forces the practice of pedagogy to open up and reflect on itself.

Let me conclude this section on patha by making some observations on therapeutic aspects.

The patha in general is characterised by the close relationship that is established between the student and the teacher. They see their efforts moving towards a common goal—understanding Brahman. Commitment on both the sides imposes greater responsibility on the teacher and the students, a greater responsibility to utter and know the truth.[2] The knowledge imparted is also a key tool in the transformation of the self because it shows a logic different from everyday logic. This attempt exposes the false foundations of certain emotions and desires. Madhva scholars emphasise that suppression is no way out, nor can the imitations of virtues last for long. The internal transformations of the self result in one's liberation. This understanding is very similar to Greek notions of knowledge and judgment. Martha Nussbaum in her book *The Therapy of Desire* (1994) specifies how Hellenistic ethics sought to transform the individual and his desires by changing the judgement about things (1994: 86). In both Madhva and Aristotle, the trivialisation of reasons for anger results in its loss. The attachment of importance is shifted. In both, the ideal of the wise man is set over and against the love, grief and pity of ordinary mortals. This is why the sannyasis can sometimes be ill-mannered, judged by the standards of everyday life, as the following incident illustrates.

One of the devotees of a swamiji visited the matha to inform him of the death of a common friend. He went into great detail about the suffering and what a loss it meant. The swamiji did not react by providing any condolences, nor did he sympathise. He just nodded his head and accepted the information without much ado. The devotee was taken aback by the lack of reaction. In a strikingly similar way, Socrates, in the face of his own death pursued the search for understanding without fear, resentment or mourning (Nussbaum, 1994: 93). He preached complete detachment. Loss of loved ones, fortune or political standing could occasion fear or pity. Socrates' own attitude before his death discouraged such emotions. Xanthippe was sent away for her tears and Apollodorus was warned against displaying grief.

In both traditions, correct judgment and perception of things leads to removal of bondage from *moha* or attachment. One of the verses in praise of Madhva's philosophy by Jayatirtha, the foremost exponent of Madhvacharya, says that the bhashya removes the threefold miseries—those that pertain to body, those that pertain to the physical world and those that pertain to the controlling agents of the world.

Greeks such as Aristotle, Socrates and the Stoics, stress that there is intense connection between belief, thought and feeling.

> The orator's whole effort—whether in inspiring anger or in calming angry people down is directed towards this complete cognitive structure (Nussbaum 1994: 90).

Thus, philosophy in these traditions is not meant for academic practice only but is inextricably related to the process of living.

In highlighting the similarities between the Hellenistic and the Madhva traditions, two important differences need to be pointed out. Firstly, the Madhvas do not involve themselves in the detailed accounts of emotions or feelings during patha. They are talked about but are not dealt with through individual experiences and narratives. The transformation is somehow sought 'automatically', more through the perlocutionary force of the words of Shastra and the guru. In upannyasa, as we shall see, feelings are more elaborately dealt with but it is not meant to transform people; only to incite them to take up the study of Shastra in earnest.

Furthermore, unlike the Greek transcendence, Madhva tradition is rooted in the Vedas. The rationality grounded in this empirical world is substantiated (not always contradicted) by the wisdom of the *agama* or verbal testimony (the scriptures). That is why bhakti (devotion to Brahman) becomes an important component of gyana or knowledge as one of the scholars highlighted, 'To have gyana without devotion is like a blind man having a torch in his hand; he can show light to others but it is of no use to him.' On the other hand, there is insistence that bhakti without gyana is irrelevant to Brahma Mimamsa. Greater gyana leads to greater bhakti and vice-versa.

The next section outlines the context of the upannyasa. The upannyasa offers an alternative to the transmission of traditional knowledge. The unique context specifies the function and the interpretation of the text, which is different from patha.

The Upannyasa

Upannyasa (a way of being near God) or pravachana (pleasant words), unlike patha, is an informal way of talking about Shastra. The sannyasis, non-sannyasi scholar teachers of the matha and sometimes pandits from outside Udupi, belonging to other mathas of the sect, give lectures on various topics or texts. A few complex polemic texts such as the *Nyaya Sudha* or the *Tattva Prakashika*, and other similar texts that are, even in patha taught to advanced students, are seldom used in upannyasa.

The upannyasa or pravachana is given in a large room where a number of people, both male and female, are seated in separate rows. Dress codes are not strictly observed. The student-teacher relation does not exist and the people disperse without any necessary interaction with the lecturer. Thus, upannyasa is basically a monologue. There is no overt interaction between participants and the guru. The dialogic aspect is internalised as we shall shortly see. The *Mahabharata*, the *Bhagavad Gita* and the *Bhagavata Purana* are often the texts around which upannyasa revolves.

The sannyasis or pandits of the Udupi matha are also invited to give lectures in towns other than Udupi.

Seldom does the complete *Upanishad* feature in an upannyasa. There are only references made to certain shlokas from various *Upanishads*. The upannyasa opens with a mangalacharana, which usually includes a verse, first in praise of Brahman and then in praise of Madhva and his successive major commentators; ending with homage paid to the guru, from whom the lectures have been learnt directly.

A grihastha-guru in a public lecture elucidates the reason and ways of liberating oneself from sorrow, referring to the shlokas or verses from the *Ishavasya Upanishad* dealt with in the previous section on patha. This version in upannyasa also matches a discussion in another upannyasa by a sannyasi-guru on the ways of attaining moksha (salvation).

On this particular occasion, in the garden in front of his house, the guru is giving upannyasa. 'P' sits on a deer skin mattress and is surrounded on two sides by men and in front, his wife and other women are seated.

The upannyasa is not a detailed exposition of the text and often, similar thoughts are connected by references from different texts. His exposition is filled with examples from daily life and there is no cross-questioning to test the undersanding. Some of the listeners are regular and enjoy his attention. Some wear shirts and trousers, while some men remove their upper garments. The listeners need not be Madhva Brahmins.

Example 1

The guru: In the *Ishavasya Upanishad*, the seers have outlined ways of overcoming this world of misery. We all want joy, yet all our methods prove futile. The birth of a child causes great joy. Parents conduct great sacrifices and rituals to get a son. But when the child grows up, he wants to live his own life influenced by modern times and individualism. He throws his parents out. Some others think money gives happiness, yet fail to recognise that the same money gives them blood pressure and unnecessary tensions. Where is happiness? In whom or what can it be found? It is found without doubt in Brahman. The *Upanishad* uses the word *vijanata*, i.e. one who is aware of Brahman knows this as certainty.

The next shloka gives the qualities of Brahman to prove and to give confidence to those who seek Him. He bestows grace on those who understand Him and He is to be understood as *shukram, akayam, avranam, shuddham, apapam.* Shukram means He is without sorrow and therefore can give us happiness. Further, His body is bliss. He does not have a body like ours, subject to the circumstances of this world. He is transcendental and beyond the effects of this universe.

One who understands Him in this way becomes blessed and attains qualities similar to Bhagavan. One can understand this by observing the effect on a person who lives with good and saintly people. On the other hand, those who keep the company of evil human beings become evil. This is one of the reasons why sannyasa in our mathas is given at a young age, so that good qualities might be ingrained into the individual when his mind is mouldable. Contrary to this, many feel that sannyasa should be given when the person is old enough to decide for himself.[3] Anyway, the point is that to become similar to someone you have to be in constant touch with that person. If you are in constant touch with Brahman who is beyond misery and full of bliss, you too shall attain His qualities.

Some, however, feel that to become like Him is to become one with Him. This is incorrect. (He points to the women sitting in the group.) Most of you here are learning music or at least sing bhajans, so you can easily understand this example. There is an instrument that emits a certain tone continuously and you wish to tune your *tamburi* (instrument) with it. After some effort, both the *svaras* (notes) are in harmony. It is so harmonious that they are indistinguishable individually. All you hear is a single sound that is pleasant to the ear. This is the proof that your tamburi is in tune. But note that the instrument emitting the continuous sound does not become the tamburi nor does the tamburi become the drone. Thus, one must understand that to be similar does not mean to be one.

The guru ended the upannyasa by elaborating on the ways of liberating oneself from bondage.

The upannyasa for *Tattva Prakashika* is not given by following the text. However, the concepts involved are explained in the upannyasa. In this example, a sannyasi-guru tries to explain who a Vaishnava is.

This is the same swamiji who gave patha on the idea of Vishnu, discussed previously.

Example 2

Swamiji: A Vaishnava is one who lives a regulated life. He needs to forsake the eating of meat and drinking of intoxicants. Along with this, there are five symbols or actions that characterise a Vaishnava. He should believe in Vishnu as the greatest; Vishnu's symbol (the counch and the disc) should be accepted and should adorn the body; he should take on and keep the name of Vishnu; should perform worship of the *saligrama* (a black coloured

> fossilised stone, a symbol of Brahman) and should live in *Vishnu Kshetra* (a place inhabited by Vaishnavas).
>
> Those involved in the search for truth should accept these symbols. They create well-being and help us live a correct life. We should remember the stories of Dhruva and Prahlada who, by their devotion to Vishnu, were able to get His grace and win over this world. It is to be noticed that both were very young when they saw Vishnu—5 to 8 years. So, those among you who are young have a greater chance of seeing God. (There is laughter in the audience. Some of them who have young children accompanying them hug them and give knowing looks.)

The swamiji goes on to explain the various ways one can become a good devotee. Thus ends the upannyasa.

Bakhtin's observation of the carnivalistic genre captures the differences in the utterance of patha and upannyasa. Bakhtin writes:

> The process of posing philosophical problems as compared to the Socratic dialogue had to change abruptly, all problems that were in the least academic fell by the wayside, complex and extensive modes of argumentation also fell away, and there remained essentially only naked ultimate questions with an ethical and practical bias (1984: 115).

Carnivalisation makes possible the transfer of questions and concepts from the abstract philosophical level to the everyday. However, it is important to keep in mind that Bakhtin's sense of the carnival is used here as an aid to understand and put in relief the various ramifications of the upannyasa. The upannyasa is similar but does not overlap with the carnivalistic genre. In fact, in some instances, the carnival departs by its ability to cause reversal of levels, the obscenities and the laughter related with it. The upannyasa does not contain some of these elements. Bakhtin's understanding of carnivalistic genre is extremely useful as a tool because its rich ideas expose the way upannyasa works and helps us build the contrast with patha, but it is quite removed from the grotesque realism that Bakhtin demonstrated in his analysis of Rabelias and his world.

The upannyasa lecturer uses everyday examples and deals with current issues. In the *Ishavasya* upannyasa, the reference made to the age of taking up sannyasa deals with the ongoing debate among the various sub-mathas. Bakhtin says that genre includes the 'journalistic' genre which portrays ideological issues of the day. He says, 'they are full of allusions to the great and small events of the epoch; they feel out new directions in the development of everyday life' (1984: 118).

The example of musical notes being harmonious yet different and the keeping of good company elucidate a philosophical idea without going into polemic debates. There are also no names taken (for e.g. the name of Advaita or Shankara) nor is there an elaboration of the opponent's viewpoint with its detailed refutation as in patha. The reason given by the gurus is that they did not want to offend advaitis who may be present in the audience.

Not only are followers of Shankara present in the audience, but also other non-Madhvas. There are therefore non-vegetarians seated along with the vegetarians. It is usual to find women and children seated along with men. There are people who have not got their upanayana (thread ceremony) performed sitting along with those who have. There are even disbelievers.

The audience on the occasion of the *Ishavasya* upannyasa comprised about 40 people, fifteen of whom were women and five of them were accompanied by their children. Most of them were Madhvas, but the group included Smarthas, Gaud Saraswat Brahmins and Gowdas (non-Brahmins). In places outside Udupi, when the gurus go on sanchara (travel), the audience is much more varied. For example, in an upannyasa by a swamiji of Udupi given in Bangalore, there were, besides the Madhvas, many Smartha and Iyengar men and women with their children. Among the non-Brahmins and non-vegetarians castes were a few lower-caste members and a couple of north Indian Punjabi Khatris who had settled in Bangalore.

Such a gathering, as Bakhtin suggests, unites and integrates differences. There is a sense of unity of polaric opposites. As Bakhtin explains it, there is a coming together of 'the tempted with the tempter, the believer with the non-believer, the righteous man with the sinner, the beggar with the rich man and so forth' (1984: 135). The utterances here become carnivalistic because there is in the audience the 'other', a homology of the carnival.

There is great creativity in the exposition of Shastra, since the utterer does not follow a text word by word or sentence by sentence. There is a sense of freedom that a guru feels and he is able to incorporate many adventurous ideas quite foreign to the textual matter.

For Bakhtin, the carnivalistic genre is fully liberated from those limitations of history and memoirs that were so characteristic of the Socratic dialogue and this allows an extraordinary freedom of plot and philosophical invention (1984: 114), as will be evident in further illustrations.

Although the upannyasa is a monlogue, it keeps in mind the heterogeneity of the listeners and there also is a constant dialogue with what Bakhtin calls the 'absent other'. For example, the guru delivering the upannyasa on the *Ishavasya Upanishad* knows that it is very easy to misinterpret the Upanishadic statements. They seem to give the idea of oneness of Brahman and the soul. Some of his expositions could be paraphrased like this:[4] The [absent and imagined] 'other' with whom the dialogue could be taking place and is internalised is named 'The Others'.

> The Others: What do you feel about the ongoing hot debate between various sub-mathas on the age at which sannyasa should be given?
>
> Guru: Sannyasa should be given at a young age.
>
> The Others: Why?
>
> Guru: So that good qualities might be ingrained into the individual when his mind is mouldable.
>
> The Others: Shall we return to the discussion of the *Upanishad* you were mentioning?
>
> Guru: Anyway the point is...
>
> The Others: We have apprehensions and doubts about what you say. We feel we are (our soul is) Brahman.
>
> Guru: This is incorrect.

The Others: Can you give an example to help clarify the issue?

Guru: Most of you here are learning music (and he goes on to give an example).

The upannyasa on Vaishnavism clearly shows how the level of philosophical abstraction evidenced in the patha on Vishnu and the Vaishnava is changed into the more tangible symbols and images.

To the listeners of the upannyasa, the lecture seems to be highly religious; it tends to proclaim Vishnu as greater than the other gods. The icon Vishnu as separate from other icons comes to mind. There is no clarification to show what Madhva meant when he used the word 'Vishnu' and hence Vaishnavism. The interpretation of the upannyasa, by not involving the critical element, leaves open and flexible the connotations of the word Vishnu. One may think of Vishnu as one among the trinity—Brahma (the creator), Vishnu (the maintainer) and Mahesh (the destroyer), or think that by upholding Vishnu, one opens up the quarrel between those who believe in Vishnu and those who believe in Shiva as the greatest.

Jack Goody makes an interesting observation while differentiating discourse in literate and pre-literate societies. He argues that writing and the development of literacy made discourse more permanent than words uttered, which gave greater scope for critical activity. This in turn enhanced rationality, scepticism and logic (1977: 37).

The oral mode without the aid of written material (in the hands of the listeners) as in upannyasa allows the interpreter of a text or concept to get away with inconsistencies. It is not done deliberately. However, there is no means of checking the process of interpretation. The audience by and large is not like the group of students in patha. They need not know the text that is being followed or be familiar with the implications of the concepts enunciated. The enforcement of stereotypes is unquestioningly accepted by the lay audience.

Goody suggests there may be different shades of meaning given to the same word, without it being recognised by the orator or the listener as it is not noted down and cross-checked. He writes:

> By means of rhetoric, through the gift of the gab, the tricks of the demagogue are able to sway an audience in a more direct way than the written word... The oral form is intrinsically more persuasive because it is less open to criticism (though not, of course immune to it) (1977: 50).

Within the framework of the carnivalistic genre, what makes this possible is:

> ...the transfer of ultimate questions from the abstractly philosophical sphere, through a carnival sense of the world to the concretely sensuous place of images and events (Bakhtin, 1984: 134).

According to Bakhtin, one of the hallmarks of the carnivalistic genre is the increased use and application of the comic element as compared to the Socratic genre.

Towards the end of the upannyasa of Vaishnavism, the orator tried to involve people by making a witty comment about young children being able to see God. It was also a provocative comment to highlight the child-like innocence that is so often missing in adults.

Carnival laughter or ritual laughter is meant to provoke an idea or a truth as shall be clear from the following examples.

A shloka of the *Bhagavad Gita* explains that what a person thinks of when he is dying is important and decides his next birth. It emphasises a rigorous discipline throughout life in preparation for such a moment of crisis when thinking of God is realisation.

> *Anta kale ca mam eva*
> *Smaran muktva kalevaran*
> *Yah prayati samad bhavam*
> *Yati nasti atra samasayah* (*Bhagavad Gita*, 8.5)
> (And whoever, at the end of his life, quits his body remembering me alone, at once attains my nature. Of this there is no doubt).

A grihastha scholar, explaining this to an audience, gave the following example to elucidate the point.

Example 3

> The grihastha scholar: It is like asking a photographer to take a nice photo. The photographer says the photo will be just like your face and nothing better. There is nothing like a good photo. The person who wants his photo to be clicked says 'No… please tell me how to sit and pose for a photograph, I do not know.' The photographer replies, keep your chin up and smile just enough to reveal two of your teeth and not more than that. Then the photographer moves behind the camera and says ready, and the person sitting upright, just as the shutter is released, yawns uncontrollably. His face at the last moment is captured in the camera. When the photo came out, the person asked, 'Why is it like this?' 'Well, it depends on what you look like at the moment the shutter is released,' replies the photographer. Therefore, Yama is the great photographer… (There is much laughter in the audience).

Bakhtin, talking about Christianity, points out that much was permitted in the form of laughter in the Middle Ages. It included parody of sacred texts and rituals. Laughter here combines the aspect of death in this world and the conditions of rebirth.

> Combined in the act of carnival laughter are death and rebirth, negation (a smirk) and affirmation (rejoicing laughter). This is a profoundly universal laughter, a laughter that contains a whole outlook on the world. Such is the specific quality of ambivalent carnival laughter (1984: 127).

Laughter also fuses ridicule with rejoicing. Stories during upannyasa counter the orthodox practices followed by many fanatical Brahmins. A guru narrated an incident about a Madhva who was fanatical about madi, a state of purity after having had a bath, when the person should not touch or be touched by anyone.

Example 4

> Guru: The Brahmin used to think madi was a way of being near God, but every time someone touched him and he had to have a bath again, he became angry and instead of uttering the name of God, started cursing the one who touched him by mistake.
>
> There were many occasions in the day when children used to tease him or adults used to touch him unknowingly and he had to have a bath. Eventually, he had so many baths a day that he developed pneumonia and the doctor advised him not to take a bath for a whole week.
>
> (There is laughter in the audience).

Another important feature of the upannyasa is the highlighting of events in what Bakhtin calls the 'carnival square'. The scenes taking place in the square are considerably more complex and intricate, with greater assortments, carnivalised contrasts, eccentricities and fundamental crownings and decrownings.

> The human souls are laid bare, either terrible souls as in the neither world, or else bright and pure ones. People appear for a moment outside the usual conditions of their lives, on the carnival square and there opens up another—more genuine—sense of themselves and of their relationships to one another (1984: 145).

The tales from *Mahabharata* often involve such descriptions:

Shishupala is insulting Krishna in front of everybody in the royal hall. Krishna forgives him a hundred times as a promise made to Shishupala's mother but when Shishupala crosses the hundredth insult, Krishna kills him. This event takes place during an important festival (the Rająsuya yagña) in Indraprastha, the kingdom of the Pandavas.

Another often quoted story from the *Mahabharata* is gambling in the game of dice. The scene is right in the middle of the royal hall in the presence of all, where evil reaches its zenith. This is an example given to depict the sudden change of fate and the decrowning. In these events, the public square is the royal hall. The example of Rama having to leave for the forest just before his crowning is coupled along with the *Mahabharata* story to show how even the gods have to face sudden twists in fate.

Bakhtin writes:

> Their behaviour at the roulette table in no way corresponds to the role they play in ordinary life. The atmosphere of gambling is an atmosphere of sudden and quick changes of fate, of instantaneous rises and falls, that is crowning/decrownings. The stake is similar to a crisis: a person feels himself on the threshold (1984: 171).

This sense of the threshold pervades the events of the upannyasa. The orators leap to points of crisis and at turning points in the epics.

The death of demons happens in the public square substituted usually by the royal palace or the open ground. The death of demons at the hands of Lord Narasimha in the story of Prahlada from the *Bhagavata* is a good example. Lord Narasimha kills the demon King Hiranyakashipu in a very dramatic way. It is the incarnation of the Lord in the man-lion form. This ferocious form emerges from a pillar in the royal hall and kills the demon when it is evening (neither day nor night), on the lap (neither on the ground nor in the sky), in the verandah (neither inside nor outside), by the nails of his hand (neither by weapon nor hand) and finally neither by man nor animal, but a combination of both. The demon had a boon that he would not be killed in any ordinarily perceived circumstances.

Could there be a better example of a decrowning, a change in fate, an event at a threshold and an event where there is a combination of opposites, of paired images all happening in the public or the carnival square? The ten avatars of the Lord in itself stand at the threshold of time. Each avatar heralds the end or beginning of a new era. Bakhtin says, 'Carnival is the festival of all annihilating and all renewing time. Thus might one express the basic concept of carnival' (1984: 124).

A hero is one who is trying to move beyond given circumstances, one who has deviated from the normal way of life. Krishna and Rama, along with the other characters of these epics, are fighting to establish a new social order. Besides these changes that the hero tries to bring about, there are some who combine in themselves many opposites. These oxymoronic juxtapositions abound in the upannyasa. The participants on the threshold live life according to extraordinary rules. These heroes move beyond accepted ways of living life and seek transformations and themselves become symbols of the transformations.

These oxymorons naturalise and exist through a combination of the wise and the stupid, the sane with the insane. The *Bhagavata* characters such as Shukacharya, Jadbharata, Ajamila, Raikva, all combine in themselves opposing poles and personalities and stand beyond the ordinary.

The upannyasa orator tells how Shukacharya, who is coming to give a discourse on the *Bhagavata* to Parikshita, the grandson of Arjuna, is followed by road urchins.

Example 5

The sannyasi-guru describes, 'He has matted hair and ash is smeared all over his body. He looks and behaves like a mad man and is not concerned about what people are saying about him. The knowledgeable, however, know what a wise man he is, for he has received instructions from Brahma. He is the one who shall liberate the soul of Parikshita with his words soaked in secret wisdom.'

Here is an example of a man 'who is alone in his knowledge of the truth and who is therefore ridiculed by everyone else as a madman' (Bakhtin, 1984: 151).

In this understanding of the upannyasa as similar to (but not the same as) the carnivalised genre, we have seen how it differs from patha as the Socratic genre. The same concepts or texts, sometimes even in the same voice, are uttered differently, depending on the addressee. However, all this does not imply that we are dealing with a frozen tradition made up of conservative Brahmins who have fixed answers to questions (Goody 1968: 15).

The transmission of traditional knowledge is a creative process and keeps its doors open to the winds of change. The re-articulation of Shastra is an attempt to make it intelligible and acceptable to the present. With patha, the acceptance of women students and foreigners (as mentioned in the previous chapter) by grihastha gurus emphasises the need to reclaim tradition in a new light with new actors and meanings. Wilhelm Halbfass says that the Hindu philosophical authors legitimised their new explanations by emphasising the need to adapt to present circumstances (1988: 364).

The upannyasa stands as an illustration of the effort of philosophical gurus to reach out to the masses. The movement more clearly entails a bridge-building between the heritage of the past and the need to make sense of the present circumstances. The relevance of transcendental structures and its significance is discovered anew in relation to the distinctive features of new situations. Welbon observes, it is 'not today finding itself in yesterday but today finding its sense—and the sense of its tomorrows—with yesterday's help' (1986: 314).

Truth and Reliability

Making 'sense' of today with the help of yesterday or re-claiming and re-articulating the past is not an enterprise that can be understood as a single monolithic project. For, not only is the past re-interpreted, but it is re-articulated in various ways. This feature leads us to pursue the question of reliability of various utterances, a line of inquiry which Bakhtin does not directly address.

Bakhtin himself says, 'We are not, of course, concerned, here with the performed social and philosophical idea present in the works' (1984: 155). Thus, Bakhtin does not deal with the subject-matter of utterances or the truth and rationality of utterance. These concerns are taken up by Pascal Boyer in his book *Tradition as Truth and Communication* (1990).

Boyer, while rejecting the argument that there is traditional continuity because of an underlying theory in the minds of the natives,[5] argues that traditional notions and concepts are not universally shared because there is no common or shared definition among all the natives.

Among the listener group in general, we observed that philosophical concepts are expressed and understood in various contexts. For example, there is no 'one' shared definition to Vishnu in the utterances and in the minds of the listeners.

Boyer goes on to differentiate the 'styles' of utterances according to different contexts. He stresses the need to examine actual communications and to distinguish between several interrelated 'registers' or styles of discourse. So, although like Bakhtin, Boyer recognises different generic types also dependent on the addressee, he concentrates on the conditions under which utterances are rendered reliable and true.

The various styles Boyer highlights can be grouped into two major types.

> The interaction described here implies that there is a principled division between those discourse registers, on the one hand, which simply use a term in a correct way and convey the common stereotypes about it, and on the other, the registers in which there is supposed to be a description of what the entity designated really is (1990: 44).

The upannyasa on Vishnu, rather than explaining the philosophical input, maintained the stereotype idea that the Vaishnavas as a group of believers are antagonistic to the Shaivites. Further, I shall argue that these various styles of discourse can be arranged according to reliability and truth factor.

The characteristic features of the common discourse given by Boyer correspond in many ways with the discourse of the upannyasa. Boyer writes:

> There are no formalised circumstances for this kind of speech, neither is the audience 'restricted' in any sense. Anyone can hear what the 'common wisdom' has to say… However, no one can draw any definite conclusions from this discourse (1990: 30).

Members of the sect also make a contrast between patha as *tattva jignyasa, shastra jignyasa* or *Brahma Mimamsa* and upannyasa as Shastra in general. The terms associated with patha emphasise vichara (reflective thought) through a detailed cross referential study, which aims at bringing about a transformation in self-understanding. Upannyasa is more generalised and thus primarily addressed to the lay follower or to a motley group, often comprising non-Madhvas—basically, a listener group. Most of the members in the audience of the upannyasa do not have the same level of sustained interest as those who are students in patha. One of the members in the listener group remarked, 'We don't have so much time that we spend years learning Shastra. We can't ignore the needs of our family.' A woman who listens to upannyasa regularly said, 'I get *samadhana* (peace of mind) after listening to the learned men. Words of wisdom help us move our mind away from the hassles of samsara (life in the family).' Many others felt that in the age of Kali, this much attention to spirituality was more than enough, a popular stereotype reinforced by the gurus in the upannyasa.

Although there are members in the audience who might be interested in pursuing patha or those who have already had patha, upannyasa is mainly addressed to the lay follower. So, besides the mixed (in terms of caste, sect and gender) composition of the addressee, the addressee also has a different objective which defines his or her level of interest. These factors condition the utterance of the guru.

Now, for the members of the caste who are not permitted to be students of sannyasis or other gurus, it does seem that the opportunity and knowledge by which the self can be transformed is denied.[6] This was one of the important factors which prompted Narayana Guru Swami (1855–1928) in Kerala to revolt against the Brahmin orthodoxy (Rao 1987).

To return to the discussion on the creation of truth, the way in which texts are discussed in patha represents to the people and the tradition a correct way of attempting to find the truth. The gurus in patha, use written texts and writing material, give detailed meaning of sentences and concepts with a constant check on understanding. There is a systematic evaluation of para-paksha, the opponent's view and the establishment of truth. Boyer also says, traditional truths require a combination of specific action and specific actors who perform them in particular situations (1990: 60). Boyer gives primary importance to the process whereby specific utterances are interpreted. This he says guarantees reliability. Truth for him is created not only because it is uttered by an expert in a place of authority, but also because the utterances have certain characteristics which make them reliable. Boyer uses certain psychological theories in understanding cognitive abilities of the native which I shall not discuss here?[7]

The context of the utterance in the pedagogic process in Udupi specifies whether a statement is more or less reliable. These features have led some Madhvas (although very rarely) to prevent their students in the initial stages from attending discourses meant for the lay person, as they fear the students might get the wrong impression of Shastra. Although there is this distinction, the gurus do see upannyasa as having a purpose to serve.

An example given by a saint guru throws light on this: 'First give the child (here implying the lay follower or listener) jaggery (the stuff of upannyasa) and then when it opens its mouth for more after having enjoyed the taste, let the mother (guru) give medicine (*Brahma Mimamsa*). The metaphor of Shastra in patha as medicine gives a clue to the greater reliability of *Brahma Mimamsa* and difference from the framework of upannyasa.'

Upannyasa is also considered lower in the hierarchy of Shastric transmission by many gurus. As a research anthropologist, whenever I asked a question related to Shastra, the genre in which the question was asked specified the answer. For example, if the question on the nature of jiva (soul) was asked while the patha on the topic was going on, then the guru would go on to enunciate the doctrine of difference (bheda) and how attribute and substratum are related. This was usually done with the help of a text or several texts which contradict advaitic and other theories. The argument would then move to the nature and existence of the soul with relation to Brahman. There were occasions for rebuttal along the way by other students. In contrast, when the same question was asked outside the context of the patha, in upannyasa, the answer would quite typically include the following: The jiva is distinct from Brahman and is finite in contrast to the infinite Brahman. It is eternal but ever-dependent on Brahman. This answer in itself does not in any way specify the uniqueness of the philosophy. It can easily be fitted into different religious teachings.

Lotman and Pjatigorski (1977), in their analysis of the function of texts, underline that a single text may serve different cultural functions. A single scientific text about a powerful new medicine could fulfil three different cultural functions—functioning as a scientific text for one part of the collective, as a religious text for another part of the collective, and as a magical text for a third part of the collective.

Shastric texts have a polyfunctional usage and their transmission varies even though the transmitter is the same. The upannyasa, unlike the patha, does not deal with the intricacies of debate on the topic. There is no rigorous philosophical refutation of the opponent's position. This, as the sannyasi teachers explained, is because during an upannyasa, there are many members among the audience who belong to various sects. It would hurt the feelings of those present, if for example, one were to go to great lengths proving Shankara wrong. The gurus did emphasise that they do not deviate from Dvaita mata (Kannada for doctrine, view). However, this process of simplification as also of beautification does dilute the philosophical content of the text. Upannyasa vulgarises the potential implications of significant topics. A saint stressed that they could not treat difficult topics as it would require training in Shastra for the student. Thus, the lecturer-guru at upannyasa can only talk about the text, not talk the text itself.

The main function of an upannyasa as a method of spreading Madhva's philosophy is to create a following. A means of perpetuating the sect; both in terms of its material as well as ideological concerns through donations and creating an interest in the lay follower. Patha does not aim to achieve this.

Thus, the nature of truth and the degree of reliability is constructed traditionally and differs according to contexts and keeping in mind the 'other' or the addressee.

Boyer does provide a framework for understanding the creation of truth. However, there are certain limitations with some aspects of Boyer's analysis. He asserts that although the examples are taken from pre-literate societies, his framework stands good for oral communication in literate societies as well (1990: viii). This creates problems with respect to communication in the Udupi matha.

In emphasising the ritualised jargon of discourse, Boyer says,

> In many traditional contexts truths are supposedly contained in utterances which the listener, sometimes even the speakers can barely understand (1990: 79).

This makes the content of utterances irrelevant.

Further, utterance, more than its value in words, is supposed to establish a causal link with the event that is being described by the expert. The diviner or shaman is bypassed and the link between a certain state of affairs and the perceivable symptoms established: 'The speakers' representations are, as I said… entirely bypassed' (1990: 112).

This would mean that in Udupi the guru is bypassed. This is not the case. The guru makes possible the understanding of the text not by customisation and memorisation of mumbo-jumbo, but by exegeses where the content of the utterances is of supreme importance.

The guru contextualises his utterances and makes a conscious effort to suit the listener. Even in patha there is an effort to suit the utterances to individual levels and needs of the student. The importance of the guru's word (especially in patha) lies in opening up to the student a new way of perceiving the world and his own place in it.

The everyday examples given in upannyasa do not allow the mind to think or examine everyday life through the philosophy that a student learns in patha. It gives, ready-made, as it were, the understanding one should draw from everyday life, whether of madi or a photographer. There is no sense of discovery. A student of patha on the other hand, is encouraged to examine reality by himself and find his own amusement and satire in life through the imbibed philosophical standpoint.

The features specified in upannyasa may be termed as 'upannyasanisation'. One may discern in this process two specific movements. Firstly, it tends to popularise academic activity or the knowledge that may be called a science. Popularising involves speaking or writing in such a way that the layman understands and appreciates. Secondly, in doing so, it inevitably reduces its own degree of reliability. The process of simplification and dramatisation produces a lesser degree of truth about the way the specific academic discipline is practised.

However, this twin process is not altogether undesirable, for it is the way a specific person in one discipline can grasp another discipline. For example, if Stephen Hawking had not upannyasanised the complex ideas of theoretical physics into *The Brief History of Time*, we would have been deprived of an understanding of the growth of knowledge in recent physics. As we have seen, many gurus feel the desirability of upannyasanisation.

In general, it occurs when sociologists choose to write in newspapers about caste, the Mandal Commission or Hindutva, or when a classical singer on stage starts playing or singing popular bhajans—this happens in most charity concerts where attracting the audience is important.

Lotman and Pjatigorski (1977: 125) highlight that the

function of a text is defined as its social role, its ability to meet certain needs of the collective that creates the text. They further add that the concept of a text has a different meaning in the study of culture than in linguistics. The cultural idea of a text originates at the moment when the fact of linguistic expressiveness ceases to be perceived as sufficient for an utterance to be transformed into a text. This feature grasps the relational aspect of a text brought out explicitly by William Graham and is relevant for the texts in patha and upannyasa.

> It is seldom, if ever, enough simply to open a sacred book and read as one would read the instructions on a package; rather, one must hear it read and expounded in a special context to grasp its meaning. Furthermore, this recognition means that scripturality arises not from the formal acts of religious leaders or church councils, however important their eventual roles in confirming the sacrality and boundaries of scripture but rather in the interaction of persons and groups of persons with a text or texts. Put succinctly, it is not a literary genre but a religio-historical one, and must be understood as such (1987: 5,6).

The implications for an analysis of patha and upannyasa are clear. We need to distinguish the contexts in which Shastra is articulated. It is a dialogic activity suited to different intentions and conceptions.

The two types of genres create their own intersubjective sphere very similar to Bourdieu's field or structure. Bakhtin's conception also consists in considering inter-subjectivity as logically preceding subjectivity. He says, 'Becoming conscious of myself, I attempt to see myself through the eyes of another person' (1978: 130).

Thus, Bourdieu and Bakhtin both reject the understanding of discourse independent of a specific situation and function. Bourdieu in *The Logic of Practice* writes:

> Language as conceived by Saussure, an intellectual instrument and an object of analysis, is indeed the dead, written, foreign

language referred to by Mikhail Bakhtin, a self-sufficient system, detached from real usage and totally stripped of its functions, inviting a purely passive understanding. The illusion of the autonomy of the purely linguistic order that is asserted in the privilege accorded to the internal logic of language at the expense of the social conditions of its opportune use, opened the way to all the subsequent research that proceeds as if mastery of the code were sufficient to confer mastery of the appropriate usages or as if one could infer the usage and meaning of linguistic expressions from analysis of their formal structure, as if grammaticality were the necessary and sufficient condition of the production of meaning, in short, as if it had been forgotten that language is made to be spoken and spoken pertinently (1990: 32).

Notes

1. Madhva's bhashya regarding this matter states, '*Ahurapy uttama strinam adhikaramtu vaidike yathorvashi yami chaiva sachyadyashcha tathapare*' (They say that women of superior talents have adhikara, i.e. capacity to study Veda. Urvashi, Yami, Sachi and many others may be taken as example).
2. P.V. Kane says that the 'one striking point about the imparting of knowledge (particularly Vedic) in the educational system of India was the great prejudice against learning from books' (P.V. Kane 1930–62, p. 347). This certainly cannot be universally justified.
3. The guru is referring to a current debate that revolves around the age at which sannyasa should be given in the Udupi astha matha. Some sub-mathas practise the giving of sannyasa to adults contrary to the tradition of bala-sannyasa (sannyasa at a young age, say 8 to 14 years).
4. Bakhtin performs a similar exercise with one of Dostoevsky's novels (1984: 210).
5. Boyer studies the Fang of Gabon, Cameroon and Equatorial Guinea. His focus is on 'witchcraft power' called *evur* and its various renderings.
6. This issue has been discussed earlier in Chapter 4 and will be highlighted in the concluding chapter.

7. In my analysis of the styles of discourse in the Udupi matha, I am not totally dealing with the native's perception in the deciding of the truth factor (most of the upannyasa audience may see the utterances as true and reliable as they are not exposed to patha). My understanding stems more from the point of view of tradition.

6

The Sannyasi and the Householder: Continuities and Discontinuities

Introduction

So far, I have concentrated on the institutional aspects of the matha with an emphasis on the organisation of the matha, sociology of food and knowledge. The actor's perception was examined with regard to these aspects. Now it is time perhaps to move directly to the study of renunciation and its articulation by various actors in Udupi, in order to arrive at their self-understanding of renunciation.

The conceptualisation of renunciation in India has been a very vexed issue for anthropologists, in the study of sectarian traditions as well as in contrast to the householder. Dumont recognised the importance of renunciation, arguing that the heart of Hinduism is revealed in the interaction between the renouncer[1] and the man-in-the world (1960: 37). Though Dumont emphasised that the renouncer revitalised the caste system and the ideology of hierarchy inherent in it, he sees the institution of sannyasa in opposition to the caste system and outside it. In a similar way, there is a contrast posed between caste and sect. Dumont posits an analogy between the church-sect dichotomy in Christianity and the caste-sect dichotomy in India.

Van der Veer, writing more recently, expresses his discomfort in using the word sect as it may 'easily obscure the fact that there is no Hindu Church' (1988: 66). Rao, on the other hand, in support of Dumont, stresses that the creation of sects in the Indian context is not always against a centralised order or institution (1984: 165). From this point of view, the use of the word sect does not pose a problem even though there is no Hindu Church. Rao, however, criticises Dumont for treating the sannyasa ashrama as simply revitalising the ideology of hierarchy within the caste system since he feels that the emphasis in the ideology of the renouncer is on egalitarianism and not on hierarchy (Rao 1984). In this discussion, it is important to note that Van der Veer and Rao are talking about two different sorts of sects. Van der Veer is highlighting the Ramanandi 'monastic order' as he prefers to call it (1988: 68) which was formed without protest against some orthodoxy. Other similar orders include the Radhasoamis, Brahmakumaris, followers of Sai Baba, Kabirpanthis, and others. Rao, on the other hand, is focussing on sects which arise out of social protest movements. Under this category, one can include Buddhism, which primarily arose as a sectarian movement against the Brahminical tradition, the social and religious sects created during the Bhakti movement and the protest movements during the British Raj. Nevertheless, at the ideological level, the two kinds of sects are the same, sharing the value of egalitarianism through renunciation. The latter point has been stressed by Rao (1984), Van der Veer (1988) and Heesterman (1985).

In contrast, the Madhva Brahmin sect in Udupi more or less reproduces the hierarchy of the caste system as was demonstrated in the study of the distribution of prasada in the main Krishna matha. In recent times, certain sannyasis have been trying to change rigid rules. However, membership is still significantly based on ascriptive criteria. In the light of this differentiation of sects, the Dumont-Rao debate gets dissolved. Dumont (1970) is talking principally of the brahminical sects (Smartha, Iyengar, Madhva), while Rao is talking about the sects born out of social protest. In the sects born of social movements, change, involving both social and ritual status (usually upwards), is implicated. In the brahminical sects, especially in the formation of the Madhva sect, a rise in the ritual status was not a substantive concern. Even tentatively put, we have at least three different sorts of sects: (a) Religious groups arising out of protest which place themselves outside the hierarchy and rules; (b) Monastic and non-monastic orders (Vallabha, Kabirpanthis) formed without protest, not strictly within the brahminical hierarchy although sometimes claiming links to it. The group also includes orders such as the Brahmakumaris and Radhasoamis, which claim to be non-Hindu orders; and (c) Sects within brahminism which to some extent preserve the hierarchy of the caste system. These are brahminical in that the sannyasi-pontiff or head of a matha is never a non-Brahmin.

The third type, which of course includes the Udupi matha, will be worked out in detail later in this chapter. For the present, let us deal with the question of the value of renunciation and how the Madhva Brahmin householder as a special category relates to it.

Sannyasa, Sannyasi and Householder

The two ashramas of renunciation and of the householder in Udupi form a larger part of the same traditional set-up. In spite of being separate categories, they share certain attributes and form a relationship which provides for channels of interdependence and criticism. The values that they share are derived from their common traditional heritage and this can be articulated through the concept of *vairagya* (detachment). The concept of vairagya invites us to understand sannyasa as a value or a virtue.[2] In this sense, it will be useful to distinguish between sannyasa within the ashrama (order or institution-formal renunciation) and sannyasa as a value. The latter, I shall argue, gives an ambivalent character to the Brahmin householder.

The sannyasi principally is a renouncer within an institutionalised set-up. The institution of sannyasa, as one of the swamijis of Udupi pointed out, came about due to the Buddhist monasteries. 'The sannyasis did not belong to a specific matha in the past. It is only after Buddhists formed their organised monasteries that in Hinduism the concept of matha and related sannyasa came about. Before that, though, there was sannyasa ashrama as a stage of life, they were not bound by an institution.' This explanation for the institutionalisation of sannyasa in Hinduism is also highlighted in more academic writings.

Das, quoting Dutt (1960), gives a similar explanation:

> Although the *parivrajaka* tradition of wandering from home into homelessness was very ancient as Dutt (1960) has argued, the wandering sects do not seem to have been organised into monastic orders before the emergence of Buddhism (Das 1982: 136).

This suggests that the institutional form of renunciation in Hinduism is a recent phenomenon, as Ghurye (1964: 11) also suggests.

Let me first discuss in general this institutionalised form of sannyasa. Sannyasa in the view of the sannyasis of Udupi was formulated as a state of mind in a congenial environment which promoted the process of attaching oneself more and more to Brahman. This was coupled, they said, with the sense of detachment from mundane and worldly interests. Most of the examples I have collected of what sannyasa means contain quotations from the *Bhagavad Gita*. This was what the gurus and even lay householders quoted as justifications in the primary encounters. The *Bhagavad Gita* was quoted because there is an inbuilt assumption that this is a familiar text and by referring to it, concepts could become easily comprehensible. It would, however, be wrong to assume that this is the only text followed.

In my own presentation, I have also relied heavily on the *Bhagavad Gita* as I encountered it in the matha but towards the end of the chapter, there is an attempt to construct the concept of sannyasa in its more complex ramifications.

One of the swamijis explained:

Vairagya or detachment comes ultimately due to the prasada or grace of God. The way to attain His prasada is to always work with His thought in your mind. The *Bhagavad Gita* gives it very well, I am sure you have read it. *Raga dvesha vimuktis tu, vishayan indriyaish charan, atma vashyair videyatma, prasadam adhigacchati* (2.64). (A person free from all attachments and aversion and able to control his senses through regulative principles of freedom can obtain the complete prasada or grace of the Lord). You see, this explains the lifestyle to be followed by a sannyasi. If one wants to be *stitha pragnya* (a term used by Krishna [2.54] to denote a mind in equilibrium), then one must devote oneself to knowing God. The more you know Him, the more you love Him. Only by knowing that He is the doer of all can we rid ourselves from the desire to have a particular sort of result. Sannyasa provides the way through which one can try to achieve detachment. It requires great practice.

The essence of this short discussion with a sannyasi was repeated when I asked a grihastha or a householder as to what sannyasa meant to him. All the grihastha scholars I talked to in the Madhva sect denied vehemently that sannyasa was peculiar to the sannyasa ashrama. 'Did not Krishna teach sannyasa-yoga to Arjuna? And was Arjuna not a grihastha?'

The householder's understanding of renunciation also highlights a state of mind or an epistemology for life, as this reply to what is sannyasa from a Brahmin householder stresses: 'Sannyasa is a way of reaching God, it can be adopted and should be adopted by all those seeking liberation from misery and disappointment we encounter in everyday life. It is, of course, very difficult, but as Krishna says, with practice and His grace, we can attain His knowledge and be free from the samsara (life of householder or life in general, i.e. free from rebirth).' The Madhva Brahmin grihastha scholar went on to quote the same shloka or verse from the *Bhagavad Gita* that the swamiji had quoted earlier.

So, the conception of sannyasa as a process and a theory of knowledge is common to both the sannyasi and the Brahmin grihastha or householder. The renouncer is not against brahminism. For Heesterman, the true Brahmin is 'the renouncer or the individualised sacrificer' (1985: 41–42) and this is true sacrifice. True sacrifice for the Udupi Madhvas is the life devoted to seeking the knowledge of Brahman and living a life in His consciousness. This is the reason why the Brahmin householder among all other castes gains importance. According to Heesterman:

> The pre-eminence of the Brahmin is not based on his priesthood, but on his being the exponent of the values of renunciation (1985: 44).

Das (1982: 46–47) points out that Dumont has neglected the meditating category of the Brahmin and is therefore, obliged to oppose the relation between caste order and ascetic order. She too shows that by treating sannyasa as a value, one can see that the renouncer ideal is followed by the Brahmin householder as well and there is an overlap between the state of the householder and the renouncer.

The attitude of indifference is shared by the sannyasi and the Madhva Brahmin householder in Udupi. Householders are encouraged to develop this attitude with respect to all events of life. It is supposed to be an outcome of life dedicated to God and His knowledge. In a public lecture, a grihastha scholar quoted the *Bhagavad Gita* to explain this sense of detachment or aloofness.

We should understand what Krishna told Arjuna (*Bhagavad Gita* 2.14). He said:

> O son of Kunti, the non-permanent appearance of happiness and distress and their disappearance in due course are like the appearance and disappearance of winter and summer seasons. They rise from sense perception. O great one in the dynasty of

> Bharata, listen carefully; one must learn to be indifferent (*titikshu*) to them without being disturbed.

The scholar stressed that 'the word titikshu occurring in the verse should not be translated as tolerance, for if it were so, the term used would have been *sahinshu* (lit. tolerance). The term used means a sense of indifference. Tolerance of misery is not a virtue, it is a sign of helplessness.'

The sannyasis also emphasise their effort in attaining this state of mind. All the gifts given to them, they say, are not for themselves, but are to be recirculated back into society. A similar explanation is given by the sadhus studied by Robert Lewis Gross. The sadhus of north India 'explained that none of the money they had collected was for their own personal use but was for the benefit of all mankind' (1992: 115). For the Udupi sannyasi, the conceptualisation of sannyasa does not exclude the management of the matha resources.

Many householders feel uncomfortable about sannyasis managing the complex affairs of the matha. They ask, 'Are these sannyasis not leaving one family lifestyle and joining another? What with all the headaches of managing people, money and other resources.'

When I posed the same question to a sannyasi-pontiff, he answered by quoting the eleventh verse of the eighteenth chapter of the *Bhagavad Gita*:

> It is, indeed, impossible for an embodied being to give up all activities. But he who renounces the fruits of action is called one who has truly renounced.

One renounces the idea that action is to attain a result and thereby shifts the focus from the result on to the action. This prescribes active participation but with a difference.

To further the understanding of sannyasa, let us see how it is related to the attainment of salvation. For the followers of Shankaracharya, the sannyasa-ashrama is a necessary prerequisite before attaining *kaivalya* (salvation). During my stay at Shringeri, where one of the *pithas* or mathas of Shankaracharya is located, I spoke to the head pontiff there who informed me that moksha, kaivalya or salvation was only possible for one who took sannyasa.

On inquiring from the Madhva monks about the status of the householder vis-a-vis salvation, they clearly stated that moksha was not the monopoly of any caste, ashrama or gender. One can remain in the same caste or ashrama and strive towards moksha. It is only in advaita that sannyasa is a necessary stage before moksha.

To substantiate this fact, one of the householder scholars quoted a shloka from *Bhagavata*:

> Priyavrta, son of Svayambhu, was told by the *chaturmukha* (four faced) Brahma—
> *Bhayam pramattasya vanestyapi syat*
> *Yatah sa aste saha shat sapatnah*
> *jitendriyasya atmarter budhasya*
> *grahasthramah kim nu karoti avdhyam?*
> (*Bhagavata* 5th part, 1st chapter, 17th verse).

(Even though one goes out to roam in the forest (as a sannyasi), he may still be fearful as he still has the six enemies (lust, anger etc.) with him. One who overcomes these defects and dwells in the self, such an intelligent man even though a grihastha is fearless. So, what is wrong in being a grihastha?)

Madhvacharya commenting in his bhashya (interpretation or commentary) *Srimad Bhagavad Tatparyam* writes:

> *Brahmadhyaha yagnyavalkyadyaha muchyante stri sahinah*
> *badhyante kechnai tesham vishesham cha viddo viduhu*
> *iti satyasamhitayam.*

[(Madhva draws support from another text—*Satyasamhita*) Brahma, Yagnyavalkya and others have got moksha with the help of (and with) their wives. For some, a woman is the reason for bondage, but the correct way is known to those who have wisdom].

This also points out the fact that detachment or vairagya is perceived as more significant than sannyasa-ashrama and the Brahmin is charged with the duty of following renunciatory values. The wife is not necessarily a temptress who will lead her husband astray, but rather a partner on the path of spirituality. This idea was also the reason why the students of the grihastha guru, mentioned in an earlier chapter, got married. This being the case, the renouncer cannot be constructed as an individual outside the world, for as Das points out, 'It is he who provides the measure of things' (1982: 136). The question that arises at this point in discussion is—what is special about sannyasa ashrama if sannyasa or vairagya is open to all ashramas?

The answer given by a swamiji of the Udupi matha to the question specified that a sannyasi within the ashrama has lesser obligations towards family and related matters. Hence, he has no obligatory kin bonds. Therefore, there is room for absolute dedication to Brahman. One can concentrate on a way of life that continuously strives to know God and one is helped by *indriya nigraha* (the control or channelisation of the sense organs). This logic was substantiated with another quotation from the *Bhagavad Gita* Krishna has said:

> The giving up of activities that are based on material desire is what great learned men call the renounced order of life (sannyasa). And giving up the results of all activities is what the wise call renunciation (tyaga or vairagya) (*Bhagavad Gita* 18.2).

This verse shows the importance of renouncing desire and the attachment to desires. The definition of sannyasa here is abstaining from those activities involving sense gratification.

For a sannyasi to have the notion of karma or individual action leading to *papa* (demerit) or *punya* (merit) is to have ignorance. The goal of sannyasa is karma-sannyasa, that is, to rid oneself through inquiry, of the doership of actions, to understand that all action and even states of mind are caused by Brahman. A bidi-sannyasi visiting Udupi explained:

> Sannyasa becomes the constant endeavour to rid oneself of the illusion that one possesses or owns. It is detachment by attaching everything to Brahman. It is not a passive giving up through repression only, but an active understanding through the logic of the Vedas. For you, the giving up of material object is visible

to the eye (since sannyasis give up certain comforts) but you cannot perceive the giving up of ownership over one's sense organs. This is the final stage of sannyasa that is depicted in the stories of Jadabharata and others. Our aim should be to follow their example.[3]

When I asked the Adamar matha senior swamiji who is involved in various social activities such as education for the poor, running orphanages, etc., as to the difference between a sannyasi doing social work and say, a person like Gandhi (who equally believed he was doing God's work), he thought for a moment and answered:

> The sannyasi himself works or at least claims to work, always with the consciousness of Brahman (Paramatma) as the ground and cause of all there is. He tries to live his life as he understands it through scriptures. In the case of Gandhi, there was the added dimension of the nation. He worked with 'India consciousness'. When he fasted, there was an effect and the effect was the intention for which he went on fast. One can establish a cause-effect relation between fasting and the stopping of riots. In the case of the sannyasi, fasting or work is for Brahman and through Brahman. The cause-effect relation cannot be as clearly established as the effect is, what you may call, the transcendental effect.

Another point of variance emerged when the swamiji pointed out that Gandhi must have encountered certain hindrances due to the time and thought he was obliged to devote to his family. Erik Erikson in his penetrating analysis of Gandhi's life stresses, 'Gandhi at times minded having to become a householder, for without his becoming committed to a normal course of life by child marriage, he might well have been a monastic saint instead of what he became: politician and reformer with an honorary sainthood'. (1970: 299).

The statements of the sannyasis of Udupi primarily show that sannyasa within the sannyasa-ashrama has scope for a greater degree of detachment than for the householder. As one grihastha explained, 'Just as you have the amateur level and professional level in sports, so also these swamijis are professional sannyasis.' He also explained that the sannyasi is not affected by the impurity caused by death or birth and can continue *adhyayana* (study and teaching of Shastra) unhindered.

Sannyasis are considered as greater adhikaris (possessing greater capacity to understand God) in the pursuit of godliness and stand as an example of superior vairagya or detachment. What Oldenberg observes in this passage on the Buddhist monks is true of the collective life of the sannyasis organised into a matha:

> A monastic order appeared then to the religious consciousness to be the reasonable natural form, in which alone the life of those who are associated in common struggle for release could find expression (Oldenberg 1882: 152, quoted in Tambiah 1982: 303).

The matha appears as a space where the ideas of renunciation can be institutionally practised. The difference in the conceptualisation and practice of the virtue of renunciation is a matter of degree between the householder and the sannyasi.

The relation between the renouncer and the householder is articulated from within each sect's philosophical framework. Depending on what this framework is, the renouncer may be seen in sharp contrast to the householder, as in the Aghori sect studied by Jonathan Parry (1994) and the Dashanamis by Gross (1994), or they may be like the Ramanandi sect studied by Peter Van der Veer (1988), wherein the Ramanandi sadhus and the Brahmin householder differ in a matter of degree based on the involvement with the divine play of Rama and Sita. Even though the Ramanandis, like the Udupi matha Madhvas, draw a clear distinction between the sannyasi and the Brahmin householder, they do not contrast (as opposed) the sannyasi and the Brahmin householder when it comes to philosophical understanding.

Burghart (1983) also shows that across different sects, the rules concerning which social relationship must be severed in order to obtain release differ. Contrary to the Ramanandis, the Kabirpanthis who are all householders also consider themselves to be ascetics. The Kabirpanthis take an entirely neutral attitude towards the Ramanandi preoccupation with separation of householder. This the Kabirpanthi's point out that for them, the house/houseless distinction does not correspond to the non-ascetic-ascetic distinction.

Burghart concludes by saying:

> In the intersectarian discourse concerning the nature of transience some ascetics might find themselves classified by others as 'householders', and householders as ascetics, and indeed the very category of householder might be naturalised so that it no longer stands in any specific relation to the ascetic (Burghart 1983: 643).

In short, for Udupi matha Madhvas, the difference between the Brahmin householder and renouncer seems to be a matter of degree and as Heesterman says, the secret of the renouncer's ascendancy over life in the world seems to lie in his impartiality (1985: 43). This greater degree, of vairagya (which is the essence of the sannyasi's life), is characterised variously as 'aloofness' by Das (1982: 135); 'intensity of involvement' by Van der Veer (1988) and 'transcendence' by Madan (1987: 97–98).

Apart from this difference in degree between the formal renouncer and the Madhva Brahmin householder, there is at another level a sharper distinction, more obviously perceived and that is the difference in insignia, dress, codes of behaviour. These symbols place the renouncer in sharp contrast to the normative pattern of life followed by the householder. The sannyasis are unmarried, maintain celibacy and renounce all social obligations to their family, lineage and natal village. The sannyasis of Udupi as elsewhere perform *atma shraddha*, that is, perform their own funeral rites. However, they do not, as in advaitic traditions, accept prasada (sacred food) in their left hand. This Olivelle (1991) and Bharati (1970) argue is done in advaitic traditions to symbolise the impurity of the dead. Bharati also highlights that the sannyasi is considered superior to the demigods as he has renounced the world and has chosen to be outside its attractions whereas the deity in the temple by accepting offerings and giving boons is still involved in the world. The contrary stance of the Udupi sannyasis stresses the significance of the renouncer's participation in society and thus legitimises his involvement with 'this world' which is real, and not only with the 'other world'.

The renouncers have few possessions except their own clothes and stick, and individually they own no property. Furthermore, the sannyasis are non-productive in a worldly economic sense, since they do not engage in manual agricultural labour, craft manufacturing, industrial work or commercial activity. This, of course, is not to say that their activities that their have an economic aspect. As Godelier points out, whether it is the offering of a priest to his God or the gifts of the faithful to a priest (in this case the swamiji), all these social relations have an economic aspect in the exchange of goods and services. This is regardless of whether money plays a part or not (Godelier 1972: 256).

Some of these transactions of donations are highlighted in the chapter on social organisation. Without going into much detail here, I would like to mention that in spite of this economic aspect, the contrast between the householder and the sannyasi can be maintained.

Firstly, the money or other resource given to the matha is not for the sake of the sannyasi or his immediate circle, but for a larger collective moving beyond the caste barrier. Secondly, the sannyasi himself has very few personal requirements and leads a simple life. As a final contrast, a sannyasi lives separately from the householders in his own monastic institutions.

The sannyasi in his appearance can be distinguished by the saffron robe and the stick (which matches the height of the young individual at the time of initiation). The gopichandana (yellow clay) markings and the tulsi (sacred basil) wood necklace around his neck distinguish him as a Madhva. He does not have a *juttu* (top knot) or the yajnopavit (sacred thread) which (like the ochre robe and the stick he possesses) differentiates him from the twice-born householder.

All the sannyasis of Udupi in the past as well as today have the title '*tirtha*' attached to the name given to them after initiation.[4] According to Vishnutirtha, the author of the

Sannyasapaddhati, tirtha means one who purifies and secondly one who knows Shastra and perhaps therefore has the ability to purify. One of the scholars said that tirtha meant one who takes or leads (you) to. This was specially true, he said, of Anandatirtha, the other name of Madhvacharya. This other name 'means one who leads you to ananda or bliss.'

In the discussion so far, we have tried to understand that renunciation is articulated at two levels; one at the level of being the world of corporeality, physical and tangible objects; the other at the level of consciousness, meanings and perceptions.

In the consciousness of vairagya, there is a similarity between the sannyasi and the householder, but in the outward appearances and ways of life, there is a sharp discontinuity. Thus, the sannyasi-Brahmin householder distinction is characterised by an epistemological continuity and an ontological break.

In logical extension, it means a sannyasi (defined as one within the sannyasa-ashrama) may not have vairagya, while as a grihastha may be a 'sannyasi', in the sense of someone having vairagya. A sannyasi who dons the ochre robe may do so with the intention of deceiving people. The Udupi sannyasis criticise those 'fake' sannyasis who take up sannyasa-ashrama to enjoy the benefits of the monastery and misuse the resources for personal gain (for an ethnographic account discussing the issue of fake saints, see Narayan 1991). Such sannyasis were understood as having no vairagya. So just by taking up sannyasa-ashrama one need not develop vairagya. On the other hand, a householder may have great vairagya. These grihasthas are often highlighted in the *Bhagavata* as persons with great Vishnu bhakti (devotion to Vishnu).

Vishnutirtha in his *Sannyasapaddhati* discusses these issues, and he concludes by saying, '*Vishnu bhakti vihino yo yatishcha shvapcha adhama*' (A *yati*, i.e. sannyasi in the ashrama, without Vishnu bhakti is worse than a *shvapacha* or dog-eater or a low caste: 1.38).

As T.N. Madan points out:

> It is through detachment rather than formal renunciation that all dualities are transcended (1987: 93).

Interdependence and Hostility

Apart from the two ashramas sharing the sense of vairagya, there is on the one hand, a sense of interdependence on various other issues and a restrained sense of hostility on the other hand mainly due to the particular lifestyle followed by saints. Let me first highlight a few important areas of interdependence. There are numerous occasions when the saints of Udupi receive donations from devotees. Although they are not entirely dependent on the donations (since each matha has property attached to it), it helps the saints in working towards the benefit of the society at large.

The sannyasis, besides providing religious and philosophical teaching (dealt with in earlier chapters), give medical, psychological and other advice regarding marriage and vocation to devotees who seek such counsel. However, in the Udupi matha, unlike in Shringeri and other places (Gross 1992: 167–8), the saints do not encourage or practise astrology or the art of healing through mantras. The performance of miracles is seen to distract the mind from the actual goal of *Bhagavat* bhakti (devotion to God).

The sannyasis are also dependent for their food and performance of rituals and rites on the Brahmin householder. This is because, as is generally true of other sects, the sannyasis have to renounce fire and the performance of yagnyas (rituals involving the sacred fire) as also the cooking of food. Patrick Olivelle writes:

> The lack of a sacred fire in particular is the hallmark of a renouncer (1992: 62).

However, a bidi-sannyasi visiting Udupi justified his cooking food for himself, saying, 'In sannyasa (ashrama) one takes fire inside oneself (*atma samarohana*), therefore, a sannyasi is not one without fire and so I can cook.' Gross (1992) mentions the use of a sacred fire—*dhuni*—among the sadhus of north India. The swamijis of the Udupi matha (all non-bidi sannyasis) do not associate with any sacred fire, except the arti (the flame waved in front of an icon during worship). They ask the purohits (Brahmin priests) to conduct the rituals for the matha or for themselves.

Another area of interdependence is focussed around a ritual occasion every evening after the sannyasi has worshipped the deities. This is a prayer called the *mantrakshate* mantra, asking Brahman to give good health, wisdom and other qualities or attributes to the sannyasi, so that he can perform his function and help the others reach liberation (from misery). This prayer is recited by Brahmin grihastha and brahmacharis who hold the coloured rice in their hands (given from a bowl filled with it). After the mantra, the rice is returned to the bowl and the sannyasi, with great devotion and respect puts it on his head, as a blessing from society. A sannyasi also said that this mantra 'strengthens our resolve to work for others and to keep to the right path so that we may show it to others.' This highlights the interdependence of the saint with at least the Brahmin society and the fact that the Brahmin householder looks up to the sannyasi to show the path towards 'freedom'.

Apart from this benign alliance, some sociologists (Dumont 1960; Madan 1987) stress that there is another side to the relationship due to the threat posed by the sannyasi through the establishment of an alternative lifestyle (usually by negating the sexual life of the householder). In Udupi, there is a warning against moha or excessive attachment to worldly pleasures, but sannyasa is not the only suggested alternative.

In a public lecture delivered by a swamiji of the Udupi matha, there is a warning against moha (attachment or affection) articulated in this way:

> When you [referring to men] come home from a long visit and hug your wife in the night and say, 'You are my dearest and you are closest to me' remember that God living inside you [with emphasis] is closer and should be more dear, as He is the one who is always going to be with you and save you.

There are stories told by the gurus that stress that Brahman is the one who can save us or liberate us from the miseries of this world. The story of Gajendra Moksha from the *Bhagavata* tells of a king cursed to be born as an elephant. When caught in the jaws of the crocodile, he shouts to his family (the elephant herd) for help. Initially the wives, children and others try to pull him out, but when they see that he cannot be rescued, they say, as the guru, improvising humorously, put it, 'Please go. We cannot save you, but do write a postcard when you reach heaven.' The men and women listening, laugh but the message is driven home.

In these examples, the sannyasi or the gurus who are householders as well do not ask the one in the grihastha ashrama to give it up and take sannyasa, the emphasis is rather on adopting vairagya within the householder's lifestyle. The change required is not necessarily of a different lifestyle, but of an attitude. It highlights the fact that the life of a householder can become a trap which makes one forget God, but the way out is not necessarily through formal renunciation. The wife is not to be shunned as one who will cause moha. She can partake of the wisdom which discourages excessive attachment. So, the threat posed is for the householder who gets carried away by moha, the web of affections. T.N. Madan talks of the fear of the renouncer due to the contrast with the householder and the illusion of worldly affairs that the renouncer propagates (1987: 93). In Udupi, this fear is not visible because the renouncer does not stand in such a sharp contrast as in other orthodox traditions and he does not negate the world of the householder. Further, the world, both the living and the non-living, is real in Dvaita philosophy, reality that is dependent on Brahman. The world of the householder cannot be contrasted to the liberating world of the renouncer as the illusory versus the real, as in many advaitic traditions.

Thus, there is no visible hostility towards the renouncer when it comes to matters of vairagya or the value of renunciation. However, regarding certain other matters, this hostility becomes more pronounced.

Dumont does talk of the 'subdued hostility' (1960: 45) towards renunciation. And this subdued hostility in Udupi often involves women. Potentially, a woman is more threatening to the renouncer than to the householder. Patrick Olivelle, quoting the *Sannyasa Upanishads*, writes that the renunciatory ideal portrays a woman as a temptress of whom the sannyasis should be especially careful. Ascetics are constantly admonished to stay away from women:

> Passion does not die with age. Old men continue to lust and old women continue to arouse lust (Olivelle 1992: 77).

'The dominant woman' (O'Flaherty 1980: 77) or the *apsara* sent to destroy the *tapas* of the sages (Dimmit and van Buitenen 1983: 259 and Marglin 1982: 167) is treated in many sectarian texts, as also in popular usage.

In the generation of sannyasis before the present one, sexual relations with women were prevalent, and this in some cases is common knowledge. In the present context, I did not find any evidence of such a relationship, most probably because unlike their previous counterparts, sannyasis who want to marry can leave the matha or give up sannyasa and are no longer under the pressure to remain with the matha 'at all costs'. Nevertheless, rumours continue to exist about some of the sannyasis, and they run the risk of being called womanisers. Acknowledging this, one of the sannyasis confided that he kept the doors open when talking to women.

On inquiring from those who thought a particular swamiji had a relation with a woman and what proof they had, most said they simply knew or else had heard it from somebody. One of them could not understand how one could abstain from sexual indulgence altogether and hence thought it obvious that even a sannyasi must 'fall' once in a while.

Another incident highlights how the swamijis are prone to caricature. During a festive occasion in a village near Udupi, saffron clothes were spread on the ground to dry. The saffron cloth of a sannyasi is not supposed to be touched by anybody except his Brahmin helper in a state of madi or purity. As people consciously sought to avoid stepping on it, one wondered why it had been put to dry here where there was a crowd. Soon, a stray dog sniffing for food and oblivious of the state of madi walked over the saffron cloth.

The two men behind me immediately commented, 'The dog can walk over the madi cloth of the swamiji, but we can't, Ah! what sort of madi is this?' I wanted to find out from the gindi (the man who washes swamiji's clothes) as to why he had risked drying the clothes there. I was surprised when he told me that those saffron clothes did not belong to the swamiji at all.

The cloth in fact belonged to a grihastha Brahmin. It is quite common for a non-sannyasi Brahmin to wear a saffron coloured cloth around the waist and as an unstitched piece over the upper part of the body. But the way the cloth is worn around the waist to cover the lower part of the body is often very different from the way a sannyasi would wear it.

Similarly, there are those who think that all is well with the sannyasis, except that they eat such heavy food—five types of sweets made for offering to Krishna taken as prasada. 'Food does have an effect, how can they work if they feel lazy after consuming such heavy food every day? Energy must be channelised otherwise it heightens their desires.'

In the chowki, where the five types of sweets are served, it is not generally correct to assume that the sannyasis also eat all of that. Furthermore, the swamijis other than the paryaya swamiji seldom eat at the chowki. They eat in their own mathas and the food is nutritious, but very simple.

There were other issues that reduced 'the renouncer to a caricature of his ideal self,' (Madan 1987: 42). But unlike the pandits of Kashmir, in Udupi, this is not such a widespread phenomenon. Nevertheless, the incidents mentioned do highlight a sort of dual relationship that exists between the renouncer and the non-renouncer. At one level, there is reverence for the sannyasi, but again at the same time, there are occasions when the non-renouncer refuses to give the sannyasi the credit for his detachment.

The conceptualisation of the renouncer–non-renouncer distinction can take place from another perspective, that of the relation between the sect and caste—the Madhva sect and the Madhva Brahmin caste.

Sect and Renunciation

Most of the anthropological literature on sect and renunciation suggests that the taking up of sannyasa is a voluntary act that ignores all caste affiliations. The renouncer has generally been understood as beyond caste or varna. (Babb 1987; Burghart 1983; Das (1977) 1982; Gross 1992; Heesterman (1964) 1985; Olivelle 1992; Rao 1979, 1984; Srinivas and Shah 1968; Uberoi 1967; Van der Veer 1988).

Thus, most of my reading had prepared me to accept the Udupi sannyasis as having no caste status. This seemed problematic in the face of active involvement with the caste hierarchy, evidenced in the restriction of entry to non-Brahmin castes for the chowki prasada, in the selection of Madhva Brahmin students of saints in the matha and as we shall see in more detail, in the initiation into sannyasa for the mathas of Udupi. They certainly seemed to revitalise the caste hierarchy, but were they part of it or did they stand outside?

The sannyasis of Udupi categorically stated (except two who after some thought agreed with the rest) that they were Brahmins. 'Just as when you take up the grihastha ashrama, you do not cease to be a Brahmin, similarly, if we take up the ashrama of sannyasa, we do not stop being Brahmin,' they said.

The Udupi sannyasis (and sannyasis in all the mathas of the Madhva sect) today are selected from among the Madhva Brahmin sub-caste. This incidentally is also true of the five Shankaracharya or Advaita mathas in Kanchi, Shringeri, Dwarka, Puri and Kashi, as their head pontiffs are chosen from among the Smartha Brahmin sub-caste.

Das (1982), through her study of myths (in the context of Gujarat), writes:

> By sannyasa being a voluntaristic category, it is meant that the occupant of any status within the society is free to become a

> sannyasi, or to put the same argument negatively, no one can involuntarily be a sannyasi. In this sense, sannyasa is different from the category Brahmin, in that membership of the category is not pre-determined (Das 1982: 45).

In Udupi, the sannyasis do not belong to various caste groups, they are chosen from within a sub-caste. However, this should not imply that the status of a sannyasi is a pre-determined like the status of the member of a caste group, in this case the Madhva Brahmin. In sannyasa, though there is a fixed group from which selection takes place, it is not pre-determined by birth as to who is to be a sannyasi. There is selection and in this sense, it is voluntary but within a caste group. One may refuse to be a sannyasi having been offered sannyasa,[5] but you cannot refuse to be a Brahmin.

J.P.S. Uberoi (1967) and M.S.A. Rao (1979, 1984) claim that the social system of caste seems to have been surrounded by a penumbral region (Uberoi 1967) of non-caste or even anti-caste where there are renunciatory religious orders whose principles repudiated the ascribed statuses resting on caste and birth. Srinivas and Shah (1968) are more careful in stressing that though caste distinctions may prevail in sects, the membership in a sect, unlike that in a caste, is not hereditary but comes through initiation. So, often the strait-jacketed division between caste and sect based on birth and choice respectively needs to be specifically contextualised.

Besides, those sannyasis who go on to become mathadipatis (pontiffs of the Udupi mathas) and are responsible for the reproduction of the mathas both ideologically and materially, there are those who are given sannyasa by the Udupi sannyasi and belong to the matha of Udupi, but are free from the burdens of running the matha and its ancillary units (as has been pointed out in Chapters 2 and 4). The bidi-sannyasis have to be Madhva Brahmins, but recently, a couple of non-Madhva Brahmins and a Brahmin woman have been made bidi-sannyasis of the Madhva matha. The senior Pejavara swamiji recently gave sannyasa to a prominent female political member of the Bharatiya Janata

Party. There were objections from some of the sannyasis of Udupi as for example, the Kaniur and Krishnapura swamijis. They felt that such changes can be brought about only by one as great as Vadiraja Swamy (one who changed the paryaya system in Udupi and tried to incorporate the non-Brahmin castes in the mainstream of the Udupi matha). When I asked the Pejavara swamiji why he had gone out of the way and given sannyasa to a woman, he replied, 'She was deeply interested in leading a life devoted to service in the name of God and she wanted to be initiated by a Madhva sannyasi. Besides, she had been asking me since a very long time. I did not want to refuse a person so keenly interested.' He went on to tell me that he did not think there was anything wrong in initiating women into sannyasa. He even suggested that if there were any more women who expressed their wish to become sannyasinis, he would consider it favourably. The woman to whom sannyasa has been given will be recognised as a Madhva sannyasi. However, this swamiji would not accept a woman as a pontiff of the Udupi matha. The institution of bidi-sannyasa, by allowing women into the sannyasa ashrama, provides flexibility in the rules for initiation into sannyasa.

Unlike the selection process of the Udupi swamijis, these bidi-sannyasis come on their own and ask for sannyasa. They can take sannyasa even after marriage. Unlike the pontiffs of Udupi matha, they are not required to have a strong background of the Shastras (Vedanta and related knowledge). These bidi-sannyasis are dispersed and often have only a name-sake relation with the guru matha and the swamiji, although they are formally Madhvas. This is the only way through which sannyasa-ashrama can be taken voluntarily in the Madhva sect. Even then, so far entry has been restricted more or less to the Madhva Brahmin caste or varna. The institution of bidi-sannyasis is a feature accommodated for the individual desire to take up the sannyasa ashrama by relaxing the rigid rules constituent of an orthodox institution, but it still remains bound by ascriptive criteria, although the current trends suggest that this might happen in the near future.

The renouncer transcends the duality of caste and sect by belonging to both. By arriving at this understanding, it is important to note that the status of the renouncer is not at par with that of the Madhva Brahmin non-renouncer. This is because sannyasa becomes the principle of internal segmentation of the caste. The position of the sannyasi is hierarchically superior to others. As we know for Dumont:

> a certain hierarchy of ideas, things and people is indispensable to social life (Dumont 1970: 20).

Dumont's opposition between pure and impure is purely a matter of religious values. This hierarchy based on religious values is restricted to the caste system. If an extension were to be made of the value of hierarchy into the sectarian domain, then the epistemological continuity of the concept of sannyasa or vairagya could be seen as a hierarchical placing of religious values.

The greater degree of vairagya among the sannyasis of the ashrama places them in a hierarchically superior position. The greater religious value comes by the virtue of being closer to God or Brahman.

As we have already observed, proximity to Brahman leads to greater vairagya and is the reason for his ascendancy over the householder. This ascendancy is maintained by scriptural support and as a living force in the eyes of the lay followers. There have been instances in the history of the Madhva sect where the sannyasis of Udupi have acknowledged vairagya in the non-sannyasi. This, however, has not happened in the recent past. The story told about Kanakadasa (16th century), a person born in the shepherd caste, is an example of how caste distinctions were overcome due to the greater proximity or understanding of God.[6] This, however, is constituted only at the level of narrative, and is neither present at the level of social life nor in the opening up of the matha to low caste members.

One may ask, 'If non-Brahmins were admitted as students of sannyasis in the past, why don't they do so now?' This enquiry requires a separate study. A study which would look into the reasons why membership to a group open to all is closed eventually to the chosen few, in short why a sect tends to adopt values of caste in India. Toomey also points out:

> In the strict sense, institutionalisation of a sect is a corruption of the founder ascetic's ideals (1986: 60).

Nevertheless, there are Madhva mathas outside Udupi with non-Madhva Brahmins as members. The Gaud Saraswat Madhva mathas give membership to Gaud Saraswat Brahmins and the International Society for Krishna Consciousness (ISKCON) has universal membership.[7]

I shall also briefly touch open notions of time and space that are based on the principle of promixity to God. Time and space are also organised into hierarchical units.

The time of festivals or birth anniversaries of the gods and great saints is more auspicious and sacred[8] than other days. The days of impurity due to death or birth (for the grihastha) are the days on which no important work or festival is conducted, for it is not auspicious. Eliade (1957) mentions that people divide their time between the sacred and the non-sacred. M.N. Srinivas's work on the Coorgs (1952) is also a good study of the notions and practices of auspicious (*mangala*) time. For the sannyasis, though, one cannot demarcate the inauspicious time so clearly, one can certainly say that the time of festivals, etc. is more sacred for them.

Apart from the everyday division of time into the sacred and the profane or just the mundane (for the swamijis), there is the hierarchical understanding of blocks of time as well, called *yugas* (eras). These are four in number that move in a cyclical order:

Kritayuga	17,28,000 years
Tretayuga	12,96,000 years
Dvaparayuga	8,64,000 years
Kaliyuga (*present time*)	4,32,000 years
One *Mahayuga*	43,20,000 years
1000 *Mahayugas* = 1 *Kalpa*	

There is *pralaya* or total destruction after each kalpa which is equal to a day of Chaturmukha Brahma's life.[9]

The understanding of the classification or labelling of these times, is based on the type of awareness that existed in terms of an individual's relation to God. There was great proximity to God in the Kritayuga which went on diminishing in the later yugas.

In the previous yugas, all human activity was understood more clearly as divine play. Mircea Eliade writes:

> Life is lived on a twofold plane; it takes into account the ordinary human existence and at the same time, shares in a transhuman life, that of the cosmos or the gods (1957).

For example, the Hindu, following the *Upanishads*, would consider the relationship with his wife in these terms—that she is earth and he heaven; that she is the *shakti* (feminine force) and he is the *purusha* (the male creator). He is at the same time fully conscious of his humanity and hers. This relation and experience, according to Eliade, is no longer present in modern times; it is an experience no longer accessible in a 'desacralised society'.

For the sages in India, the continued loss of this experience is a consequence of the loss of the correct knowledge of God. So, the arrangement of the yugas can be viewed according to the degree to which society was 'Brahman conscious'.

In the *Brahma Sutra* bhashya, Madhvacharya, quoting from the *Skanda Purana* writes (translating from Sanskrit):

> Knowledge came from Narayana. For some time it sustained. This period is called Kritayuga. Next, to some extent, doubt and illusion vitiated knowledge. This period is Treta. Next, knowledge as such disappeared. This is Dvapara. This was helped by a special circumstance, namely the curse of sage Gautama.[10] The condition of ignorance was such that even the divinities could not help the situation. They could only pity men seeking knowledge. So having been requested by them, Narayana the defectless, Bhagavan the most complete, Mahayogi the omnipotent appeared as the son of Parashara the father and Satyavati the mother. Their son (Vyasa) divided and classified

the Vedas into four main branches, further condensed them into 24, 101 branches, then 1000 branches and finally 12 branches. Next in order to fix its meaning, he composed the *Brahma Sutras*.

Jayatirtha, commenting on the bhashya, explains that all this was done for the benefit of mankind who did not respect the logic of the times and acted irresponsibly (by not preserving knowledge and incurring the wrath of Gautama).

The *Bhagavata* calls the last yuga of kali a bad time for those interested in knowledge of Bhagavan. It describes a time vitiated by evil forces that prevents the understanding of Brahman, yet it also therefore specifies that even a little effort towards knowing God yields greater results.

I shall not go into details of sacred and profane or inauspicious space here. It is sufficient to mention again that the proximity to an icon or the space where gods and great saints lived and live creates a hierarchy in spatial units (dealt within the chapter on food). There have been studies in terms of right and left, clockwise and anti-clockwise [see Das (1982: 91–113), Kausik (1979), Seneviratne (1985)], for a non-sectarian, but for a general understanding of the religious division of space, time and people in Hinduism, see Madan (1992). Milner, in a recent study (1994), develops the thesis of 'resource structuralism' which, among other things, demonstrates how status is ordered by differing forms of 'association', with the renouncer and the Brahmin getting highest status by their closest relation to God.

In Udupi the hierarchical understanding of concepts and people orders the everyday living of the members of the sect. It is reflective of Dvaita philosophy which strikes out at the advaitic notion of equality and non-difference (abheda). These notions prevalent among lay members are upheld and propagated by the sannyasis and other gurus of the matha. Burghart, in emphasising that Dumont's Brahmin counterparts shaped his conception of caste, calls Dumont an 'European Brahmin' (1990: 268). It might be added that due to the significant role hierarchy as an ideology plays in Dumont's framework, he is an European Madhva Brahmin.

Let me now turn to the process though which initiation into the sannyasa-ashrama takes place. What qualifies one to attain a hierarchically superior position?

The Process of Recruitment

As we have seen, a sannyasi has to be born a Madhva. The sannyasis heading the matha, when looking for a successor, consider only those who are male Madhvas and are further born in an orthodox family, which still values the traditional way of life (in eating, bathing, sleeping, study, etc.). Apart from this criterion, the sannyasi should be a celibate. Traditionally, sannyasa is given to a young boy between the age of 8 to 14. This practice of bal-sannyasa (childhood sannyasa) is followed in Udupi since the time of Madhvacharya. As stated in the earlier chapter, there has recently been a debate about the age of taking up sannyasa. Some insist that the individual should know what it means before he is initiated into the sannyasa-ashrama. Whatever be the age of the individual at the time of initiation, two things are mandatory at the outset. One, he should not have been married and second, the Brahmin should have completed his upanayana or sacred thread ceremony. This makes him twice born and eligible for instruction from a guru.

Another important matter looked into is astrological feasibility of sannyasa. The horoscope should be favourable for renunciation. It should point out whether or not an individual has the potential for vairagya, the keen sense of detachment imperative for sannyasa.

The pontiff looks around for suitable families and Madhva Brahmin boys and asks for their horoscopes that are then given to the astrologer traditionally affiliated to the particular sub matha(s).

During my stay, I spoke to an old astrologer of great repute, Ganapathy Achar, who has been selecting horoscopes for some of the Udupi mathas. He had been given three to four *jatakas* (horoscopes) by a senior swamiji of the matha for selection.

These jatakas were of Brahmins in the age group 18–21 years, since the swamiji involved felt that sannyasa should only be given to a mature person. The discussion began with Ganapathy Achar emphasising the importance of astrology. He said, '*Shabda shastra mukham, jyotisham chakshusi*' (If *shabda shastra* or Vedanta is the face, then *jyotisha* or astrology is the eyes).

Jyotisha is divided into three basic parts, *Ganitha, Hora* and *Samhita*, each having many sub-parts. The one useful for Ganapathy Achar is a sub-part of Hora called jataka or horoscopy. It has been written over the ages by sages Parashurama, Vishnugupta and others.

The Hora is called *Braht Jatakam* and the one used by astrologers has been compiled by Varahamihiracharya (5th century AD). Besides the chapters on marriage, children, death, etc., the text has a chapter exclusively for sannyasa called *pravrajya yoga* (pravrajya also means sannyasa).

Ganapathy Achar further said, 'You see, in general, if one constellation has four or more planets, then the jataka is good for sannyasa.' He went on to give six other characteristics that figure in a sannyasi's horoscope. According to him, the jataka must not be good in the eyes of the world. There must be the *drishti* (aspect) of *shani* (the planet Saturn associated with bad fortune) with respect to marriage, children and other related points considered important for a happy grihastha life.

It is also possible to ascertain whether or not a person is capable of vairagya (detachment). An astrologer can say whether the person will continue with transcendental and spiritual matters throughout his life or not.

I did ask him why some sannyasis left the ashrama[11] if one can know the conditions of sannyasa in an individual through his horoscope. The reply was that human beings (astrologers) can make mistakes in reading horoscopes. 'There are many secrets of human nature which only great sages of the past knew in detail,' he said.

After the horoscope is satisfactory, the final step is the consent of the parents and in particular the mother before *diksha* (initiation) into sannyasa takes place. This is more important when the boy to be initiated is too young to decide for himself;

but if the individual is old enough, then his own decision becomes more crucial. The acceptance is marked by the receiving of special mantrakshate (coloured rice) given by the pontiff. Once the Brahmin boy takes the mantrakshate, he is bound and the acceptance is considered final.

The following illustrations aim to amplify the variables.

The junior Phalimar swamiji took sannyasa at the age of 23, having been born on the 14th of May 1956. He comes from Mullibagalu, a town in Karnataka, and is a Madhva Brahmin. He told me how he was initiated into sannyasa.

> I was a student of the senior Phalimar swamiji and was interested in knowing about Brahman, although I used to play a lot of cricket. One fine day, the swamiji, seeing my disinterest in worldly matters, asked me to take sannyasa. He must have seen my horoscope also; anyway, he knew a lot much about me.
>
> My mother opposed the proposal. We have a lot of land and many temples to look after. But swamiji convinced her and I was happy. You must know that the mother's consent is important. That was really what I wanted to be—in constant thought of God. Whenever I think about Shastra, I completely forget the world. But I soon realised that I had to involve myself in some of the worldly affairs since I am with this matha. I have tried to compromise and do my best. I get great satisfaction in teaching my students. I like *Bhagavad Gita* the best, although I enjoy *vyakarna* (grammar) and *tarka* (logic) very much.

The Kaniur senior swamiji selected a junior swami, insisting that sannyasa should be given at a young age. The junior swamiji was 14 when he was given sannyasa. He is now studying Shastra from his guru, the pontiff of Uttaradi matha (a non-Udupi Madhva matha).

It has been the custom in this sub-matha of Udupi to select a junior swami from among the kinsmen of the swamiji. Since at least the last four generations, the senior swamiji has selected one of his brothers' sons.

The Kaniur swamiji said, 'I selected my successor from among my younger brothers' sons. There were two, I selected the more intelligent one. His jataka also showed that this person should be given sannyasa'. He proceed to give me the details of his horoscope.

The mother of the junior swamiji of Kaniur felt proud to declare that her son was a sannyasi. 'You see, it is a great merit for the whole family if there is a sannyasi in the house. Even the ancestors become happy.' The same feeling was expressed by the mother of the Shirur matha swamiji. She even described the initiation ceremony. 'My son was very young (8 years) and I had to comfort him, as soon after the tiring ceremony he developed fever,' she said. The sannyasis even though they are supposed to sever all ties with the family, have a special relation with the mother and continue to maintain links with the family. B.D. Tripathi's study of sadhus in different orders (mainly in north India) also suggest that they do not sever ties with their families and maintain a link with their caste.

The mother of the Shirur swamiji, who is now a widow, lives in the Shirur matha at Udupi. Everyone including the father bows before the sannyasi, but the mother is prohibited from bowing down to her 'son'. When I asked the Shirur swamiji's mother why she was staying in the matha when the sannyasi was supposed to break off with his family after initiation, she replied, 'I am alone and don't have any other relatives whom I can stay with. Where else can I go?' She had a large room for herself in the matha and when I met her for the first time, she had a couple of woman relatives visiting her. On various occasions, she expressed anxiety over the fact that her 'son' would be the paryaya swami after the present one completed his tenure. She once said, 'You see the swamiji (when referring to her son, she used the term *swamigalu* in Kannada) is still young (about 30 years) and everyone does not have the same goodwill towards the matha, some people may do him harm.' She immediately added, 'Well', of course, he can manage, but it is good that he has the support of the experienced and wise Sode matha swamiji.' The Sode matha is the traditional ally (dvanda matha) of the Shirur matha as designated by Madhvacharya, hence the Sode matha is customarily bound to assist the Shirur matha. The relation between these two mathas is not only bound by traditional prescriptions but also by a bond of mutual trust and affection. The Shirur swami consults the Sode swami on matters relating to the running of the matha. In other mathas, the head pontiff of the matha takes the decisions or the junior swamiji has the help of his senior. The Shirur matha is the only matha in Udupi which has only one junior swami, without any senior swamiji. The other mathas that have only one swamiji, namely Krishnapura and Sode, have senior sannyasis who are experienced in the art of managing the mathas.

There have been a few studies on the life histories of Indian monks or sadhus (Balfour 1897; Ghurye 1954; Gross 1992; Jha 1971 and Miller 1976), and most have concentrated on sannyasa as a release from oppressive social and psychological conditions. This in Udupi is seldom the case. Robert Lewis Gross writes:

> Whatever the rigours and deprivations an ascetic life may represent, it correspondingly offers certain compensations. It definitely legitimises a means of avoiding anxiety producing situations related to marriage, sexuality, procreation, family responsibility and economic support (1992: 417).

These motivations did not feature as the major reasons for taking sannyasa in Udupi. It was rather the notions of punya (merit), spiritual salvation and the recognition one gets when one becomes entitled to do Krishna puja at the main matha that seemed to be the prime motives. The non-predominance of the motives mentioned by Gross could be a result of the restriction imposed by the sect in closing the sannyasa-ashrama to a specific group and the absence of being able to voluntarily take up sannyasa.

The mainstream institution of bala-sannyasa in the Udupi matha in addition to denying voluntary initiation also distinguishes itself by going against the accepted notion of sannyasa-ashrama as the final stage in the life of a human, taken at old age in the scheme of *varnasharama dharma*. *Brahmacharya* (the first stage in the varnasharama dharma when sannyasa diksha is given in Udupi) is usually understood as a state of learning when all the physical and mental faculties are agile. Old age signifies a stage in life where one has learnt through experience the ephemeral nature of life that could result in detachment. But old age is also a stage in life where physical and mental faculties are at a low.

Bhartrahari in his *Vairagya Shatakam* (Swami Madhvananda, 1990) stresses the advantage in taking sannyasa at old age and gives reasons as to why sannyasa should be taken as a means of salvation. He emphasises the need to understand old age as a stage in which one can easily renounce desires.

In more modern discourse, gerontologists signify this stage as a state of ambiguity. For Minois (1987), ambiguity is the phenomenological universe of old age, a time of both maximal experience and of maximal debility. The experience can fuel the knowledge of the futility of worldly pursuits in the background of traditional sectarian upbringing and this can be the pull factor towards vairagya. Maximal debility can foster the idea of non-productive activity. One can do little for society and oneself. This can be a powerful push factor. Together the push and pull factors can incite one to take sannyasa ashrama.

Cole writes:

> Aging like illness and death reveals the most fundamental conflict of the human condition: the tension between infinite ambitions, dreams and desires on the one hand, and vulnerable, limited, decaying physical existence on the other, the tragic and ineradicable conflict between the spirit and the body (Cole 1992: 239).

The logic of sannyasa in the Udupi matha tries to resolve these conflicts. One of the sannyasis commented, 'By taking sannyasa in old age you can do nothing, but if it is taken at a younger age, then you can strive towards God all your life and work with the ambition of doing something for society.' Ingrained within this ethos is the fact that sannyasa-ashrama is not a life lived in seclusion but a way of life that is deeply interactive with society.

Bal-sannyasa is a celebration of the realisation of Madhvacharya at a young age as he took sannyasa in his childhood (so did

Shankaracharya) soon after his upanayana. Madhvacharya took sannyasa to authorise his stance and voice and through this to set right the misconception in society. Today also, what the sannyasi says carries weight because he is a sannyasi, a *jagadguru* and the sannyasis of Udupi have interacted intensely with the society and circumstances of their times. Sannyasa-ashrama, as the fourth and final stage of life taken at old age, is more a form of retirement and less of 'renouncement'.

Even the philosophical outlook of Madhva's thought favours an early beginning of Shastra when the mind is alert and responsive to plan and live a fruitful life. Interestingly enough, Deleuze and Guattari begin their book by saying:

> The question what is philosophy can perhaps be posed only late in life, with the arrival of old age and the time for speaking concretely (1994: 1).

The time to speak concretely here is when the hair turns grey and wrinkles gather on the face—the typical face of the wise sage. But the scholars in Udupi feel philosophy needs to be understood as life goes on, so that ideas can interact with the on-going process of existence. The first chapter of the *Brahma Sutra* bhashya, called *Jignyasadhikarna*, deals with questions regarding the nature of philosophy. And this epistemological outlook determines further study and lifestyle. The conclusions to be reached are not a function of old age.

The focus on bal-sannyasa, however, does not exclude the possibility of taking up sannyasa-ashrama in old age. This is made possible by the institution of bidi-sannyasis. There are no rigid rules for them and most people take up formal renunciation after their marriage towards old age. The matha thus provides space for those male Madhva Brahmins wanting to take sannyasa ashrama at old age. These bidi-sannyasis, because of the relaxed rules of sannyasa, remain on the periphery of the Udupi matha. These sannyasis on the fringe have a relatively passive and sedentary life.

The last section offers an interpretation of vairagya as the Madhvas understand it.

The Meaning of Vairagya

This concluding section deals with the meaning that Madhva's philosophy attaches to vairagya or sannyasa in general. The previous explanations in the chapter have rested mainly on ethnographic encounters with the sannyasis or householders. The meaning that unfolded in the more specific discussions, especially during patha (instruction of particular texts of Madhva's tradition) and a comparative study of the scriptures yielded a more definite and complex understanding. This understanding is part of the studentship of a sannyasi, which is not easy to convey in an interview or a conversation (even though spread out over a period of time). Further, various scholars have tried to grapple with the issue. For example, as T.N. Madan (1987) suggests, if Dumont calls renunciation 'a sort of universal language in India' (1970: 52 in Madan 1987: 98), then it can be best understood through the concept of transcendence, whereas for him it implies a movement beyond choices.

Whether it be novels, myths or the *Upanishads* themselves, works that lie at the confluence of sociology and Indology have tried to focus on the value of renunciation.[12] In the discussion of the *Sutra Anandmayabhyasat* in the *Brahma Sutra* bhashya of Madhva and in *Tattva Prakasika*, its commentary by Jayatirtha, the cause of bondage is shown to be *lokaprasiddhi*, i.e. that which is 'generally' understood. The bondage is created by the ideas that have found wide usage in the world. But when we inquire into the truth of the worldly usages, it is found that the meanings are distorted.

Herein lies the possibility of a critique of intersubjectivity as that which permanently situates a being-in-one-kind-of-world. The movement beyond the first being in the world is not for Madhva a mere transition of perspectives, it results in ananda or joy. This 'second order' reality is not only an epistemology but also a way of being. This state of joy corresponds to a being-in-the-world different from the first.

Adhikara (the capacity to study) is the necessary

presupposition of jignyasa (inquiry). It is a state that makes the subject-matter doubtful (*sandhigadha*). Thus, adhikara is a condition where adhyayana (study) becomes indispensable. Madhva shows how definition of the adhikara on the basis of birth does not explain the background for jignyasa decisively. Therefore, he feels that it is the quality (guna) which defines adhikara leading to adhyayana and results in changes in personality. Madhva discerns three levels of adhikara—adhama (lower), madhyama (middle) and uttama (superior). Those that have 'middle' or 'higher' level of adhikara means the person has *santa* (his mind fixed in Brahman and therefore peaceful), *danta* (non-repressed control over the senses born out of understanding), *uparata* (withdrawn from the objects of the world), *titiksu* (not mere tolerance, as often it is a sign of helplessness, but indifference) and *samhita* (the ability to evaluate and move beyond the cause of misery). It is not that these gunas (abilities) are not there before the study commences, but that adhikara shaped by these gunas leads to its further refinement and enhancement.

It is this re-formation of the self that Shastra attempts. Milton Singer, in one of his books, (1984) points out the need to develop wider and inclusive personalities and identities that can counter the growing despondency and threats of dangerous wars. He finds in the Indian ethos and philosophy a way out of despair and depression, a way to preserve the planet earth (Singer 1984: 155–188).

Madhva states that *atha* in the phrase *Athato Brahma jignyasa* means the desire to be happy. The bhashya is *Atha-sabdao mangalarthah.* (The word atha signifies mangala, auspicious disposition consisting in the fact that jignyasa is the outcome of joy.) So, by the use of the word *atha* in the *Sutra*, the author intends to show that jignyasa is not the outcome of (and also does not lead to) pain. Nothing is laboured. This disposition is what is called punya and dharma in the correct sense of the term and it is *shreyas* in the Upanishadic sense and it is mangala in the bhashya sense.

Adhikara is the recognition of the fact that the self is capable of opening up by appropriating a reality that is different from one's present. It suggests that the self is to be arrived at through the detour of interpretation.

Madhva stresses that adhyayana should be Vedic in nature. Transcendental knowledge is for him an outcome of the study of Shastra that commences with Veda. It is the source of valid knowledge about Brahman. Badarayana, in writing the *Brahma Sutras*, throws light on the esoteric Vedic statements. The *Sutras* thus become the guides that can help us solve the apparently contradictory statements in the Veda. The first *Sutra* shows how the inquiry into Brahman is indispensable for an adhikara whose quest is to know the cause of all that is and this quest is an expression of joy or ananda.

Madhva's acceptance of Veda does not mean he relies on an 'authority'. Madhva emphasises that Veda, if at all, is to be accepted as pramana (source of valid knowledge). This distinction becomes crucial in the evaluation of other interpretations or bhasyas of the *Sutra* and the Veda. That is, whether you question the validity of the apparent statements of the Veda and inquire into the meaning or you accept the Veda or the *Shabda Pramana* as an authority that cannot be questioned.

In Madhva's philosophy, the use of the English term 'authority' with respect to the Veda is to adopt an anti-intellectual step because it often stands outside the arguments of reason. Authority implies implicit faith or belief; consequently and popularly any Vedic philosophy is thought to be based on an 'authoritative text'. If intellect asks us to inquire, authority asks us to believe. Veda as pramana is a system of knowledge that is coherent within and with elements outside. If the reality of the world is experienced, then its absence (Advaita) cannot be accepted even if some Vedic statements seem to support it. The reality of the world is perceived emphatically and 'perception' (as a means of knowledge) for Madhva is *prabala* (strong). Veda does not contradict or disregard the knowledge gained through *pratyaksha* (perception) or *anumana* (inference).

It complements and enriches it further. It must be noted that as Veda, Veda is not pramana but as pramana it is Veda.

Veda (in the light of the *Brahma Sutras*) is for Madhva a way of transcending the *lokaprasiddhi* (the first belonging or the inter-subjectivity). It is a language of reason that is beyond empirical reasoning.

The *Kena Upanishad*, also called *Talvakra*, proclaims that, that which is real is beyond and different from what we see, hear or think ordinarily. Brahman as the cause of all is also the cause of the self. The relation between self and Brahman reveals the actual source of thought and action, which is Brahman. The first part of the *Upanishad* says one should know Brahman to be the cause and 'not that which men follow after here' (*Tadeva Brahman tvam viddhi nedam yadidam upasata*).

The truth for Madhva is that which gives rise to a correct understanding of Brahman and hence this world. The outcome of such a theory sees the world as essenceless (*asara*) and transient (*anitya*). This knowledge comes from knowing that Brahman is *sarvottama* (the very highest) and *sarvakarta* (all doer, the cause of all). The disinterest in that which is not the source of anything in this world is the outcome of a detailed study that emphasises vichara—reflection or contemplation. The detachment from the first belonging and attachment to Brahman is the appropriation of knowledge that is given in the text. This understanding gives rise to higher adhikara and a transformed self.

Adhikara is a way of life that sees the need for constant vichara as means of self-understanding. Once the connection between understanding and being-in-the-world is understood, vairagya or detachment first and foremost means, detachment from false consciousness, or wrong knowledge. It is the ontological status of such a detachment that is termed as sannyasa. Renunciation is not primarily the abstaining from sexual activity, or the donning of a special dress. These are the ways of being which characterise the philosophy of reflection. If it is not so, then the dress, way of life of a sannyasi and so forth become merely imitation of symbols, wherein repression of desires takes more of one's time than the will to jignyasa.

This 'will', too, is the product of Brahman's grace (prasada). The sign of prasada is the process of jignyasa. Thus, adhikara and with it vairagya, peace, control of the senses, etc., are the result of the all-causing Brahman. Transcendence in its conceptualisation seeks to move beyond the world. Yet this renunciation, so necessary to the sannyasa ashrama, has another side and that is its relation to the social world in its trying to sacralise and maintain it. In this sense, asceticism is somewhat Janus-faced. Jonathan Parry writes:

> The symbol of asceticism thus points in two opposite directions at once. It offers a route of escape from the world, yet it generates a power that is necessary to sustain it (1994: 270).

In sustaining the world, the institution headed by ascetics interacts with many of the institutions and values of the modern world. The concluding chapter seeks to analyse the interactions that define the emerging status of a tradition.

Notes

1. The renouncer, in contrast to the Brahmin householder, for Dumont is 'dead to the social world, has escaped the network of interdependent caste relations, is and becomes an end for himself as in Western social theory, on the condition that he is cut off from ordinary social life. That is why I have called this person an individual outside the world' (Dumont, 1970: 235).
2. The break-up of the Sanskrit word sannyasa as given by the saints is *sam + nyasa—nyasa* meaning the process of detachment from the world and *sam* meaning done nicely, together formulated as a state of mind in a congenial environment done so that the process leads to attachment with God.
3. The story of Jadabharata is portrayed in the *Bhagavata*. A king who through successive births emerges as a vairagi (a detached person) and by attaining the knowledge of Brahman (Brahma gyana), renounces even the love for his own body.
4. This is true of all the swamijis of the Madhva matha in India (except the sannyasis of ISKCON).
5. The Pejavara swamiji had offered sannyasa to a Madhva Brahmin

youth and he had declined. This had happened just before the present junior swamiji was given diksha (initiation). Sometimes, parents of young boys also refuse to allow their sons to take sannyasa.

6. Vyasatirtha had many students, but he used to give special attention to Kanakadasa, who was born a Kurba (shepherd caste). The others, most of them Brahmin students, used to observe this and get jealous: 'How can a low-born get more attention?' Vyasatirtha noticed the hostility among the students. He decided to teach them a lesson to make public Kanaka's greatness. On the day of ekadashi (eleventh day of the lunar forthnight), a day for fasting he called all his students including Kanaka and said, 'I know how difficult it is to fight the pangs of hunger. I am giving you a banana each, you can eat it provided you find a place where no one sees you.'

   The students eagerly took the banana and started searching for secret places. In the evening the guru, Vyasatirtha after patha (instruction) asked them where and how they ate their bananas. Some said they went to a dark corner, others hid behind a tree or had gone into the woods. When it was Kanaka's turn, he showed his uneaten banana and said, 'I am sorry I did not eat my banana'. On enquiring he said, 'Respected guru, I searched a lot but I could not find a place where no one was present. Wherever I went, Bhagavan (God) was always present, watching me. You had said I should eat without anybody knowing, I could not do so as Bhagavan was everywhere.' This incident opened the eyes of the other students and put them to shame. Thus, Kanaka was praised by his guru for having *aproksha* (the deep and intuitive knowledge of Bhagavan). Kanakadasa was able to achieve a hierarchically superior position as compared to his other Brahmin classmates.

   Kanakadasa was also hailed by Vadiraja Swamy (also 15th century) of the Sode Udupi matha and given an important place in the matha's ideological scheme.

   The point is that the devotion and understanding of Bhagavan creates reverence and acceptance in the eyes of the lay followers as well as the sannyasis of Udupi, who till today sing the bhajans (devotional songs) composed by Kanakadasa.

7. A.C. Bhaktivedanta, the founder of ISKCON, draws the succession of disciples from Madhvacharya. Moreover, some Madhvas consider the ISKCON as part of the Madhva sect.
8. The usage in both Kannada and Sanskrit for auspicious and inauspicious is mangala and amangala respectively.

9. The information is derived from the *Bhagavata*.
10. It is said that sage Gautama protected learned Brahmins when they were in need of protection. But the Brahmins, owing to envy instead of being grateful to Gautama, brought discredit to him by making him kill an artificial cow which was their creation. They even abused him. When Gautama came to know this, he cursed the Brahmins and took away the power of knowledge from them.
11. Some of the sannyasis in recent years have been lured by the world outside the matha and have given up sannyasa to live the life of a householder. Lakshmimanogna Tirtha of the Shirur matha left the ashrama to become Rajagopal Achar, married and got himself a job at a bank. He is now an artist and author, well-known in literary circles as Arya, his pen name.
    The most dramatic of all abdications was that of Vishvavijaya Tirtha, the junior swamiji of the Pejavara matha, in 1987. He had gone to the USA for six months, with the consent of his guru, senior Pejavara Swamy, to promote Madhva philosophy and collect money for a 350 bed hospital in Udupi. While he was away, the Phalimar swamiji publicly questioned the propriety of a sannyasi crossing the seas. Ostensibly, stung by criticism, the junior swamiji announced his abdication, after meeting his guru in Bangalore. He was disgusted with 'the narrow-mindedness, the selfishness and the orthodoxy around the mathas'. He said he wanted to free himself from all this.
12. Most of these studies have tended to focus on the advaitic philosophy to understand the renunciatory values. The notions of the world as illusion, and of salvation as implying 'becoming Brahman' (*aham Brahma asmi*) is part of this understanding. The following discussion also therefore, stands as an alternative means of comprehension.

7

Conclusion: The Udupi Madhva Matha in Contemporary India

The changing forms of Indian traditional culture under the impact of modern forces has been the focus of anthropological and sociological scrutiny for some time now. Since the works of M.N. Srinivas (1967) and Milton Singer (1972), the assumption of the incompatibility between modern and traditional cultures has been debunked. The thrust in most of the research has been to show how traditions constantly adapt and adopt the values and norms of the modern world (Khare 1970; Lele and Singh 1993; Rudolph and Rudolph 1967; Shils 1961; Singh 1973; Srinivas 1992).

Traditional institutions perpetually re-formulate themselves in interaction with the external world, or with what Shils (1981: 240) calls 'exogenous factors'. This constant innovation is the key to a tradition's survival over a long period of time. Because tradition is constantly changing it becomes necessary for us to inquire periodically into the question of its current place in the contemporary world. Traditions change because the circumstances to which they refer change (Shils 1981: 258). Inquiry into the present form of a tradition not only contextualises the traditional institution, but also highlights the dynamic forces at work in the modern world.

Establishing Relevance

The Udupi Madhva matha as a traditional space has demonstrated its flexibility to adapt to changes over time. Initially, the main Krishna matha was not open to all castes. It was Vadiraja Swamy's effort in the 16th century which allowed entry to all castes for Krishna darshan. The inclusion of prasada that Kanakadasa of the shepherd caste used to offer to the deity was an attempt to include the lower castes into the mainstream ideology of the matha. Today, once again, the question of negotiating boundaries between various castes and faiths has come up as a contentious issue. This issue—whom to include and which groups to exclude—keeps emerging and seems to be an important factor for the survival of this institution as was seen in the distribution of prasada in the chowki and in other eating places in the main Krishna matha.

The following example further reinforces the point:

While giving a lecture in Kannada to a mixed gathering, the Pejavara swamiji was asked a question by the Dalit novelist, Devanoor Mahadev. Devanoor said:

> Our Pejavara swamiji goes out into our settlements bestowing tirtha (sacred water) and prasada to our pious folk, but this is not enough. We do not want this from his Holiness. We are humble human beings. I have a straight and simple question for the swamiji. Is he ready or willing to take one of our Harijan boys as his shishya (student)?

The closely-packed audience shifted uncomfortably. A direct question like this is rarely asked. Swamiji immediately took up Devanoor's question—

> Our young friend here has asked me a straightforward question.

> I congratulate him on his candour and courage. He has given voice to the wounds of the Shudra masses, trodden upon since centuries. I am a sannyasi, I must renounce all caste prejudice. I personally do not believe in or recognise any such distinctions. These castes and creeds and high and low divisions must all go because they create exploitation. I am sure, with time, this will vanish. I know fully well, what I have been doing is too inadequate but I have severe limitations. I am like a captain leading a troop. I cannot march way ahead leaving my troop behind. If I go too far, the enemy may take me captive or my own troop may shoot me down suspecting me to be a deserter. I have to be cautious, I can only advance thus far and no further. I have to take my troop along with me. My young learned friend must understand my peculiar position and condone what little I do.

This particular swamiji said that it would be some time before the groups/castes excluded from becoming formal students would be taken in by sannyasis. Other swamijis justified their stand by pointing out that although they did not personally have students of lower castes, they were running schools especially meant for the scavenger caste. The paryaya swami, as we have seen, had encouraged women and members of all castes to write the *Bhagavad Gita* verses for the Gita Mandir that he was constructing, provided they give up smoking and drinking of alcohol for at least the time they are writing the verses. Although these attempts redefine traditional practice, many are dissatisfied that nothing has been done at the institutional level to incorporate women and non-Brahmins as formal students. It is perhaps to answer this demand that non-sannyasi gurus have started including women and non-Brahmins in their classes (patha).

To involve non-Brahmin and women, both the pontiffs and the pandits have adopted more endearing and effective forums and integrative strategies. The upannyasa emerges as a more liberal form where the sannyasis and the scholars take on the mantle of modern intellectuals and seek to transform and reinterpret tradition tailored to the needs of the city dweller, often using their images and categories in a humorous and dramatic fashion. The discourse in the upannyasa is structured to suit the multi-sectarian, multi-cultural gathering. Opposing schools of thought often refuted in formal classes are not criticised. These are often urban locales and require interpretations that negotiate boundaries between worshippers of different faiths and beliefs. In this sense, the discourse is a way of dealing with the current nature of plurality in India. The traditional institutions in India increasingly need to contend with the polycentric social and cultural backdrop of their existence. One of the intentions of the gurus of the matha in addressing these audiences is also to create a following which has repercussions on the resources a charismatic or a good orator is able to gather for his matha.

The work of interpretation is thus important for the continued survival of a traditional institution. This re-articulation redefines the place of an institution and establishes its relevance. For Anthony Giddens, this renewal of ideas is more significant for the integrity of a tradition than its longevity. He writes:

> The integrity of tradition derives not from the simple fact of persistence over time but from continuous 'work' of interpretation that is carried out to identify the strands which bind present to past (Giddens 1994: 64).

The forward movement by linking the past to the present echoes the orthogenetic process put forward by Singer. The orthogenetic, in contrast to the heterogenetic, is a process where the core of tradition does not undergo change. Singer writes:

> Because an indigenous innovation emerges within, the system is not associated with the alien and the strange and it is not regarded as a threat to tradition and requires no special segregation and neutralisation. It is permitted to develop on its own merits or demerits, so to speak, its eventual acceptance or rejection is not posed as a dilemma of either accepting or rejecting all the basic institutions, values and beliefs of the traditional system (Singer 1972: 396).

Singer portrays the lifestyle of businessmen in Madras (now Chennai) to show their involvement with modern, capitalist values and hence, disproves Weber's thesis of 'other worldly' Indian behaviour. The context of the Udupi matha can further sharpen the critique as it exposes a traditional institution's interaction with modern norms and values.

The Tenor of Transformations

Max Weber, while classifying types of social action, says traditional action is that which is 'determined by ingrained habituation' and this implies an 'unthinking acceptance of ancient custom' (1978: 25,30). Actions and thought in the Udupi matha are not a blind, dogmatic, unchangeable acceptance of traditional norms. This involves active debate which seeks to reformulate and recontextualise the practice of tradition. These transformations occur without the aid of a charismatic leader or prophet and affect the everyday living of the members of the sect. Conscious departures from tradition need not have prophetic sanction as Weber stresses (1978: 37). He further adds:

> In times of strict traditionalism, a new order—one actually regarded as new—was not possible without revelation unless it was claimed that it had always been valid though not yet rightly known, or that it had been obscured for a time and was now being restored to its rightful place.

The 'rightful place' in tradition is often a contested issue, if at all it can gain acceptance as a new addition. It would be pertinent to recollect a few examples here. As has been mentioned before, some of the sannyasis of Udupi are changing the system of initiating young boys (10–14 years) soon after their sacred thread ceremony. Nowadays, many of the sannyasis feel that sannyasa should only be given to mature adults who are aware of their responsibilities and austerities. Their logic is that when boys grow up, they regret having given up 'good things in life' and start indulging in them on the sly. Kaniur Swamy's running a cinema hall has been criticised by some of the members of the Udupi matha, but the swamiji justifies it as a means of survival.

> Without this, my matha will suffer, I don't have lands like the other mathas. Some people criticise me and say the cinema hall gets vulgar films, but they don't see that good films like *Bhakt Prahalad* also come. How can you expect only good things to exist? Aren't the good ways accompanied by the bad everywhere.

These debates and the arguments put forward for change point out that established traditions contain, in varying ways, the potential to develop and endure. New circumstances arouse the imagination and logical powers of the members of a tradition and provide new applications of hitherto unused and unthought categories. Shils also stresses that reformulations within tradition occur because of the 'imagination' and 'creative intelligence' of the adherents involved (Shils 1981: 214). The imagination and new technique are also reflected in the administrative set-up of the matha. The next example analyses this administrative structure of the matha in the way it systematises and routinises the internal affairs and uses Weber's own framework of bureaucratic structures. It goes to show that innovation in traditional institutions incorporate rules of modern bureaucracy without necessarily losing their identity.

The matha has evolved as a space where there is an interesting mixture of traditional and modern bureaucratic management. The 'office' (the locals also call it the office) and the staff is set up according to the bureaucracy of modern times (rational- legal authority). The office is responsible for issuing passes to the students who eat in the main Krishna matha. All official business such as correspondence, maintaining files and plans are looked after by the office. It further regulates the role of officials and pays them salaries. So there is an accountant. However, his intention in accounting for the profit and investments is not to make more money but to use it for the benefit of the devotees.

The pre-modern rules described by Weber outweigh the rational-legal in this set-up. The offices are managed by trustees and companions. Unlike most South Indian temples where there are two offices, one governmental and the other traditional (Appdurai and Breckenridge 1976; Selvam 1995; Uma Shankari 1982), there is no interference from the Government in the Udupi matha. All appointments are made by the pontiff of the matha. They are also ad-hoc rather than permanent. The staff at the office keep changing after each paryaya. In other non-paryaya mathas, the officials work voluntarily (mostly after retirement) and change frequently. The working sphere does not necessarily entail the separation of public and private spheres of existence. Added to this, loyalty in this system is not devoted to impersonal and functional purposes, but is more dependent on a disciple's faith to a person. The bureaucratic management of people and resources remains more traditional than modern, intensified by sacred taboos and traditional status-group privileges (Gerth and Mills, 1970: 199).

A more marked systematisation is seen in the procedure of worship (puja). The list handed out at the reception office in the matha specifies the name of the puja and the amount it will cost to have the puja performed. This orders and controls the action of the devotee as also the accounting of money collected by the performance of the pujas (a receipt is handed to the devotee after payment in cash).

This listing of the puja by the office brings about a certain amount of social control and discipline (the time of worship orders the inflow of devotees and the set procedure for worship leads to economy of time and energy). These remain stable even when the paryaya swamiji changes. Only the higher-level officials change while most of the lower-level workers, such as gate keepers and cleaning staff, generally remain the same. The bureaucratisation embodied in the office of the matha as Weber says, can be:

> ... made to work for anybody who knows how to gain control over it. A rationally ordered officialdom continues to function smoothly even after the enemy has occupied the territory; he merely needs to change the top officials (Weber 1968: 989).

The matha members display a strongly shared sense of

traditional culture, character and status on the one hand and an ability to articulate and represent the matha in ways akin to modern culture and administrative procedures on the other. The matha pontiffs and other members do not replace one dimension by the other. For example, a sannyasi may actually give greater play to the voluntary (non-kinship) modes of affiliation based on one's educational background, occupational skill, and economic status, although he is not prepared to open the matha at the administrative level beyond the birth-ascriptive caste membership. The modern social features interact without 'levelling the sacred and hierarchical caste order and replacing it' (Rudolph and Rudolph, 1967: 36). Khare's excellent work on the Kanya-Kubja Brahmins exposes the connection of tradition and modernity in an organisational set-up. Khare has analysed the administrative procedures among the Kanya-Kubjas according to the Weberian framework and his conclusions also highlight the flexibility of tradition's capacity to adopt modern structures of bureaucracy (Khare, 1970: 161–194). It is important to note that in this understanding, the process of change is not evolutionary. Modern innovations tend to reinforce traditional norms. Tradition, by being in constant communication with the current trends in the modern world, informs and constructs its own identity. This identity is regulated by the 'guardians' and 'experts' of tradition (Giddens 1994: 82). An emphatic way in which guardians regulate the changes was illustrated in Chapters 4 and 5—'The Cultural Production of Knowledge' and 'Styles of Discourse in the Production of Knowledge', respectively. Certain interpretations are allowed whereas other ways of understanding Madhva's philosophy are barred in the traditional set-up. Therefore, though a tradition is not the mechanical following of precepts in an unquestioning way, it is also not infinitely mutable. There is a conscious effort on the part of the pontiffs and other experts of the matha to give direction and meaning to changes within their tradition. As Shils observes, experts in traditions are like intellectuals in the modern world. They are not only the ones who interpret and transform tradition, but claim a special right to, and responsibility for, the cultivation of truth in science and scholarship as well as the transmission of cultural heritage of persons according to the needs of the society (Shils, 1961: 10).

This construction and communication of tradition in the hands of regulative forces (the experts and guardians) defines the way in which transformations occur. These occur without the necessary aid of 'prophetic revelation'. Appadurai adds that the changes occur in an undramatic fashion and agrees to the fact that the past is a rule-governed, therefore finite, cultural resource. He writes:

> As with other kinds of cultural rules, anything is possible but only some things are permissible (Appadurai 1981c: 218).

The Logic of Emerging Perspectives

From the discussion so far, one can reasonably argue that the members of the matha are able to reflect on the past and their own practices which results in the transformation and critique of the tradition. This critique is possible because of the contextualisation of the matha in the modern world. It enables the members to reflect on their tradition. Contrary to this view, Hans George Gadamer argues that authority is linked with tradition and that any understanding necessarily remains within the inescapable realms of tradition and authority. Gadamer writes:

> Tradition has a justification that is outside the arguments of reason… (1975: 247).

The implication of Gadamer's theory would inhibit any critical attitude by the members of the matha towards their own tradition (much like Weber's understanding of traditional action).

Paul Ricouer takes up this issue and critically evaluates Gadamer's hermeneutics of tradition (1981). Ricoeur's hermeneutics suggests that when two world-views (in this case traditional and modern) meet, they get transformed and enlarged. This provides a vantage point from which a critique can take place, implying that perceptions and viewpoints are not closed and shut. Applying Ricoeur's understanding, one may argue that the exposure to modern values results in a movement beyond traditional ideas. The return from this movement back to tradition results in the incorporation of contemporary norms. It provides scope for reflection on the past and one's present status in society. Interaction with the external world results in the 'opening up' of tradition. The members of the matha transform their world with the understanding of their surroundings. The movement from tradition—the 'distanciation' leads to a new 'belonging' and these are the twin arches of the hermeneutic bridge referred to by Ricoeur (also see the 'Introduction' to this book). It involves the expansion of one's own horizon through the incorporation of a new mode of being.

As it emerges, the adherents of the matha with their openness not only find new ways of making sense of their world, but also provide themselves with new tools of self-understanding. To further elucidate this point, let me briefly dwell upon the involvement of members of the matha in political ideology at the national level and how it leads to new formulations, associations and a distinct understanding of their status.

Most of the members of the sect are either active or passive supporters of the BJP (Bharatiya Janata Party) and the VHP (Vishwa Hindu Parishad). The senior Pejavara matha swamiji belongs to the Dharma Sansad of the VHP. As Nandy points, out the Dharma Sansad 'is a synod of saints and seers of all faiths prevalent in Hindu society' (1995: 91). For the Pejavara swamiji, this forum enables the restoration and preservation of dharma. He thinks it is one of the ways the present generation can be made aware of 'the correct way of living in the modern world' as it can reach the masses. He even participated in the meeting of the Dharma Sansad held in Udupi in 1985. His participation was criticised by other saints of the matha, but his argument was that the Sansad provided a platform where members of different sects could interact for a common cause. This forum, in this sense, is quite remarkable as it has enabled alliances with the

Shankara mathas, a union previously inconceivable (see also Nandy, 1995: 91). The Pejavara swamiji further added, 'I agree that mathas should stay away from politics, but if political parties start interfering with religion, we have to speak out.' Thus, for this swamiji, the involvement with politics is an active encounter. For other members, these political parties imply a certain ideology which they are sympathetic towards. A bidi-sannyasi staying in one of the Udupi mathas said, 'I am sympathetic towards the BJP. I do not know much but favour their Hindutva. By Hindutva, I mean dharma and there is a peculiarity to dharma in India. Outside India, life tends to be materialistic.'

This trend, visible in the Udupi mathas, is a movement towards the restoration of brahminical power. As one of the senior pontiffs explained:

> We do not wish to repeat the mistakes of our forefathers. We must give equal status to the lower castes but we must at the same time realise the potential of great minds that are now migrating to America.

This conversation took place soon after a Brahmin clerk working in an office came to swamiji for help for his wife, also working in the same office with him, on a temporary basis. She was apparently replaced by a candidate from the reservation quota, inspite of her seniority. The clerk had said, 'It is not the time for us Brahmins.'

The swamiji could not do much except write a letter of recommendation. The alliance of the swamijis (some active, some passive) with the BJP suggests that this party is seen as a vehicle for social protest but a protest coming from the traditional elite who feel dispossessed by the forces that have shaped public life in the last fifty years.

The effort to restore classical brahminism and Vedanta is not restricted to the 'semi-modern' or the 'westernised Indian' who seek to create a Hindu nation as implied by Nandy (1995: 58), rather it is the primary motive of the sectarian tradition in India. Nandy also says that the formulation of Hindutva in constituting a nation is divorced from traditional notions:

> In other words, the Hindus who would constitute the Hindu *rashtra* are not expected to be Hindus in the traditional sense. The traditional Hindus are seen as too diverse, feminised, irrational, unversed in the intricacies of the modern world, and too pantheistic, pagan, gullible and anarchic to run a proper state (1995: 63).

This, according to Nandy, is a reaction to and a compensation for the modern Hindu's distance from the lived traditions of Hinduism in whose hands it is an instrument of political mobilisation which seeks to masculinise the self-definition of the Hindus.

Within the lived tradition, Hindutva assumes a different form, and seeks to re-establish its conception of dharma based on traditional understanding. This traditional understanding is not insulated from modern or western ideas and values. The members of the matha, in perceiving Hindutva as a vehicle of preserving brahminical identity at a national level, give a new input which gives to Hindutva a pan-urban formulation resulting in the opening up of the initial impetus which went into creating a national ideology. The traditional members of the Udupi matha see themselves as capable of contributing to the running of the State. They are interested in the political process but have distinct aims and motivations.

The conceptualisation of Hindutva by the Udupi sannyasis and other members of the sect is neither a violent stand against the Muslims (the politics of the twentieth century) as Gyanendra Pandey suggests (1993: 1–23), nor is it the process of recuperating the lost masculinity by positing 'a generalised Oedipal relation between the Mother-nation and her sons' (Hansen, 1996: 140). It is the concern with the decline of the brahminical social order (see Frankel and Rao, 1990) that has prompted some of the saints of the matha to forge an alliance with modern political parties. This alliance alters the traditional role played by the pontiffs of the matha and permits a greater understanding of their own relevance and status in the contemporary world.

Tradition, in its effort to grapple rather than gloss over

worldly modern structures, emphasises its grounding in the here and now of existence. Indian thought is not (as Weber, speaking more in the framework of Advaita says), 'in the last analysis indifferent to the realities of the world' (Weber, 1962: 162). Soteriological concepts and theories within the Madhva sect do not disregard the reality of the world. They rather stress the 'proper' relation with this world for salvation.

In self-representation, these transformations are attributed to the ill-effects of the age of Kali (the age of darkness). The gurus also specify that tradition is not what it used to be. And in this sense, there is deterioration, but on the other hand, it is understood as circumstantial and not altogether negative and there are ways in which the interpretation of texts accommodates this 'degeneration'. The members of the matha stress that in earlier yugas (epochs), one had to do great tapas (penance) for many years, but now in the Kaliyuga, due to the (bad) times, there is a concession granted by the gods—for just by taking His name or by gaining little knowledge, one can get salvation (moksha). One of the scholars of the matha maintained that tradition continues as long as the (prescribed) texts are transmitted properly and as long as there is a wish to understand them 'correctly'. His implication was that reading of the sacred texts will automatically ensure a form of traditional practice which could vary with the times. He insisted that if Madhva's philosophy has to survive, it cannot remain closed and shut, reflecting the matha's ability and desire to reproduce itself materially and ideologically. This does not imply that the laws of Manu or some other primer set ages ago still regulate life. It is rather, as another pandit of Udupi said, '*Dharma Shastras* should be perceived as similar to the constitution, it loses its relevance if there are no amendments.'

The flexibility of the living traditions to adapt and change is not a corruption of tradition. In my view, it is more profitable to see tradition as being carried forward with certain traits of modernity. This forward movement displaces any understanding of tradition as static or frozen. Thoughts and ideas do not exist independent of society, closed within texts. Ideas penetrate society and social relations and these in turn penetrate ideas. In this situation, one cannot expect a tradition devoid of modern meanings, nor modernity bereft of traditional moorings (see Borden 1989; McCarthy 1994). This is the reason religious ideas remain central to society and as long as this is the case, a sectarian perspective allows an analysis which seeks to point out the unique and the universal in a particular context and its relevance in the contemporary world. At one level, the desacralised, 'deteriorating modern world' (Gross, 1992: 462) is, not entirely favourable for researching religious transcendence making one wonder how long these systems will survive, yet paradoxically this very desacralisation provides fertile ground for the mathas to establish their relevance. For many throughout the world, traditions promise some sort of release and peace (or escape, for the sceptic) from hazards and tensions of our fast moving, complicated and stressful modern lives.

Traditional systems are successfully pursuing adaptive strategies which suggest that there is a demand for spiritualism. This can be evidenced in its more commercial forms in the cable television network which devotes a channel to public lectures on Hindu religious subjects; therapeutic spiritual courses conducted by various gurus, costing upto Rs. 85,000 per head (Deepak Chopra's course held in Goa cost that much, as reported in a leading newspaper of Delhi); and in the incorporation of yoga and meditative techniques in the corporate sector. Most of these gurus who give discourses and conduct courses have themselves had training in traditional institutions such as mathas or gurukulas for many years before they confront the lay audiences.

Religion will persist situated in different contexts and presenting itself in different guises. It is necessary for us to assess the occasions in which religious expressions arise and to understand their contemporary usage.

Glossary

Note: Most of the words included in this list have been used frequently in the text. Although many of these terms have more than one meaning, the one relevant to the textual discussion is given here. This glossary also gives the pronunciation of the word through diacritics.

abheda (abheda)	Non-difference.
achada (acāda)	Traditional practice and custom.
acharya (acārya)	Teacher; scholar; sometimes a surname.
adhikara (adhikāra)	Capacity to learn or acquire knowledge.
adhina (adhina)	Dependent.
ananda (ānanda)	Joy.
anhika (ānhika)	Meditation.
anvaya (anvaya)	The correct order of words in a verse or sentence.
apauruchesheya (ápauruceṣeya)	Authorless, referred to the Vedas.
arghya (arghya)	Offering of water.
ashrama (aśrama)	The stages in the traditional Hindu life cycle.
astika (āstika)	Those schools of thought that accept the Vedas as a source of valid knowledge.
bala-sannyasi (bāla-sannyāsi)	Those *sannyasis* who have taken up *sannyasa* before their marriage.
bhajan	Devotional songs.

bhakti	Devotion emerging from the knowledge of Brahman.
Bhashya (Bhāśya)	The interpretation by the Vedantic saints.
Bhashyakara (Bhaśyakāra)	The Bhasya givers.
bheda	Difference or distinction.
bhiksha (bhikṣa)	The food offered to a sannyasi.
bhojan	Food.
bhojanshala (bhojanśāla)	The place where sacred food is distributed to students and devotees.
bidi sannyasi (bidi-sannyāsi)	Free *sannyasi* not bound by the responsibilities of looking after the matha.
brahmachari (brahmachāri)	The first stage in the tradition Hindu life cycle, is expected to be celibate.
chatur masya (cātur māsya)	The fourth month period during the rainy season when saints do not travel. A time usually for intensive *patha*.
chowki (cowki)	The place where saints and Brahmin devotees take prasada.
chintane (cintane)	The revision class in *patha*.
chullah (cūlah)	Traditional firewood stove.
dakshina (dakṣina)	Religious gift in cash or kind.
darshana (darśana)	An act of viewing; a philosophical system supposed to be based on the realization of the founder.
devaru	God.
dukha	Sorrow.
dvadashi (dvādaśi)	The twelfth day of the lunar calendar.
dvanda	Duality; confused mind.
dvanda matha	The eight mathas of Udupi were grouped into four pairs by Madhva so that each matha in the group could support the other if required.
dvija	Twice-born.
ekadashi (ekādasi)	The eleventh day of the lunar calendar, which is the prescribed day for fasting.
gopichandana	Yellow clay in the form of a ball.
grihastha	Householder.
guna purna (guṇa pūrṇa)	Full of attributes and encompassing all attributes.

gurukula	Schools for imparting traditional knowledge.
jataka (jātaka)	Horoscope.
jignyasa (jigñyāsa)	The spirit of inquiry.
jiva	Soul.
gyana kanda (gyana kāṇḍa)	That part of Veda which according to Advaita leads to knowledge of Brahman as against the part that deals with rituals.
karma kanda (karma kāṇḍa)	According to Advaita, that part of Veda which deals with rituals.
kavya (kāvya)	Poetry.
khandartha (khandārtha)	The meaning of words.
madi (maḍi)	Purity.
mandir (mandir)	Temple.
mangala (mangala)	Auspicious.
mangalacharana (mangalācaraṇa)	The verses in praise of Brahman and the guru usually at the beginning of a text.
matha (maṭha)	Monastery.
mathadhipati (maṭhādipati)	The person in charge of the matha who is allowed to worship the idol at the main Krishna matha.
moha (moha)	Intense or undue attachment to transient things.
naivedya (naīvedya)	Offering made to God.
nastika (nāstika)	Those schools of thought that do not accept the Veda as valid source of knowledge.
nirguna (nirguṇa)	Without qualities.
nitya (nitya)	Eternal.
niyamana (niyāmana)	Maintaining.
panchanga (pancānga)	Traditional Hindu calendar.
paryaya (paryaya)	The pontiffs of the sub-mathas of Udupi undertake the responsibility of worshipping Krishna and manage the main matha by rotation for a period of two years.
patha (pāṭha)	Classes held to impart traditional knowledge.
phalahara (phalahāra)	Eating of fruits.
prakrti (prakṛiti)	Nature.
pramana (pramāṇa)	Source of valid knowledge.

prasada (prasāda)	Consecrated food offered to a deity of powerful being, then distributed.
puja	Worship, particularly a systematic adoration of one's deity and related rituals.
punya (puṇya)	Religious merit.
purohit	Ritual expert or priest.
purva paksha (pūrva-pakṣa)	The prior text to be refuted.
rasa (rasā)	Flavour.
shakti (śakti)	Power.
samhara (samhāra)	Annihilation.
samskara (samskāra)	Association, impression, fixed notion, habitual reaction formed by one's past.
sanchara (sancāra)	Travel.
sandhya vandana (sandhyāvandana)	The customary worship of the twice-born.
sannyasa (sannyāsa)	Renunciation of the world; asceticism.
sannyasi (sannyāsi)	A renouncer who has undergone the sannyasa initiation.
saru	Pulses in spicy and watery tamarind gravy.
shastra (śhāstra)	Source of traditional knowledge.
satvika (sātvika)	good, pure.
satya	Real or true.
seva	Service.
shibira (śibira)	A camp organised by mathas to instruct students.
siddhanta (siddhānta)	Established doctine.
simhasana (simhasāna)	(lit. lion seat) The place where the pontiff sits in the matha.
shishya (śiśya)	Student.
shloka (śloka)	Verse.
srishti (sriṣti)	Creation.
svarupa (svarūpa)	One's own essence.
svatantra	Independent.
swami (swāmi)	The renouncer as referred to by the researcher.
tapas	Penance.
tarka	Logic.
tatvanyasa (tatvanyāsa)	Meditation.

tirtha	Sacred water; place of pilgrimage; a prefix used in the name of ascetics initiated in the Madhva sect.
upanayana (upanayāna)	The sacred thread ceremony of the twice-born male.
upannyasa (upannyāsa)	The transmission of traditional knowledge in a public lecture given to a large, multi-sectarian audience.
vairagya (vairāgya)	Detachment; a life of discipline that leads to freedom from bondage.
vanaprastha (vānaprastha)	The third stage in the traditional Hindu life-cycle.
vichara (vicāra)	Thought process; reflexive thought.
vidhi	Procedure.
vidwan (vidwān)	Learned scholar.
vrata	Abstinence.
vrindavana (vrindāvana)	Burial ground of the pontiffs.
vyakarna (vyākarṇa)	Grammar.
yajnopavit (yajñopavīt)	The sacred thread worn across the torso by the twice-born male.
yuga	Age or era.

Bibliography

Acharya, U.R. 1989, *Udupi: An Introduction*. Udupi: Sri Krishna Matha.

Appadurai, Arjun and C.A. Breckenridge. 1976. 'The South Indian Temple', *Contributions to Indian Sociology*, 2: 2, 187–200.

Appadurai, Arjun. 1974. 'Right and Left Hand Caste in South India', *Indian Economic and Social History Review*, 11: 216–60.

Appadurai, Arjun. 1981a. *Worship and Conflict Under Colonial Rule: A South Indian Case*. Cambridge: Cambridge University Press.

Appadurai, Arjun. 1981b. 'Gastro-politics in Hindu South Asia', *American Ethnologist*, 8: 494–511.

Appadurai, Arjun. 1981c. 'The Past as a Scarce Resource', *Man* (n.s.) 16, 201–19.

Augé, Marc. 1977. *The Anthropological Circle*. Cambridge: Cambridge University Press.

Augé, Marc. 1992. *Non-lieux: Introduction a une anthropolgie de la surmodernite*. Paris: Seue.

Babb, Lawrence A. 1975. *The Divine Hierarchy: Popular*

Hinduism in Central India. New York: Columbia University Press.

Babb, Lawrence A. 1987. *Redemptive Encounters*. Delhi: Oxford University Press.

Bakhtin, Mikhail and Medvedev. 1978. 'Introduction' in *The Formal Method in Literary Scholarship*, (ed.) by A.J. Wehrle. Baltimore, The John Hopkins University Press.

Bakhtin, Mikhail. 1984. *Problems of Dostoevsky's Poetics*. Manchester, Manchester University Press.

Balfour, Henry. 1897. 'Life History of an Aghori Fakir', *Journal of the Anthropological Institute*, 26: 340–357.

Beal, Anne. E. 1995. 'Reflections on Ethnography in Morocco: A Critical Reading of Three Seminal Texts', *Critique of Anthropology*, 15: 3, 289–304.

Bharati, Agheyananda. 1970. *The Ochre Robe*. New York: Doubleday and Company.

Bhartrhari. 1990. *Vairagya Shatakam*. Tr: Swami Madhvananda. Calcutta: Calcutta Advaita Ashram.

Bhat, P. Gururaja. 1975. *Studies in Tuluva History and Culture*. Manipal: Author.

Biardeau, M. 1965. 'Ahamkara: The Ego Principle in the Upanishads', *Contributions to Indian Sociology*, VIII, 62–84.

Borden, C. 1989. *Contemporary India: Essays on the Uses of Tradition*. Delhi: Oxford University Press.

Bourdieu, Pierre. 1984. *Distinction: A Social Critique of the Judgment of Taste*. London: Routledge and Kegan Paul.

Bourdieu, Pierre. 1986 (1977). *Outline of a Theory of Practice*. Cambridge: Cambridge University Press.

Bourdieu, Pierre. 1988. *Homo Academicus*. Oxford: Polity Press.

Bourdieu, Pierre. 1989. *La noblesse d'Etat*. Corsps et Grander Ecoler. Paris: Editions de Miniuit.

Bourdieu, Pierre. 1990. *The Logic of Practice*. Stanford: Stanford University Press.

Boyer, Pascal. 1990. *Tradition as Truth and Communication: A Cognitive Description of Traditional Discourse*. Cambridge: Cambridge University Press.

Breckenridge. C.A. 1976. 'Worship and Endowments in South India'. Ph.D. Dissertation, University of Wisconsin.

Buhler, G. 1886. (Trans) *The Laws of Manu*. Delhi: Motilal Banarssidas.

Burghart, Richard. 1983. 'Renunciation in the Religious Traditions of South Asia', *Man*, 4: 635–668.

Cantlie, Audrey. 1980. 'A Commensal Relationship with God: The Nature of Offering in Assamese Vaishnavism' in M.F.C. Bourdillon and Fortes (eds.), *Sacrifice*. London Academic Press, pp. 107–125.

Cantlie, Audrey. 1981. 'The Moral Significance of Food Among Assamese Hindus' in A.C. Mayer (ed.), *Culture and Morality*, pp. 42–62. New Delhi: Oxford University Press.

Clifford, James. 1986. 'Partial Truths', in Clifford and Marcus (eds.) *Writing Cultures: The Poetics and Politics of Ethnography*. California: University of California Press, pp. 1–26.

Cole, T.R. 1992. *The Journey of Life: A Cultural History of Ageing in America*. Cambridge: Cambridge University Press.

Das, Keshava. 1968. *Upasane: A Souvenir*. Udupi: Kaniur Matha.

Das, Veena. 1982. *Structure and Cognition: Aspects of Hindu Caste and Ritual*. Delhi: Oxford University Press.

Das, Veena. 1995. *Critical Events: An Anthropological Perspective on Contemporary India*. Delhi: Oxford University Press.

Deleuze, Gilles and Felix Guttari. 1994. (Tr. from French by Burchell and Tomlinson). *What is Philosophy*. London: Verso.

Dimmit, C. and W.J.C. van Buitenen, (eds.). 1983. *Puranic Myths*. New Delhi: Rupa.

Dumont, Louis. 1957. 'For a Sociology of India', *Contributions to Indian Sociology*, 1: 7–22.

Dumont, L. and D. Pocock. 1959. 'Pure and Impure', *Contributions to Indian Sociology*, No. 3: 9–39.

Dumont, Louis. 1960. 'World Renunciation in Indian Religions', *Contributions to Indian Sociology*, 4: 3–62.

Dumont, L. 1970. *Homo Hierarchicus: The Caste System and its Implications*. Chicago: University of Chicago Press.

Durkheim, E., 1961. *Elementary Forms of the Religious Life*. New York: Collier Books.

Durkhiem E. and M. Mauss. 1993 (1903). *Primitive Classification*. (ed.) by R. Needham, Chicago: The University of Chicago Press.

Dutt, S. 1960. *Early Buddhist Monasticism*. Bombay.

Eck, Diana L. 1981. *Darsan: Seeing the Divine Image in India*. Chambersburg, Pa.: Anima Books.

Eck, Diana L. 1983. *Banaras: City of Light*. London: Routledge and Kegan Paul.

Edgerbon and Langness. 1974. *Methods and Styles in the Study of Culture*. San Francisco: Chandler and Sharp.

Elaide, Mircea. 1959. *The Sacred and the Profane: The Nature of Religion*. Tr.: Willard R. Trask. New York: Harcourt Brace Jovanovich.

Erikson, E. 1970. *Gandhi's Truth: On the Origins of Militant Non-violence*. London: Faber and Faber Ltd.

Ferro-Luzzi, G.E. 1978. 'Food for the Gods in South India', *Zeitschrift fur Ethnologie*, 13(1): 86–108.

Foucault, Michel. 1988. *History of Sexuality Vol. 3—The Care of the Self.* New York: Vintage Books.

Fuller, Christopher J. 1992. *The Camphor Flame: Popular Hinduism and Society in India*. Princeton, N.J.: Princeton University Press.

Frankel, F.R. and M.S.A. Rao (eds.) 1990. *Dominance and State Power in Modern India: Decline of a Social Order*. Delhi: Oxford University Press.

Gadamer, H.G. 1975. *Truth and Method*. London: Sheed and Ward.

Garfinkel, Harold. 1967. *Studies in Ethnomethodology*. Englewood Cliffs, N.J.: Prentice-Hall.

Geertz, C. 1971. 'Deep Play: Notes on the Balinese Cockfight' in C. Geertz (ed.). *Myth, Symbol and Culture*. New York: W.W. Norton and Company, pp. 1–38.

Gerth and Mills. (ed.). 1970. *From Max Weber*. London: Routledge.

Ghurye, G.S. 1964 (1953). *Indian Sadhus*. Bombay: Popular Prakashan.

Giddens, Anthony. 1994. 'Living in a Post-traditional Society', in Ulrich Beck et al. *Reflexive Modernisation: Politics, Tradition and Aesthetics in the Modern Social Order*. Cambridge: Polity Press.

Godelier, M. 1972. *Rationality and Irrationality in Economics*. New York: Monthly Review Press.

Goldman, Robert P. 1978. 'Fathers, Sons and Gurus: Oedipal Conflict in the Sanskrit Epics', *Journal of Indian Philosophy*. 6: 325–92.

Goody, Jack. 1968. *Literacy in Traditional Societies*. Cambridge: Cambridge University Press.

Goody, Jack. 1977. *The Domestication of the Savage Mind*. Cambridge: Cambridge University Press.

Goody, Jack. 1987. *The Interface Between the Written and the Oral*. Cambridge: Cambridge University Press.

Govindacharya, B. 1984. et al. *Udupi: Past and Present*. Udupi: Pejavara Matha.

Govindacharya, B. 1985. 'Dvaita in Karnataka' in Krishna Swamy (ed.) *Avalokana: A Compendium of Karnataka Heritage*. Bangalore: Directorate of Kannada Culture.

Graham, William A. 1987. *Beyond the Written Word: Oral Aspects of Scripture in the History of Religions*. Cambridge: Cambridge University Press.

Gross, Robert Lewis. 1992. *The Sadhus of India: A Study of Hindu Asceticism*. New Delhi: Rawat Publications.

Halbfass, Wihelm. 1988. *India and Europe: An Essay in Understanding*. Albany: State University of New York Press.

Hansen, T.B. 1996. 'Recuperating Masculinity: Hindu Nationalism, Violence and the Exorcism of the Muslim Other', *Critique of Anthropology*. 16:2, pp. 137–72.

Hawkins, Stephan. *A Brief History of Time*. London: Bantam Press.

Heesterman, J.C. 1985 (1964). 'Brahmin, Ritual and

Renouncer', in J.C. Heesterman (ed.) *The Inner Conflict of Tradition*. Chicago: University of Chicago Press.

Heesterman, J.C. 1985. *The Inner Conflict of Tradition*. Chicago: Chicago Press.

Hirschhop, Ken. 1989. 'Introduction' in Ken Hirschhop and David Shepherd (eds.). *Bakhtin and Cultural Theory*. Manchester: Manchester University Press.

Husserl, E. 1970. *Logical Investigations*. (Translated by J.N. Findlay). London: Routledge and Kegan Paul.

Jha, Makhan. 1971. *The Sacred Complex in Janakpur*. Allahabad: United Publishers.

Jopphe, Christian. 1986. 'The Cultural Dimension of Class Formation and Class Struggle: On the Social Theory of Pierre Bourdieu', *Berkeley Journal of Sociology*. 31: 53–78.

Kamath, S.U. (ed.) 1983. *Karnataka State Gazetteer*, Part 2. Bangalore: Government of Karnataka.

Kane, P.V. 1930–62. *History of Dharmasastra* (*Ancient and Medieval Religious and Civil Law*). Government Oriental Series, Class B, no. 6, 5 vols. Poona: Bhandarkar Oriental Research Institute.

Kaushik, Meena. 1979. *Religion and Social Structure: A Case of the Doms in Benaras*. Delhi University: Ph.D. Thesis.

Khare, R.S. 1970. 'Tradition and Modernity of the Modern Kanya-Kubja Organisation' in R.S. Khare, *The Changing Brahmans: Associations and Elites among the Kanya-Kubjas of North India*. pp. 161–94. Chicago: University of Chicago Press.

Khare, R.S. 1974. 'Hindu Transactions: Diversity and Dualism in Bruce-Kapferer' in M. Singer and B.S. Cohen (eds.). *Transaction and Meaning*. Philadelphia: Institute for the Study of Human Issues.

Khare, R.S. 1976. *Culture and Reality: Essay on the Hindu System of Managing Foods*. Simla: Indian Institute of Advanced Study.

Khare, R.S. and M.S.A. Rao (eds.). 1986. *Food, Society and*

Culture: Aspects in South Asian Foods Systems. North Carolina: Carolina Academic Press.

Khare, R.S. 1992. 'Food with the Saints: An Aspect of Hindu Gastrosemantics' in R.S. Khare (ed.). *The Eternal Food*. New York: New York Press, pp. 1–26.

Lele, Jayant and Rajendra Singh. 1993. 'Modernising Intellectuals or Commuters between Cultures', in Chandrasekhar Bhat, Laxmi Narayan and K. Ranga Rao (eds.). *Sociology of Development and Change: Essays in Memory of Professor M.S.A. Rao*. New Delhi: Orient Longman, pp. 322–49.

Lotman, M. and Pjatigorski, A.M. 1977. 'Text and Function' in David P. Lucid (ed.). *Soviet Semiotics: An Anthology*. pp. 125–35, London: John Hopkins Press.

Madan, T.N. 1965. *Family and Kinship: A Study of the Pandits of Rural Kashmir*. Bombay: Asia Publishing House.

Madan, T.N. 1975. 'On Living Intimately with Strangers' in A. Beteille and T.N. Madan (eds.) *Encounter and Experience: Personal Accounts of Fieldwork*. Delhi: Vikas Publishing House, pp. 131–56.

Madan, T.N. 1987. *Non-Renunciation: Themes and Interpretations of Hindu Culture*. Delhi: Oxford University Press.

Madan, T.N. (ed.) 1991. *Religion in India*. Delhi: Oxford University Press.

Madan, T.N. 1994. *Pathways: Approaches to the Study of Society in India*. Delhi: Oxford University Press.

Marglin, Frederique A. 1982. 'Kings and Wives: The Separation of Status and Royal Power' in T.N. Madan (ed.) *Way of Life: King, Householder, Renouncer: Essays in Honour of Louis Dumont*. New Delhi: Vikas, pp. 155–82.

Marglin, Frederique A. 1985. *Wives of the God-King: The Rituals of the Devadasis of Puri*. Delhi: Oxford University Press.

Mariott, McKim. 1955. *Village India: Studies in the Little Community*. Chicago: University of Chicago Press.

Marriott, McKim. 1968. 'Caste Ranking and Food Transactions' in M. Singer, B.S. Cohen (ed.). *Structure and Change in Indian Society*. Chicago: Aldine Publishing Company, pp. 133–72.

Marriott, McKim. 1989. 'Constructing an Indian Ethnosociology', *Contributions to Indian Sociology*, n.s. 23: 1–39.

McCarthy, Paul. 1994. *Post-modern Desire: Learning from India*. New Delhi: Promilla and Co.

Miller, David M. and Dorothy C. Wertz. 1976. *Hindu Monastic Life: The Monks and Monasteries of Bhubaneshwar*. Montreal: McGill Queen's University Press.

Milner, M. Jr. 1994. *Status and Sacredness: A General Theory of Status Relations and an Analysis of Indian Culture*. New Delhi: Oxford University Press.

Minois, G. 1987. *History of Old Age: From Antiquity to Renaissance*. Tr.: S.H. Tenison 1989. Chicago: Chicago University Press.

Moreno, Manuel. 1992. 'Pancamritam' in R.S. Khare (ed.). *The Eternal Food*. pp. 147–178. New York: New York Press.

Nandy, Ashis, et al. 1995. *Creating Nationality: The Ram Janmabhumi Movement and Fear of the Self.* Delhi: Oxford University Press.

Narayan, Kirin. 1991 (1989). *Storytellers, Saints and Scoundrels: Folk Narrative in Hindu Religious Teaching*. Philadelphia: University of Pennsylvania Press.

Nayak and B.R. Gopal (eds.). 1990. *South Indian Studies*. Mysore: Geeta Book House.

Nussbaum, Martha C. 1994. *The Therapy of Desire: Theory and Practice in Hellenistic Ethics*. Princeton: Princeton University Press.

O'Flaherty, Wendy Doniger. 1975. *Asceticism and Eroticism in the Mythodology of Shiva*. New Delhi: Oxford University Press.

O'Flaherty, Wendy D. 1980. *Sexual Metaphors and Animal Symbols in Indian Mythology*. Delhi: Motilal Banarsidas.

Oldenberg, Hermann. 1982. *Buddha: His Life, His Doctrine, His Order*. London: Williams and Norgate.

Olivelle, Patrick. 1992. *Samyasa Upanisad: Hindu Scriptures on Asceticisim and Renunciation.* New Delhi, Oxford University Press.

Pandey, Gyanendra. 1993. 'The Civilised and the Barbarian: The 'New' Politics of Late Twentieth Century India and the World' in G. Pandey (ed.) *Hindus and Others: The Question of Identity in India Today.* New Delhi: Viking, pp. 1–23.

Parry, J.P. 1980. 'Ghosts, Greed and Sin: The Occupational Identity of the Benaras Funeral Priests'. *Man*, n.s. 15: 18–111.

Pocock, D.F. 1986. 'Art and Theology in the Bhagavata Purana', in Veena Das (ed.). *The Word and the World: Fantasy, Symbol and Record.* New Delhi: Sage Publications, pp. 9–40.

Rabinow, Paul. 1986. 'Representations are Social Facts: Modernity and Post-modernity in Anthropology' in Clifford and Marcus (eds.) *Writing Cultures: The Poetics and Politics of Ethnography*, pp. 195–233. California: University of California Press.

Raghavendrachar, H.N. 1965. *Brahma-Mimamsa.* Vol. I. Mysore: University of Mysore.

Raghavendrachar, H.N. 1941. *The Dvaita Philosophy and its Place in the Vedanta*, Mysore: University of Mysore.

Raghavendrachar, H.N. 1945. *Madhva Siddhanta.* (in Kannada). Mysore.

Raheja, G.G. 1988. *The Poison in the Gift.* Chicago: University of Chicago Press.

Rao, Krishna A. 1989. *Udupi—A Great Religious Centre.* Manipal: Rotary Club.

Rao, M.S.A. 1984. 'Some Subjective Orientation in Understanding Indian Social Reality' in Ravindra Kumar (ed.). *Philosophical Theory and Social Reality.* New Delhi: Allied Publishers, pp. 155–67.

Rao, M.S.A. 1979. *Social Movements and Social Transformation.* Delhi: Manohar Publishers.

Rao, M.S.A. 1987. *Social Movements and Social Transformation:*

A Study of Two Backward Classes Movements in India. Delhi: Manohar Publishers.

Redfield, Robert. 1953. 'Primitive World View and Civilisation' in *The Primitive World and its Transformations*. New York: Cornell University Press.

Ricoeur, Paul. 1981. *Hermeneutics and the Human Sciences: Essays on Language, Action and Interpretation*. Cambridge: Cambridge University Press.

Rosaldo, Michelle Z. 1980. *Knowledge and Passion: Ilongot Notions of Self and Society*. Cambridge: Cambridge University Press.

Rudolph, L.I. and Rudolph, S.H. 1967. *The Modernity of Tradition: Political Development in India*. Chicago: University of Chicago Press.

Sartre, J.P. 1957. *Being and Nothingness*. London: Methuen.

Schutz, A. 1962. *Collected Papers I: The Problem of Social Reality*. The Hague: Martin Nijhoff.

Selvam. 1995. *Social Organisation of a Temple in Tamil Nadu*. Department of Sociology, Delhi University: Ph.D. Thesis.

Seneviratne, H.L. 1985. 'An Exploration of the Meaning of Space in a Temple of the Tooth in Kandy', *Purusartha* 8, 177–95. Paris.

Shankari, Uma. 1982. *Sociology of Religion: A Temple in Tamil Nadu*. Delhi University: Ph.D. Thesis.

Sharma, B.N.K. 1981 (1961). *History of the Dvaita School of Vedanta and its Literature*. Delhi: Motilal Banarsidas.

Shils, Edward. 1961. *The Intellectuals Between Tradition and Modernity: The Indian Situation*. The Hague: Mouton and Co.

Shils, Edward. 1981. *Tradition*. Chicago. Chicago University Press.

Singer, Milton. 1966. 'The Radha Krishna Bhajans of Madras City' in Milton Singer (ed.) *Krishna: Myths, Rites and Attitudes*. Honolulu: East West Press, pp. 90–138.

Singer, Milton. 1972. *When a Great Tradition Modernises: An*

Anthropological Approach to Indian Civilisation. New York: Praeger Publishers.

Singh, Yogendra. 1973. *Modernisation of Indian Tradition.* Delhi: Thomson Press.

Srinivas, M.N. and A.M. Shah. 1968. 'Hinduism'. *International Encyclopedia of Social Sciences.* pp. 358–66.

Srinivas, M.N. 1952. *Religion and Society among the Coorgs of South India.* Oxford: Clarendon Press.

Srinivas, M.N. 1992. *On Living in a Revolution.* Delhi: Oxford University Press.

Srinivas, M.N. 1967. *Social Change in Modern India.* Berkeley: University of California Press.

Tambiah, S.J. 1982. 'The Renouncer: His Individuality and His Community' in T.N. Madan (ed.). *Way of Life: King, Householder, Renouncer.* Delhi: Oxford University Press, pp. 299–320.

Timm, Jeffrey R. 1992. 'Tradition Hermeneutics in South Asia' in J.R. Timm (ed.) *Texts in Context: Traditional Hermeneutics in South Asia.* Albany: State University of New York Press, pp. 299–306.

Todorov, T. 1984. *Mikail Bakhtin: The Dialogic Principle.* Minneapolis: University of Minnesota Press.

Toomey, P.M. 1986. 'Food from the Mouth of Krishna: Socio-Religious Aspects of Sacred Food in Two Krishnaite Sects' in R.S. Khare and M.S.A. Rao (eds.). *Food, Society and Culture.* Carolina Academic Press, pp. 55– 84.

Trautmann, T.R. 1981. *Dravidian Kinship.* Cambridge: Cambridge University Press.

Tripathi, B.D. 1978. *The Sadhus of India: The Sociological View.* Bombay: Popular Prakashan.

Uberoi, J.P.S. 1967. 'Sikhism and Indian Society', *Transactions of the Indian Institute of Advanced Study.* Vol. 4. Simla.

Van der Veer, Peter. 1987. 'Taming the Ascetic: Devotionalism in a Hindu Monastic Order'. *Man,* (n.s.) 22: 680–95.

Van der Veer, Peter. 1988. *Gods on Earth: The Management of Religious Experiences and Identity in a North Indian Pilgrimage Centre*. Delhi: Oxford University Press.

Wacquant, Loie J.D. 1992. 'Towards a Social Praxeology: The Structure and Logic of Bourdieu's Sociology' in P. Bourdieu and Loie J.D. Wacquant *An Invitation to Reflexive Sociology*. Chicago: University of Chicago Press, pp. 1– 60.

Weber, Max. 1962. *The Religion of India: The Sociology of Hinduism and Buddhism*. Free Press.

Weber, Max. 1968. *Economy and Society: An Outline of Interpretive Sociology*. (eds.) Roth and Wittch, New York: Bedminister Press Incorporated.

Weber, Max. 1978. *Economy and Society: An Outline of Interpretive Sociology*. (eds.) Roth and Wittch, Berkeley: University of California Press.

Welbon, G.R. 1986. 'Person, Text, Tradition: India's Acharya', *History of Religions*. Vol. 1:25, No. 4. 368–377.

Primary Sources

Badarayana. *Bhagavad Gita*.

Badarayana. *Brahma Sutra*.

Badarayana. *Bhagavata Purana*.

Jayatirtha. *Nyaya Sudha*.

Jayatirtha. *Tattva Prakashika*.

Jayatirtha. *Prameya Dipika*.

Vadiraja Swamy. *Rukmanisha Vijaya*.

Madhvacharya. *Brahma Sutra Bhashya*.

Madhvacharya. *Tantrasara*.

Madhvacharya. *Mahabharata Tatparya Nirnaya*.

Narayan Tantri, Agrahara. 1976. *Paramahamsa Nama Japa Puja Karma*. Udupi: Shirur Matha.

Narayanapanditachar. *Sumadhva Vijaya*.

Narayanpanditachar. 1956 (reprint). *Yogadipika*, Udupi: Adamar Matha Madhvacharya.

Pandurangi, K.T. 1990. *Tattryopanishad.* Chirtanur: Sriman Madhva Siddhantonnahini Sabha.
Raghavendra Swamy. *Parimala.*
Raghavendra Swamy. *Prakasha.*
Rajarajeshwara. *Rama Sandesham.*
Shankaracharya. *Brahma Sutra Bhashya* or *Sharirika Bhashya.*
Satapatha Brahmana.
Ishavasya Upanishad.
Sama Veda.
Taittariya Upanishad.
Vishnutirtha. 1931 (reprinted). *Sannyasapaddathi.* Udupi. Srikrishna Press.
Vyasa Tirtha. *Tattparya Chandrika.*

Index